BLOOM'S

HOW TO WRITE ABOUT

Mark Twain

R. KENT RASMUSSEN

Introduction by Harold Bloom

BLOOM'S
LITERARY CRITICISM
An imprint of Infobase Publishing

Bloom's Literary Criticism
An imprint of Infobase Publishing
132 West 31st Street
New York NY 10001

Library of Congress Cataloging-in-Publication Data

Rasmussen, R. Kent.
   Bloom's how to write about Mark Twain / R. Kent Rasmussen; introduction by Harold Bloom.
      p. cm.
   Includes bibliographical references and index.
   ISBN 978-0-7910-9487-7 (hc : alk. paper) 1. Twain, Mark, 1835–1910—Criticism and interpretation. 2. Criticism—Authorship. 3. Report writing. I. Bloom, Harold. II. Title. III. Title: How to write about Mark Twain.

   PS1338.R37 2007
   818'.409—dc22

                                            2007007248

Bloom's Literary Criticism books are available at special discounts when purchased in bulk quantities for businesses, associations, institutions, or sales promotions. Please call our Special Sales Department in New York at (212) 967-8800 or (800) 322-8755.

You can find Bloom's Literary Criticism on the World Wide Web at
http://www.chelseahouse.com

Text design by Annie O'Donnell
Cover design by Ben Peterson
Printed in the United States of America

Bang MSRF 10 9 8 7 6 5 4 3 2 1

This book is printed on acid-free paper.

CONTENTS

SERIES INTRODUCTION

B LOOM's How to Write about Literature series is designed to inspire students to write fine essays on great writers and their works. Each volume in the series begins with an introduction by Harold Bloom, meditating on the challenges and rewards of writing about the volume's subject author. The first chapter then provides detailed instructions on how to write a good essay, including how to find a thesis; how to develop an outline; how to write a good introduction, body text, and conclusion; how to cite sources; and more. The second chapter provides a brief overview of the issues involved in writing about the subject author and then a number of suggestions for paper topics, with accompanying strategies for addressing each topic. Succeeding chapters cover the author's major works.

The paper topics suggested within this book are open ended, and the brief strategies provided are designed to give students a push forward on the writing process rather than a road map to success. The aim of the book is to pose questions, not answer them. Many different kinds of papers could result from each topic. As always, the success of each paper will depend completely on the writer's skill and imagination.

HOW TO WRITE ABOUT MARK TWAIN: INTRODUCTION

by Harold Bloom

THERE GENERALLY is no problem with *what* to write about in Mark Twain, because *Huckleberry Finn* is one of the essential American books. Only *The Scarlet Letter, Moby-Dick, Leaves of Grass,* Emerson's *Essays,* and Emily Dickinson's *Complete Poems* can compete with it in our 19th century. In the early years of the 21st century, we cannot as yet agree what in American 20th-century literature will prove indispensable. I myself would choose Faulkner's *As I Lay Dying, The Sound and the Fury, Light in August,* and *Absalom, Absalom!* as the best of our prose fiction in the last century. The poets Robert Frost, Wallace Stevens, Hart Crane, and Elizabeth Bishop also would be among my candidates: most critics would add T. S. Eliot and W. C. Williams, and some would select Ezra Pound and Marianne Moore as well. Of the poets of my own generation, the works of John Ashbery and of the late A. R. Ammons and James Merrill persuade me they are permanent. One can add the major plays of Eugene O'Neill, Tennessee Williams, and Thornton Wilder, and the principal novels of Philip Roth and Thomas Pynchon, doubtless among others.

If asked the Desert Island Question, with the condition that the one book would have to be American rather than Shakespeare, I might be compelled to choose *Leaves of Grass,* and then hope to memorize *Huckleberry Finn* before I am cast away. Scott Fitzgerald, Ernest Hemingway, and T. S. Eliot all would have chosen Huck rather than Walt, but Whitman seems to me *the* unique writer of Western Hemisphere literature, whether written in Spanish, Portuguese, French, or English. Mark Twain, like Whitman, is read throughout the world, yet Whitman breaks the new road, as D. H. Lawrence remarked. Huck Finn takes the path that Don Quixote and Sancho Panza cut in their wanderings through a declining Spain, and Twain can be thought of as the American Cervantes.

Pragmatically then the question becomes: how to write about Huck Finn, who has proved larger even than his splendid book, rather in the mode that Falstaff and Hamlet established among Shakespearean characters. Twain after all had first created Huck in *The Adventures of Tom Sawyer* (1876), where the young outcast all but runs off with the book. Eight years later came *Adventures of Huckleberry Finn*, where Twain is a master literary artist and gives us much his greatest work, never remotely to be matched by him. To write about Twain, whether in *Huckleberry Finn*, or in such more problematic achievements as *Pudd'nhead Wilson* and *A Connecticut Yankee in King Arthur's Court*, you need to ask and try to answer: What are the varieties of the comic that he extended and at least partly invented?

Much that is best in Twain's humor exploits the limits of fantasy and farce. A great but reluctant live entertainer, ambivalent though almost as successful as Charles Dickens, Twain conveyed his anxious expectations as a performer even in the freedom-loving figure of Huck Finn. I myself would urge anyone writing about Huck to work at analyzing the boy's need to evade, tell untruths, and mystify even the reader, in addition to anyone he encounters except for his raft-companion, Jim. Huck lies merely to keep in practice, weirdly bringing together Twain and the totally antithetical Nietzsche, who urged survival by "lying against time." Huck's immediate nightmare is his mad, murderous father, the drunken Pap, but his ultimate antagonist is time. How to write about Huck at last becomes each reader's personal quest for the blessing of more life, a time without boundaries.

Twain read Nietzsche, with some gusto, only after he had finished *Huckleberry Finn*, but Twain remains our authentic American nihilist, outshining such descendants as Nathanael West and Thomas Pynchon. Huck is Mark Twain's will revenging itself against time, and time's dread: "It *was*." Huck incarnates that will: He never can age into a "maturity" that merely represents death-in-life. Writing about Huck is to meditate upon your own will to live, whoever you are.

PROLOGUE

I N HER introduction to *Lighting Out for the Territory: Reflections on Mark Twain and American Culture* (1997), the distinguished scholar Shelley Fisher Fishkin recalls how she became interested in Mark Twain during her youth. She started reading his books while she was in grade school and found them to be great fun. However, it was not until high school that she began to take them seriously. During her junior year, she read *Adventures of Huckleberry Finn* for the first time and experienced a kind of awakening—what might be called an epiphany. Expecting that book to be much like *The Adventures of Tom Sawyer,* she was stunned when her English teacher announced the topic on which everyone in the class was to write an essay: "How Mark Twain used irony to attack racism in *Huckleberry Finn.*"

The assignment caught the young Fishkin off guard, but as she got into Mark Twain's novel, this challenge gradually began to make sense. Fishkin happened to be reading the book in 1965, a year when the United States was tearing itself apart over unresolved racial conflicts, whose origins went back to the era of slavery—the same era in which *Huckleberry Finn* is set. At the same time Fishkin was puzzling over news stories about such disturbing events as Mississippi civil rights workers being murdered for helping African Americans register to vote and cities across the nation erupting in deadly racial violence, she was meeting characters in Mark Twain's novel whose words and behavior helped her to understand the roots of modern American racism. The novel also helped her to appreciate the nature of irony—the use of words to express ideas that may be the opposite of their literal meanings. Among the examples of racial irony that Fishkin recalled from her first reading of *Huckleberry*

Finn is Pap Finn's outrageous tirade against an educated black man he has encountered:

> Oh, yes, this is a wonderful govment, wonderful. Why, looky here. There was a free nigger there, from Ohio; a mulatter, most as white as a white man. He had the whitest shirt on you ever see, too, and the shiniest hat; and there ain't a man in that town that's got as fine clothes as what he had; and he had a gold watch and chain, and a silver-headed cane—the awfulest old gray-headed nabob in the State. And what do you think? they said he was a p'fessor in a college, and could talk all kinds of languages, and knowed everything. And that ain't the wust. They said he could vote, when he was at home. Well, that let me out. Thinks I, what is the country a-coming to? It was 'lection day, and I was just about to go and vote, myself, if I warn't too drunk to get there; but when they told me there was a State in this country where they'd let that nigger vote, I drawed out. I says I'll never vote agin. Them's the very words I said; they all heard me; and the country may rot for all me—I'll never vote agin as long as I live. And to see the cool way of that nigger—why, he wouldn't a give me the road if I hadn't shoved him out o' the way. I says to the people, why ain't this nigger put up at auction and sold—that's what I want to know. And what do you reckon they said? Why, they said he couldn't be sold till he'd been in the State six months, and he hadn't been there that long yet. There, now—that's a specimen. They call that a govment that can't sell a free nigger till he's been in the State six months. Here's a govment that calls itself a govment, and lets on to be a govment, and thinks it is a govment, and yet's got to set stock-still for six whole months before it can take ahold of a prowling, thieving, infernal, white-shirted nigger, and—"

The irony in this passage is as powerful as any in literature. On its surface, it is an impassioned antiblack diatribe filled with racist invective. At the same time, however, it exposes the illogic of racism by subtly calling attention to the differences that separate Pap from the black professor whom he denounces. The professor appears to be a model citizen—refined, highly educated, and holding a responsible position. Nevertheless, Pap rages at the very idea that any government would allow such a man to vote and not permit him to be sold back into slavery.

What kind of citizen is Pap? By his own account, he takes pride in saying he will never vote again, in protest of a government that permits black people to vote. At the same time, he admits that when he was on his way to vote himself, he got "too drunk to get there." From earlier passages in the novel, we already know that Pap is lazy, irresponsible (he has abandoned his son, Huck), and illiterate. He might also be described as "prowling, thieving, infernal." What then, does his diatribe really attack—black people or white racist thinking? Might that passage and other, similarly ironic passages in *Huckleberry Finn* therefore be read as assaults on racism?

As you can see, Fishkin's 11th-grade essay assignment gave her a great deal to think about and helped her appreciate that analyzing literature can be much more than a busywork exercise. In Fishkin's case, one teacher's challenging essay assignment helped point her toward a career as a scholar and a teacher. It opened her mind to new ideas and made her realize how relevant literature can be to the real world in which she lived.

Fishkin's story does not end there. Many years later, after she published *Lighting Out for the Territory,* she went back to her old high school to speak and had the pleasure of seeing her former English teacher, Anthony Arciola, who by then was retired. She told him she had *finally* figured how to answer the question he had posed so many years earlier. In saying that, Shelley touched on something else relevant to essay writing: You will rarely find full answers to every question you address—a point stressed throughout this present volume. Also, whether your future leads you into an academic career like Fishkin's or in a completely different direction, you will always continue to learn.

HOW TO WRITE
A GOOD ESSAY

ALTHOUGH THERE are many ways to write about literature, most assignments for high school and college English classes call for analytical papers. These assignments require you to present your interpretation of a text to your readers. Your objective is to interpret the text's meaning to enhance readers' understanding and enjoyment of the work. Without exception, strong papers about the meaning of literary works are built on careful, close readings of the texts. Careful, analytical reading should always be the first step in your writing process. This volume provides models of close, analytical reading of selected Mark Twain works. These should help you develop your own skills as a reader and as a writer.

As the examples throughout this book demonstrate, attentive reading entails thinking about and evaluating the formal, or textual, aspects of Mark Twain's works: theme, character, form, and language. In addition, when writing about works, many readers choose to move beyond the texts themselves to consider their cultural contexts. In such instances, essays might explore the historical circumstances of the time period in which the works were written and the periods in which they are set. Alternatively, the essays might examine the philosophies and ideas that the works under question address.

However, even in cases in which you explore a work's cultural context, your essay must still address the more formal aspects of the work itself as a piece of literature. For example, an interpretative essay that evaluates Charles Dickens's use of the philosophy of utilitarianism in his novel *Hard Times* (1854) cannot adequately address Dickens's treatment of the

1

philosophy without firmly grounding its discussion in the novel itself. In other words, any analytical paper about a text, even one that seeks to evaluate the work's cultural context, must also have a firm handle on the work's themes, characters, and language. You must look for and evaluate these aspects of a work, then, as you read a text and as you prepare to write about it.

WRITING ABOUT THEMES

Literary themes are more than merely topics or subjects treated in a work; they are attitudes or points about these topics that often structure other elements in a work. Writing about a theme therefore requires that you not just identify a topic that a literary work addresses, but also discuss what that work says about that topic. For example, if you were writing about the culture of the American South in William Faulkner's famous story "A Rose for Emily," you would need to discuss what Faulkner says, argues, or implies about that culture and its passing.

When you prepare to write about thematic concerns in a work of literature, you will probably discover that your text, like most works of literature, touches upon other themes in addition to its central theme. These secondary themes can also provide rich material for essay topics. A thematic essay on Faulkner's "A Rose for Emily" might consider gender or race in the story. While neither of these could be said to be the central theme of the story, they are clearly related to the passing of the "old South" and could provide plenty of good material for papers.

As you prepare to write about themes in literature, you may find several strategies helpful. After you identify at least one theme in the work on which you are writing, you should begin by evaluating how other elements of the story—such as character, point of view, imagery, and symbolism—help develop that theme. You might ask yourself what your own responses are to the author's treatment of the subject matter. Be careful not to neglect the obvious either: What expectations does the title set up? How does the title help develop thematic concerns? For example, the title "A Rose for Emily" clearly says something about the narrator's attitude toward the title character, Emily Grierson, and all she represents.

WRITING ABOUT CHARACTER

Generally, characters are essential components of fiction and drama. Many essay writers find that analyzing character is one of the most interesting and engaging ways to explore a piece of literature. After all, most characters are human, and we all know something about being human and living in the world. Although it is always important to remember that fictional characters are imaginary creations—even if they are modeled on real people—it makes sense to begin evaluating them as you might evaluate a real person. Start by examining your own response to characters. Do you like or dislike them? Do you sympathize with them? Do they behave as you would expect real human beings to behave? Why or why not?

As you begin the process of analysis, keep in mind that emotional responses such as these are merely starting places. To explore and evaluate literary characters fully, you must return to the formal aspects of the texts and evaluate how the authors draw their characters. The 20th-century British writer E. M. Forster coined the terms *flat* and *round* characters. Flat characters are static, one-dimensional figures who frequently represent a single concept or idea. In contrast, round characters, who are fully drawn and much more realistic, frequently change and develop over the course of a work. Are the characters you are studying flat or round? What elements of the characters lead you to evaluate them as you do? Why might the author have drawn characters as they are? How does their development affect the meaning of the work?

Similarly, you should explore the techniques that authors use to develop their characters. For example, do we hear the characters' own words or do we hear only other characters' assessments of them? Or, does the author use an omniscient or limited omniscient narrator to give readers access to the workings of the characters' minds? If so, how does that help to develop the characterizations? *The Adventures of Tom Sawyer* (1876) and *Adventures of Huckleberry Finn* (1884) provide sharp contrasts in this regard.

Often you can even evaluate narrators as characters. This is almost obligatory if you wish to understand Mark Twain's *Roughing It* (1872) and *Life on Mississippi* (1883), which both use anonymous first-person narrators. However, you can also evaluate anonymous third-person narrators, such as *Tom Sawyer*'s narrator, whose persona seems to shift throughout the novel. Among the questions to ask of narrators is how trustworthy their opinions and assessments are.

You should also think about characters' names. Do they mean anything? If you encounter a hero named Sophia or Sophie, you should probably think about her wisdom (or lack thereof), since *sophia* means "wisdom" in Greek. Similarly, since the name Sylvia is derived from the word *sylvan,* meaning "of the wood," you might want to evaluate that character's relationship with nature. Why might Mark Twain have used the name Tom for both the hero of *Tom Sawyer* and the pauper boy in *The Prince and the Pauper* (1881)? And what could possibly be behind the name "Huckleberry"? You should also look at titles of works. *The Adventures of Tom Sawyer* contains a definite article in its title; *Adventures of Huckleberry Finn* does not. Could that distinction convey a subtle difference in meaning? Mark Twain's 1880 travel book about Europe is titled *A Tramp Abroad.* It is a simple title, but what does it mean? Does it allude to a disreputable vagrant or to some kind of walking trip? Might Mark Twain have selected that title merely to be provocative? Pursuing questions like these can help you develop thorough papers about characters from psychological, sociological, or more formalistic perspectives.

WRITING ABOUT HISTORY AND CONTEXT

As the opening of this chapter notes, it is possible to write analytical essays that also consider the contexts of literary works. After all, nothing is written in a vacuum. Authors live and write during real historical periods and in real cultural contexts. And, like all of us, they are shaped by their environments and the events of their times. Learning more about the historical and cultural circumstances surrounding authors and their works can help illuminate their writings and provide productive materials for essays. Remember, however, that when you write an analytical essay on a work, you should use the context to illuminate the text of the work itself and not lose sight of your goal—to interpret the text as a literary work. Use historical or philosophical research as a tool to develop your textual evaluation, not as an end in itself.

Thoughtful readers often consider how history and culture affect authors' choices and treatments of their subject matter. Investigations into the history and context of works can examine the works' relationships to specific historical events, such as the Salem witch trials of 17th-century Massachusetts or the Restoration of King Charles I to the British monarchy in 1660. Bear in mind that historical contexts are not limited to politics and world events. Although knowing about the Civil War can be helpful in interpreting some of Mark Twain's writings and a basic knowledge of Elizabethan politics can illuminate *The Prince and the Pauper*, historical context also entails the fabric of the daily lives of ordinary people. Examining a text in light of changing gender roles, race relations, class boundaries, or working conditions can give rise to thoughtful and compelling papers. Understanding the conditions of slaves in the American South, for example, is actually a key to understanding Mark Twain's thinking when he was writing *A Connecticut Yankee in King Arthur's Court* (1889).

You can begin thinking about these issues by starting with broad questions. For example, what do you know about the time period and about the author? What does the editorial apparatus in your text tell you? These might be good starting places. Similarly, when specific historical events or dynamics are particularly important to understanding a work but might be somewhat obscure to modern readers, textbooks usually provide notes to explain historical background. These are a good place to start, but if the editions you are reading provide no such notes, you will need to turn to other sources, such as encyclopedias or general histories. Online sources can help too, but be careful in selecting them as there is a great deal of misinformation on the Web. Many articles on Wikipedia are excellent, but others are unreliable. If you are unsure which are which, stick to books published by reputable presses.

With this information, ask yourself how these historical facts and circumstances might have affected the author, the presentation of theme, or the presentation of character. How does knowing more about the work's specific historical context illuminate the work? To take a well-known example, understanding the complex attitudes toward slavery during the time Mark Twain wrote *Adventures of Huckleberry Finn* should help you begin to examine issues of race in the text. Additionally, you might compare these attitudes to those of the time in which the novel was set. How might this comparison affect your interpretation of a work written after the abolition of slavery, but set before the Civil War, as is the case with *Huckleberry Finn*?

WRITING ABOUT PHILOSOPHY AND IDEAS

Philosophical concerns are closely related to both historical context and thematic issues. Like historical investigation, philosophical research can provide a useful tool as you analyze a text. For example, an investigation into the working class in Charles Dickens's 19th-century England might lead you to a topic on the philosophical doctrine of utilitarianism in *Hard Times.* Many other works explore philosophies and ideas quite explicitly. Mary Shelley's famous novel *Frankenstein* (1818), for example, explores the 17th-century political philosopher John Locke's tabula rasa theory of human knowledge, as she portrays the intellectual and emotional development of the creature that Victor Frankenstein brings to life. As this example indicates, philosophical issues are somewhat more abstract than investigations of theme or historical context. Other examples of philosophical issues might include human free will, the formation of human identity, the nature of sin, and questions of ethics.

Although writing about philosophy and ideas might require some outside research, usually the notes or other material in your text will provide you with basic information. Often, footnotes and bibliographies in the editions you use will suggest places you can go to read more about the subjects. If you identify a philosophical theme that runs through a text, you might ask yourself how the author develops that theme. Look at character development and the interactions of characters, for example. Similarly, in fiction you might examine whether the narrative voice addresses the philosophical concerns of the text.

WRITING ABOUT FORM AND GENRE

Genre, a word derived from French, means "type" or "class." Literary genres are distinctive classes or categories of literary composition. On the most general level, literary works can be divided into the genres of drama, poetry, fiction, and essays, yet, within those genres are classifications that are also typically called genres. Tragedy and comedy, for example, are genres of drama. *Form,* on the other hand, is generally applied to the shape or structure of a work.

Although you might think that writing about form or genre leaves little room for argument, many terms for forms and genres are fluid. Just as literature evolves and changes, so do its forms. For example, dramatic tragedy was once quite narrowly defined, but over the centuries play-wrights have broadened and challenged traditional definitions, changing the shape of tragedy. When Arthur Miller wrote *Death of a Salesman* in 1949, many critics challenged the idea that tragic drama could encom-pass a man as common as Willy Loman. Prose fiction changes, too, and Mark Twain's writings are notoriously difficult to assign to specific genres and forms.

Evaluating how works of literature fit into or challenge the boundar-ies of their forms or genres can offer fruitful avenues of investigation. Once again, you might find it helpful to ask why a work does or does not fit into traditional categories. For example, why might Miller have thought it fitting to write a tragic drama about a common man? Simi-larly, you might compare the content or theme of a work with its form. How well do they work together?

WRITING ABOUT LANGUAGE, SYMBOLS, AND IMAGERY

Within all literary genres, words are writers' most basic tools. Language is the fundamental building block of literature. It is essential that you pay careful attention to how authors use language and to their word choices as you read, reread, and analyze texts. Imagery is language that appeals to the senses. Most commonly, imagery appeals to our sense of vision, allowing us to create mental pictures; however, authors also use language that appeals to our other senses. Images can be literal or figurative. Lit-eral images use sensory language to describe real things. In the broadest terms, figurative language uses one thing to mean something else. For example, if you were to call a man a snake, you would know that you do not mean he is really a reptile. You would be using figurative language to communicate a negative opinion of the man. Because people think of snakes as sneaky, slimy, and sinister, the concrete image of a snake would serve to communicate your abstract feelings.

The two most common figures of speech are similes and metaphors. Both are forms of comparisons between two apparently dissimilar things. Similes are explicit comparisons using linking words such as "like" or "as." Metaphors are implicit comparisons that might be regarded as sub-stitutions, such as referring to a human being as a snake. Saying a person "acts like a snake" uses a simile; saying the person "is a snake" uses a metaphor.

Symbols, by contrast, are things that stand for, or represent, other things. Often they represent something intangible, like concepts or ideas. In everyday life we use and understand symbols easily. Babies at christenings and brides at weddings wear white to represent purity. Consider a dollar bill: Its paper has no intrinsic value. A paper bill is a symbol of something else, the government's guarantee of its monetary value. Symbols in literature work similarly. Authors use symbols to evoke more than a simple, straightforward literal meaning. Characters, objects, and places can all function as symbols. Famous literary examples of symbols include Moby Dick, the white whale of Herman Melville's novel, and the scarlet *A* Hester wears in Nathaniel Hawthorne's *The Scarlet Letter* (1850). As both of these examples suggest, a literary symbol cannot be adequately defined or explained by any one meaning. Hester's Puritan community clearly intends the letter *A* she wears as a symbol of her adultery; however, as the novel progresses, even her own community reads the letter as representing not merely "adultery," but also "able," "angel," and a host of other meanings.

Writing about imagery and symbols requires paying close attention to the author's language. To prepare a paper on symbols or imagery in a work, try to identify and trace the images and symbols and then draw some conclusions about how they function. Ask yourself how any symbols or images help contribute to the themes or meanings of the work. What connotations do they carry? How do they affect your reception of the work? Do they shed light on characters or settings? A strong paper on imagery or symbolism will thoroughly consider the use of figures in the text and will try to reach some conclusions about how or why the author uses them.

WRITING COMPARE AND CONTRAST ESSAYS

You may find that comparing and contrasting the works or techniques of an author provides a useful tool for literary analysis. For example, a compare and contrast essay might compare two characters or themes within a single work, or it might compare the author's treatment of the same theme in two different works. It might also contrast methods of character development or analyze an author's differing treatment of a philosophical concern in two works.

Writing compare and contrast essays requires some special consideration. Although such essays may provide you with plenty of material to use, they also present a built-in trap: the "laundry list" approach to writing. These papers often become mere lists of points of comparison. A strong thesis must make *assertions* that the essay attempts to prove or validate. To do that, the essay must comment on the *significance* of the similarities and differences that you observe. It is not enough merely to show that works contain similarities and differences. You must show *why* those similarities and differences are important, try to account for how they come about, and explain how they illuminate themes.

Remember, too, that a thesis should not be merely a statement of the obvious. A compare and contrast paper that focuses only on obvious similarities or differences does little to illuminate connections within or among works. Often, an effective method of shaping a strong thesis and argument is to begin your paper by noting the similarities among the works and then to develop a thesis that asserts how these apparently similar elements are different. For example, if you were to observe that Mark Twain uses the narrative voices of greenhorns in both *Roughing It* and *Life on the Mississippi*'s piloting chapters, you might analyze what makes their processes of maturing different.

Similarly, Mark Twain created many "mysterious stranger" characters, outsiders with special powers who enter communities and transform them. He made his most extensive use of such characters in a series of unfinished novels that were posthumously published, but similar "stranger" figures appear in many of his other works, including *A Connecticut Yankee in King Arthur's Court* and "The Man That Corrupted Hadleyburg." A comparison between the title characters of one or both of those works with the stranger of a work such as *No. 44, The Mysterious Stranger* could be the basis of an interesting essay. Such an essay should begin by identifying the characteristics that the stranger figures have in common and then go on to analyze the aspects of their motivation and behavior that separate them. Every time you strive to analyze similarities and differences, you should discuss significance. Again, to move beyond the obvious, your paper must move beyond the laundry-list trap.

PREPARING TO WRITE

Armed with a clear sense of your task—illuminating the text—and with an understanding of theme, character, language, history, and philosophy, you are ready to approach the writing process. Remember that good writing is grounded in good reading and that close reading takes time, attention, and more than a single reading of a text. Read for comprehension first. As you go back and review a work, mark the text to chart the details of the work as well as your reactions. Use a pencil to draw boxes around important passages, repeated words, and image patterns. "Converse" with the text through marginal notes. Mark turns in the plot, ask questions, and make observations about characters, themes, and language. If you are reading a book that you cannot mark because it does not belong to you, record your reactions in a journal or notebook. If you are handy with a computer, consider supplementing your reading of printed texts with computer searches of electronic texts for key words. Electronic texts of all the Mark Twain works covered in this volume are freely available online at Project Gutenberg (www.gutenburg.org) and at other sites.

If you have read a work of literature carefully, with attention to both the text and the context, you have a leg up on the writing process. Admittedly, at this point, your ideas are probably broad and undefined, but you have taken an important first step toward writing a strong paper.

Your next step is to focus, to take a broad, perhaps fuzzy, topic and define it more clearly. Even a topic assigned by your instructor may need to be focused appropriately. Remember that good writers make whatever topics on which they write their own. There are a number of strategies—often called "invention"—that you can use to develop your own focus. In one such strategy, *freewriting,* you spend 10 minutes or so simply writing about your topic without referring back to the text or even your notes. Write whatever comes to mind; the important thing is that you write. Often this process allows you to develop new, fresh ideas or approaches to your subject matter. You could also try *brainstorming.* Write down your topic and then list all the related points or ideas you can think of. Include questions, comments, words, important passages or events, and anything else that comes to mind. Let one idea lead to another. In the related technique of *clustering* or *mapping,* write your topic on a sheet of paper and write related ideas around it. Then list related subpoints under each of these main ideas. Many people then draw arrows to show connections between points. This technique helps narrow your topic and can also help organize your ideas. Similarly, asking journalistic questions—who? what? where? when? why? and how?—can develop ideas for topic development.

Thesis Statements

Once you have developed a focused topic, you can begin to think about your thesis statement, which is the main point or purpose of your paper. If your paper lacks a strong thesis, it is likely to develop into little more than random, disorganized observations about the text. Think of your thesis statement as a kind of road map of your paper. It tells both you and your readers where you are going and how you are going to get there.

To craft a good thesis, keep a number of things in mind. First, as the title of this subsection indicates, your paper's thesis should be a *statement,* an assertion about the text that you intend to prove or validate. Beginning writers often formulate questions that they attempt to use as theses. For example, a writer exploring the title character of Mark Twain's *Pudd'nhead Wilson* might ask what makes David Wilson a "pudd'nhead" and whether the derogatory nickname has any basis in fact. Asking questions such as these is a good strategy to apply to the invention process to help narrow your topic and find your thesis, but it cannot serve as the thesis statement because it does not tell your readers what you want to assert about Wilson.

A writer might shape the question about Wilson into a thesis by instead proposing an answer to those questions: Although the novel's brilliant lawyer David Wilson eventually convinces fellow villagers he is not the "puddinghead" they think him to be, facets of his life story suggest that either he really is a fool in other ways or that his life has been a tragic waste. Notice that this thesis statement provides an initial plan, or structure, for the rest of the paper, and the statement need not fit into one sentence. After establishing the basis for Wilson's reputation as a puddinghead and the reasons why he eventually sheds that reputation, the essay writer might next examine evidence demonstrating that Wilson is indeed either a fool or a tragic figure.

Remember that a good thesis makes an assertion that requires support because it does not state the obvious. A paper trying to formulate a thesis about Wilson by saying "*Pudd'nhead Wilson*'s title character is regarded as a fool" is simply stating the obvious. To develop your thesis, you must ask yourself a series of questions, such as: Why is Wilson regarded as a fool? Does he deserve that reputation? How does it affect his life? What does he do to change people's opinions of him? Is it possible there is something wrong about him? Such questions can help direct formulation of a fuller thesis.

As the road map analogy also suggests, your thesis should appear near the beginning of the paper. In relatively short papers (three to six pages) the thesis almost always appears in the first paragraph. Some writers fall into the trap of saving their thesis for the end, hoping to achieve a startling moment of revelation, as if to say, "I'll bet you never suspected that Wilson may be a fool, after all!" In some kinds of writing, such surprise endings serve a valid purpose. However, placing your thesis at the end of a school essay can seriously mar the essay's effectiveness. If you fail to clearly define your essay's point and purpose at the beginning, readers will have difficulty assessing the arguments leading up to your conclusion and understanding points you make along the way. Presenting your thesis at the end forces your readers to re-read your essay to assess its logic and effectiveness.

Another kind of mistake to avoid is using the first-person voice ("I"). It is not strictly wrong to write in the first person, but it is difficult to do so gracefully. Beginning writers using the first person often fall into the trap of writing self-reflexive prose; that is, they tend to write *about* their paper *within* their paper. This can lead to that most hackneyed of opening essay sentences: "In this paper I am going to discuss . . ."

A self-reflexive voice not only makes for awkward prose, it frequently tricks beginning writers into boldly announcing a topic while avoiding a thesis statement. An example might be a paper that begins:

```
Mark Twain's novel The Tragedy of Pudd'nhead Wilson
traces the career of David Wilson, a Missouri attorney
whom villagers regard as a harmless fool until he proves
himself in a spectacular murder trial. In this paper I
will consider whether Wilson really is a fool anyway.
```

The author of this paper does little more than announce a topic for the paper (the question of whether Wilson is a fool). The author may intend the last sentence as a thesis but fails to present an opinion about why Wilson may be a fool. An improved thesis would indicate *why* Wilson may be a fool, so that readers will know in what direction the paper is headed and be able to follow its reasoning.

Outlines

Developing a strong, thoughtful thesis early in your writing process should help focus your paper. Outlining provides another essential tool for logically shaping that paper. A good outline helps you see—and develop—relationships among points in your argument and ensures that your paper flows logically and coherently. Outlining not only helps to place points in a logical order, it also helps you arrange subordinate supporting points, weed out irrelevant points, and determine whether important points may be missing from your argument. Most students are familiar with formal outlines that use numerical and letter designations for each point. Remember, though, that there are different types of outlines; an informal, unnumbered outline can also be a useful tool. What really matters is that you spend time developing some form of outline—formal or informal. Think of an outline as a tool that helps you shape and write a strong paper. The more good tools you use, the easier it will be to write a strong paper.

If you don't spend sufficient time planning your paper's supporting points and shaping the arrangement of those points, you will most likely construct a vague, unfocused outline that provides little, if any, help with the writing of the paper. Consider the following example:

Thesis: After more than 20 years of being regarded by townspeople as a puddingheaded fool, attorney David Wilson proves his brilliance in a spectacular murder trial and is finally recognized as an exceptional man. However, an appraisal of his life shows that he may really be a fool or have psychological problems and that his wasted life is the true tragedy of the novel.

    I. Introduction and thesis

   II. Evidence showing Wilson really is a fool
          A. Evidence of antisocial behavior
          B. Remaining where he's not appreciated
          C. Near-bungling of his fingerprint evidence

  III. Wilson's reputation
          A. Why he's called a "pudd'nhead"
          B. His odd hobbies
          C. His background

   IV. Wilson's triumphs
          A. The duel
          B. The murder trial

    V. Tragedy
          A. What the term means
          B. Ambiguities about the novel's title
          C. Is the book really a "tragedy"?

   VI. Novel's tragic characters
          A. York Driscoll
          B. Roxy
          C. Wilson

  VII. Conclusion

This outline might be useful as a starting tool for summarizing important points. However, it will *not* serve well as a practical road map for organizing an actual essay and must be revised before proceeding. The outlined points are all relevant, but they are not arranged in an order that will direct a writer step by logical step to the essay's conclusion, namely, that even though Wilson finally wins his community's admiration and sheds his reputation as a pudd'nhead, he may still be a fool. The best way to begin is by rearranging the outline's main headings—roman numerals I–VI.

   After stating a paper's thesis, it is usually wise to proceed by defining the terms most relevant to the core issue of that thesis. This paper aims to argue that Wilson's wasted life is the novel's central tragedy, so a brief discussion of what is meant by "tragedy" (line V in the above outline) should follow the first entry. Keep in mind that many terms have multiple meanings and be careful not to lock yourself into a narrow dictionary definition that may not apply to your thesis. Find a definition that is relevant and then use the term consistently to conform to that definition.

After the paper establishes what it means by "tragedy," the next logical step would be to survey characters and determine which is the novel's true figure of tragedy (line VI). It should be obvious that the paper will eliminate all the candidates except Wilson, the rest of the paper will focus on him. A logical order in which to present evidence would be to begin by showing why people regard Wilson a fool (line III) and then show what changed his reputation (line IV). The paper would finally survey evidence that Wilson really is a fool (line II) and then wrap up its argument in the Conclusion (line VII).

The revised outline should look more like this:

```
      I.  Introduction and thesis

     II.  Tragedy
              A. What the term means
              B. Ambiguities about the novel's title
              C. Is the book really a "tragedy"?

    III.  Novel's tragic characters
              A. York Driscoll
              B. Roxy
              C. Wilson

     IV.  Wilson's reputation
              A. Why he's called a "pudd'nhead"
              B. Odd hobbies
              C. His background

      V.  Wilson's triumphs
              A. The duel
              B. The murder trial
```

   VI. Evidence that Wilson really is a fool
      A. Evidence of antisocial behavior
      B. Remaining where he's not appreciated
      C. Near-bungling of his fingerprint evidence

  VII. Conclusion

This new outline will prove much more helpful when it comes time to write the paper. As a road map, it now contains all the main highways and most of the major surface streets. However, it would be an even more useful tool if it were to add specific examples to support each point. A more complete outline might look like this:

    I. Introduction and thesis

   II. Tragedy
      A. What the term means
      B. Ambiguities about the novel's title
      C. Is the book really a "tragedy"?

  III. Novel's tragic characters
      A. York Driscoll
      B. Roxy
      C. Wilson

  IV. Wilson's reputation
      A. Why he's called a "pudd'nhead"
        1. Viewed suspiciously as an outsider
        2. Inscrutable remark about a dog
      B. Odd hobbies
        1. Palmistry
        2. Maxims
      C. His background

   V. Wilson's triumphs
      A. The duel
        1. Earns new respect
        2. Is invited to run for mayor and wins

     B. The murder trial
       1. Proves Luigi innocent
       2. Proves Tom Driscoll guilty
       3. Proves that Tom and slave Chambers
         were switched during infancy

  VI. Evidence that Wilson really is a fool
     A. Evidence of antisocial behavior
       1. living on outskirts of town
       2. never marrying
     B. Remaining where he's not appreciated
       1. A northerner in a southern town
       2. Not allowed to practice his profession
     C. Near-bungling of his fingerprint evidence
       1. Doesn't compare prints on murder
         weapon with prints in his files
         until after trial is underway
       2. Never before compares prints of
         infant Tom and Chambers

  VII. Conclusion

The outline is now like a map with all the highways, main surface streets, and connector roads and is a sufficient guide for the essayist to get started writing. However, it would be yet more helpful to add notes on relevant quotes (with page citations) and incidents on which to draw while writing the essay. Such a detailed outline would be like a road map that marks all the rest stops, places of interest, and other useful details. If you follow your outline's directions, they should lead you to the conclusion, which may require merely a summing up of the main points built throughout the essay.

Body Paragraphs

Once your outline is complete, you can begin drafting your paper. Paragraphs, units of related sentences, are the building blocks of a good paper, and as you draft your paper you should keep in mind both the function and the qualities of good paragraphs. Paragraphs help you chart and control the shape and content of your essay, and they help readers see your organization and your logic. You should begin a new paragraph whenever you move from one major point to another, and each paragraph should be able, or nearly able, to stand on its own. In longer, more complex essays, you might use a group of related paragraphs to help support major points. Remember that in addition to being adequately developed, a good paragraph is both unified and coherent. If you suspect that a paragraph may be overly long, it is probably a good idea to break it up. If you do that, make sure that the section you have broken off begins with a sentence that clearly identifies its subject.

Unified Paragraphs

Each paragraph should be centralized around one idea or point, and a unified paragraph carefully focuses on and develops this central idea without including extraneous thoughts. It may help to think of each paragraph as a mini-essay. For beginning writers, a good way to ensure that you build unified paragraphs is to include a topic sentence in each paragraph. This topic sentence should convey the main point of the paragraph, and every sentence in the paragraph should relate back to it. Any sentence that strays from the central topic does not belong in the paragraph and needs to be revised or deleted.

Consider the following paragraph about Wilson's eccentricities. Notice how it veers from the central point established by the topic sentence with which it opens:

> Among the reasons villagers consider Wilson eccentric are his odd interests, some of which reveal disturbing aspects of his personality. For example, he busies himself with hobbies such as writing enigmatic maxims, most of which are used as chapter headings credited to "Pudd'nhead Wilson's Calendar." Some of his maxims suggest that he might make an interesting case study for a psychiatrist. For example, the one heading chapter 9 reads, "Why is it that we rejoice at a birth and grieve at a funeral? It is because we are not the person involved." Is that a cry for help? On the other hand, many maxims are both clever and amusing. For example, chapter 5 opens with "Training is everything. The peach

was once a bitter almond; cauliflower is nothing but
cabbage with a college education." Linking "cabbage" and
"college education" is funny, but this maxim actually
makes a point relevant to the chapter 5 account of Tom
Driscoll's college education. It might also be read as a
subtle allusion to David Wilson's college education.

The maxim about cabbage is interesting but irrelevant to the topic sentence's point and fails to explain what the maxim has to do with Wilson's education. By sidetracking readers, the paragraph's last several sentences weaken the paragraph's argument. The cabbage maxim should be omitted and replaced by a more relevant example.

Coherent Paragraphs

In addition to shaping unified paragraphs, you must also craft coherent paragraphs, paragraphs that develop their points logically with sentences that flow smoothly into one another. Coherence depends on the order of your sentences, but it is not strictly the order of the sentences that is important to paragraph coherence. You also need to craft your prose to help readers see connections between sentences.

Consider the paragraph below about Wilson as an undiscovered genius. It expresses the same ideas as the paragraph that follows it, but neglects to help readers see relationships between points:

Wilson is an example of one of Mark Twain's favorite
themes: undiscovered genius—the notion that a person's
greatness may never become known because he never has an
opportunity to display his talent. Mark Twain's *Extract
from Captain Stormfield's Visit to Heaven* (1909) mentions
men recognized as great in heaven who are unknown to
human history because they never had opportunities
to demonstrate their greatness. Wilson's genius is
recognized at the end. During the preceding two decades,
his neighbors fail to recognize his abilities. They also
treat him as a fool. He abandons his efforts to practice
law in Dawson's Landing and lives a quiet, marginalized
existence, doing odd surveying and bookkeeping jobs,

while pursuing his hobby of collecting "finger marks"
of villagers on glass slides. That latter pursuit
reinforces the villagers' opinion of him as a fool.

This paragraph demonstrates that unity alone does not guarantee paragraph effectiveness. The argument is hard to follow because the author fails both to show connections between the sentences and to indicate how they work to support the overall point. Notice how much stronger and easier to follow the next paragraph is with better transitions to link sentences:

Wilson is an example of one of Mark Twain's favorite
themes: undiscovered genius—the notion that a person's
greatness may never become known because he never has
an opportunity to display his talent. For example,
Mark Twain's *Extract from Captain Stormfield's Visit
to Heaven* (1909) mentions men recognized as great in
heaven who are unknown to human history because they
never had opportunities to demonstrate their greatness
(Rasmussen, 60). Wilson is luckier. His genius is
finally recognized at the end. However, during the two
decades leading up to that moment, his neighbors not
only fail to recognize his abilities, they also treat
him as a fool. Through those years, he abandons his
efforts to practice law in Dawson's Landing and lives
a quiet, marginalized existence, doing odd surveying
and bookkeeping jobs, while pursuing his hobby of
collecting "finger marks" of villagers on glass slides—
a pursuit that reinforces the villagers' opinion of
him as a fool.

A variety of techniques are available to strengthen paragraph coherence. Careful use of transitional words and phrases is essential. You can use transitional "flags" to introduce examples or illustrations (*for example, for instance*); to amplify points or add other phrases of the same idea (*additionally, furthermore, next, similarly, finally, then*); to indicate conclusions or results (*therefore, as a result, thus, in other words*); to signal contrasts or qualifications (*on the other hand, nevertheless, despite this, on the contrary, still, however, conversely*); to signal comparisons (*likewise, in comparison, similarly*); and to indicate movements in time (*afterward, earlier, eventually, finally, later, subsequently, until*). Sometimes the best way to link sentences is to run them together, connecting them with appropriate transitional words. Be careful, however, not to let your sentence grow too long. The longer a sentence is, the more likely it is that something will go wrong. When that happens, the point of the sentence is certain to be less clear.

In addition to transitional flags, careful use of pronouns aids coherence and flow. If you were writing about *The Prince and the Pauper,* you would not want to keep repeating a phrase such as "the prince" or the name "Miles Hendon." Careful substitution of the pronoun "he" can aid coherence. A word of warning: Whenever you substitute pronouns for proper names, always be sure your pronoun references are clear. In a paragraph discussing both Prince Edward and Miles Hendon, substituting "he" for one or both names may lead to confusion. Make sure that it is clear to whom each pronoun refers. Generally, a pronoun for a person refers back to the last proper name that is used, but if the name for which the pronoun is a substitute is more than one sentence back, it is better to spell out the person's name. In fact, in general, when you are in doubt, spell out the name; it is better to be mildly redundant than ambiguous. Another firm rule to follow is *never* to begin paragraphs with pronouns or use any pronouns in paragraphs that require readers to refer back to previous paragraphs to identify references.

Repeating the same name over and over can lead to awkward, boring prose, but it is possible to use repetition to sustain your paragraph's coherence. Careful repetition of important words or phrases often lends coherence to a paragraph by helping remind readers of key points. However, it takes some practice to use this technique effectively. To test the flow of your prose, read it aloud. Reading silently (especially from a computer screen) will miss many problems in sentences that reading aloud will catch. If you get in the habit of reading aloud (and correcting) your own prose, your writing will improve as you develop an ear for effective use of repetition and other aspects of the rhythm of your prose.

Introductions

Introductions and conclusions present particular challenges for writers. Generally, your introduction should do two things: capture your readers' attention and explain the main points of your essay. In other words, your introduction needs to do more than merely present your thesis. You may find that starting the essay's first paragraph is one of the most difficult parts of the paper. It is hard to face a blank page or screen. Many beginning writers, desperate to begin somewhere, start with overly broad, general statements. Although it is often a good strategy to open with broad, general subject matter and then narrow your focus, it can be a mistake to begin with an overly broad and sweeping statement, such as "Color is important to everyone," or "Throughout the history of literature, many authors have used color to express their points." Such empty sentences do little more than fill blank pages but contribute nothing to advancing your argument. To gain their readers' interest, some writers begin with pertinent quotations or intriguing questions.

Or, you might begin with an introduction of the topic you will discuss. If you were to write about Hawthorne's use of color in "Young Goodman Brown," for instance, you might begin by talking about color symbolism in Western culture. Another common trap to avoid is depending on your title to introduce the author and the text you are writing about. Always include the work's author and title in your opening paragraph.

Compare the effectiveness of the following introductions:

1. Throughout history, colors have had significance. For example, think about red, white, and black. In this story, Hawthorne uses color to reflect his belief that humans are a mixture of evil and purity.

2. In many cultures particular colors carry specific meanings. Western culture is no exception. Colors convey meaning to us even though we are often not consciously aware of these meanings. White signals purity. Brides and babies wear white. Red signals danger or sexuality. Think about bullfighters' capes or Little Red Riding Hood's

cloak. Often writers incorporate these color codes
into their works to reinforce their meanings. In
"Young Goodman Brown," Nathaniel Hawthorne uses
color codes to reflect his belief that humans are
neither evil nor pure, but a mixture of both.

The first introduction begins with a boring, overly broad sentence, cites unclear, undeveloped examples, and then moves abruptly to the thesis. Notice, too, how readers deprived of the paper's title do not know the title of the story that the paper will analyze. The second introduction works with the same material and thesis, but provides more detail, and is, consequently, much more interesting. It begins by discussing cultural uses of color, gives specific examples, and then speaks briefly about the use of color symbolism in literature. The paragraph ends with the thesis, which includes both the author and the title of the work to be discussed.

The paragraph below provides another example of an opening strategy. It begins by introducing the author and the text it will analyze and then moves on to introduce relevant details of the story and set up its thesis:

The story of a 19th-century American transported to
sixth-century England, Mark Twain's *A Connecticut Yankee
in King Arthur's Court* is often credited with being
the first true time-travel story. Its 1889 publication
date follows by one year the first edition of Edward
Bellamy's *Looking Backward, 2000–1887,* a story about
another 19th-century man who travels a century into
the future, but Bellamy's book is not widely recognized
as conforming to the conventions of a science-fiction
time-travel story. Its protagonist reaches the future
merely by awakening after a long sleep, and he never
returns to his own time. It might therefore be said
that he does not actually "travel" through time. By
contrast, Hank Morgan, Mark Twain's protagonist, is
suddenly transported 13 centuries into the past and
later returns to the 19th century. Is his story, however,
any more a true time-travel story than Bellamy's? Mark

Twain offers no explanation of how Morgan travels back in time, and the method he uses to return Morgan to his own time is exactly the same as that which Bellamy uses to send his protagonist into the future: Morgan simply awakens in the 19th century after a long sleep. It can therefore be argued that *A Connecticut Yankee* is no more a true time-travel story than *Looking Backward*. To confirm that hypothesis, we must first establish what conventions constitute a science-fiction time-travel story and then determine how they apply to *A Connecticut Yankee*.

Conclusions

Conclusions present another series of challenges for writers. Possibly you have heard the old adage about writing papers: "Tell us what you are going to say, say it, and then tell us what you've said." Although this formula does not necessarily lead to bad papers, it does not necessarily lead to good ones either. It will almost certainly result in boring papers (especially boring conclusions). If you have done a good job establishing your points in the body of the paper, readers already know and understand your argument. There is no need to merely reiterate. Do not simply summarize your main points in your conclusion. Such a boring and mechanical conclusion does nothing to advance your argument or interest your readers. Consider the following conclusion to the paper about color in "Young Goodman Brown":

> In conclusion, Hawthorne uses the colors brown, pink, black, and red to tell his reader a lot about humanity. Faith's ribbons are pink, a mixture of red and white. They indicate that even at our best, humanity is not wholly good. Young Goodman Brown's last name, Brown, indicates the same about him.

Besides starting with a mechanical and obvious transitional device, this conclusion does little more than summarize the main points of the outline (and it does not even touch on all of them). It is incomplete and uninteresting.

Instead, your conclusion should add something to your paper. A good tactic is to build upon the points you have been arguing. Asking why? often helps to draw further conclusions. For example, in the paper discussed above, you might speculate or explain why color symbolism is effective in "Young Goodman Brown." Since scholars often discuss this story as an allegory, you could discuss the allegorical use of color. Another method of successfully concluding a paper is to speculate on other directions in which to take your topic, tie it into larger issues. It might help to envision your paper as just one section of a larger paper. Having established your points in this paper, how would you build upon this argument? Where would you go next? In the following conclusion to the paper on "Young Goodman Brown," the author reiterates some of the main points of the paper, but does so to amplify the discussion of the story's theological message.

> In the end, neither Faith nor Young Goodman Brown is completely pure. Hawthorne's use of pink and brown emphasizes this. But his point is larger. Brown's real problem is not that he contains both good and evil, faith and doubt, but that he has let doubt prevail. Once he returns to the village he believes himself faithful, while he doubts every other member of his community. The narrator describes Faith as joyful, the minister as "venerable," and Goody Cloyse as an "excellent old Christian," yet Brown "shrank" from them. In losing faith in others, Brown denies himself one good and necessary thing: human community. Finally, as if to emphasize that Brown's lost faith has taught him incorrectly, the narrator refers to Brown as "a stern, a sad, a darkly meditative, a distrustful, if not a desperate man."

Citations and Formatting
Using Primary Sources
As examples included in this chapter indicate, strong papers on literary texts incorporate quotations from the text to support their points. It is not enough simply to assert your interpretation without providing support or evidence from the text. Without well-chosen quotations to support your argument you are, in effect, just saying to readers, "take my

word for it." It's important to use quotations thoughtfully and selectively. Remember that the paper presents your argument, so choose quotations that support your assertions. Do not let the author's voice overwhelm your own. With that caution in mind, there are some guidelines you should follow to ensure that you use quotations clearly and effectively.

Integrate Quotations

Quotations should always be integrated into your own prose. Do not just drop them into your paper without introduction or comment. Otherwise, it is unlikely that your readers will see their function. You can integrate textual support easily and clearly with identifying tags, short phrases that identify the speaker. For example:

> The narrator calls Young Goodman Brown "a stern, a sad, a darkly meditative, a distrustful, if not a desperate man."

Although this tag appears before the quotation, you can also use tags after or in the middle of the quoted text, as the following examples demonstrate:

> "Evil is the nature of mankind," claims the devil.

> "I helped your grandfather, the constable, when he lashed the Quaker woman so smartly through the streets of Salem," the devil tells Brown. "And it was I that brought your father a pitch-pine knot, kindled at my own hearth, to set fire to an Indian village, in King Philip's war."

You can also use a colon to formally introduce a quotation:

> Aylmer's conceit is clear: "Doubt not my power."

When you quote brief sections of poems (three lines or fewer), use slash marks to indicate the line breaks in the poem:

> Emmeline Grangerford's poem about Stephen Dowling Bots ends with an allusion to the boy's fate: "His spirit

was gone for to sport aloft / In the realms of the good
and great."

Longer quotations (more than four lines of prose or three lines of
poetry) should be set off from the rest of your text in block quotations. Double-space before you begin the quotes, indent (not "tab")
them one-half inch from the left-hand margin, and double-space the
quote itself. Because the indentations themselves signify inclusion
of quotations, do not use quotation marks around cited passages,
unless the quotation marks themselves are part of the quoted text.
Use colons to introduce the passages, as in this example of a prose
quotation:

When Tom sets off to perform his chore, melancholy soon
overtakes him:

> Tom appeared on the sidewalk with a bucket of
> whitewash and a long-handled brush. He surveyed
> the fence, and all gladness left him and a deep
> melancholy settled down upon his spirit. Thirty
> yards of board fence, nine feet high. Life to him
> seemed hollow, and existence but a burden.

In that single passage, Mark Twain uses five different
phrases to describe Tom's melancholy.

Note that block poetry quotes do not require slashes to indicate separate
lines:

Emmeline Grangerford's verses about Stephen Dowling
Bots reveal her obsession with death:

> O No. Then list with tearful eye,
> Whilst I his fate do tell.
>
> His soul did from this cold world fly,
> By falling down a well.

```
She seems almost to revel in her explicit description
of Stephen's death.
```

As in these examples, it is useful to follow block quotations immediately with at least brief interpretative remarks that advance points the quotes are supposed to support. Do not assume that readers will interpret quotations the same way you do.

Quote Accurately

Always quote accurately. Any text you use within quotations marks or blocks must reflect its author's *exact* words. There are, however, some rules to follow if you must modify the quotation to fit into your prose.

1. Use square brackets to indicate material you insert in the original text to add essential information, such as a proper name after a pronoun or transitional phrase substituting for deleted text:

   ```
   As a result of his encounter in the woods,
   Brown becomes, "more conscious of the secret
   guilt of others, both in deed and thought, than
   [he] could now be of [his] own."
   ```

2. Conversely, if you choose to omit any words from the quotation (which is often a good idea to save space and remove irrelevant distractions), use ellipses (three spaced periods following a space) to indicate missing text. It is also a good idea to use an ellipsis at the end of a sentence that is incomplete:

   ```
   You don't know about me, without you have read
   a book by the name of "The Adventures of Tom
   Sawyer," but that ain't no matter. That book was
   made by Mr. Mark Twain, and he told the truth,
   mainly. There was things which he stretched,
   but mainly he told the truth. . . . Aunt Polly
   . . . and Mary, and the Widow Douglas, is all
   told about in that book . . .
   ```

Note that an ellipsis has exactly three periods and is preceded by a space. In the above example, the ellipsis following "told the truth" is preceded a period that ends a sentence. Technically that period is not part of the three-point ellipsis, but sometimes a period followed by an ellipsis is called a four-point ellipsis.

Punctuate Quotations Properly

Punctuation of quotations often causes more trouble than it should. Once again, you merely need to keep a few basic rules in mind.

1. Periods and commas should be placed *inside* quotation marks, even if they are not part of the original quotation:

   ```
   "I wish I owned half that dog."
   ```

   The only exception to this rule is when the quotation is followed by a parenthetical reference. In this case, the period or comma goes after the citation (more on these later in this chapter):

   ```
   "I wish I owned half that dog" (24).
   ```

2. Other marks of punctuation—colons, semicolons, question marks, and exclamation points—go *outside* the quotation marks unless they are part of the original quotation:

   ```
   The older man challenges the younger man's airs
   by asking, "'Dern your skin, ain't the company
   good enough for you?'" (question mark is part
   of quoted text)

   Does Huck fully understand what it means to say,
   "'All right, then, I'll go to hell'"? (question
   mark is added by essayist)
   ```

Note that both examples use double quotes to indicate quotes of text that appears within quotations marks in the original sources.

Documenting Primary Sources

Unless you are instructed otherwise, you should provide sufficient information for your readers to locate material you quote. Generally, literature papers follow rules established by the Modern Language Association. These can be found in the *MLA Handbook for Writers of Research Papers* (sixth edition). This book should be in most library reference sections.

The MLA rules for citing sources are widely available from reputable online sources. One source is the Online Writing Lab (OWL) of Purdue University. The URL (universal resource locator) for OWL's guide to MLA style is owl.english.purdue.edu/owl/resource/557/01/. The Modern Language Association also answers frequently asked questions (FAQs) about MLA style on its helpful Web page at www.mla.org/style_faq. Generally, when you cite from literary works in papers, you should keep a few guidelines in mind.

Parenthetical Source Citations

MLA asks for parenthetical source references in your text after quotations. When you work with prose (short stories, novels, or essays), include page numbers in the parentheses:

```
Wilson "often studied his records, examining and poring
over them with absorbing interest" (29).
```

Note that it is not necessary to use "page" or "p."

Works Cited Page

Parenthetical citations are linked to a separate "Bibliography" or "Works Cited" page at the end of the paper. This page lists all works cited alphabetically by authors' last names. An entry for the above reference to Mark Twain's *Pudd'nhead Wilson* should read:

```
Twain, Mark. The Tragedy of Pudd'nhead Wilson and the
Comedy Those Extraordinary Twins. New York: Oxford,
1996. Facsimile reprint; originally published 1894.
```

In this example, 1894 is the date of the book's original publication, and 1996 is the publication date for the edition actually used. The words

"Facsimile reprint" indicate that the Oxford edition is a photographically reproduced copy of the first edition.

The *MLA Handbook* includes a full listing of sample entries, as do many online explanations of MLA style.

Documenting Secondary Sources

To ensure your paper is built entirely on your own ideas and analysis, literature instructors may ask you to write interpretative papers without any outside research. If, on the other hand, your paper requires research, you must document any secondary sources (sources other than the text you are analyzing) you use. Always document direct quotations, summaries or paraphrases of other's ideas, and factual information that is not common knowledge. Follow the guidelines above for quoting primary sources when you use direct quotations from secondary sources. MLA style also includes specific guidelines for citing electronic sources. OWL's Web site provides a nice summary at owl.english.purdue.edu/owl/resource/557/09/.

Parenthetical Citations

As with the documentation of primary sources, described above, MLA guidelines require in-text parenthetical references to your secondary sources. Unlike the research papers you might write for a history class, literary research papers following MLA style do not use footnotes or endnotes to document their sources. For example, after a quotation, you would type the last name of the author of the secondary source you wish to cite and the relevant page number or numbers:

```
Mark Twain is believed to have modeled the fictional
David Wilson on a real Missouri lawyer named Samuel
Taylor Glover (Rasmussen 518).
```

If you mention the author's name in your prose, then you need include only the page number in your citation:

```
According to Rasmussen, Mark Twain is believed to have
modeled the fictional David Wilson on a real Missouri
lawyer named Samuel Taylor Glover (518).
```

If your list of cited sources includes more than one work by the same author, parenthetical citations to that author should include enough identifiable words from each title to indicate which of the author's works is cited:

> According to Rasmussen, Mark Twain is believed to have modeled the fictional David Wilson on a real Missouri lawyer named Samuel Taylor Glover (*A to Z* 518).

If the author is not mentioned, you would use "(Rasmussen, *A to Z* 518)."

Like direct quotations, paraphrases and summaries of another writer's ideas must also be documented:

> Extract from *Captain Stormfield's Visit to Heaven* mentions men whom heaven recognizes as great who are unknown to human history because they never had opportunities to demonstrate their greatness (Rasmussen 60).

Works Cited Page

As with the primary sources discussed above, the parenthetical references are keyed to a separate works cited page at the end of your paper. This example of such a page uses representative entries from chapters in the present volume. Complete lists of sample entries appear in the *MLA Handbook* and on reputable online summaries of MLA style.

WORKS CITED

Burto, Barnet Berman. *A Dictionary of Literary, Dramatic, and Cinematic Terms.* 2d ed. Boston: Little, Brown, 1971.

Pinckney, Darryl. Introduction and Notes. In *Pudd'nhead Wilson and Those Extraordinary Twins*, by Mark Twain (New York: Barnes & Noble Classics, 2005): xv–xl.

Railton, Stephen. "The Tragedy of Mark Twain, by Pudd'nhead Wilson." *Nineteenth-Century Literature* 56, no. 4 (March 2002): 519–544.

Rasmussen, R. Kent. *Mark Twain A to Z.* New York: Facts On File, 1995.

Smith, David L. Afterword. In *The Tragedy of Pudd'nhead Wilson and the Comedy Those Extraordinary Twins*, by Mark Twain (New York: Oxford University Press, 1996): 1–17 (back pages).

Plagiarism

Failure to document your sources fully and accurately can leave you open to charges of stealing the ideas of others—a practice called plagiarism. This is a serious matter and should not be taken lightly, even if you are writing a paper that only one other person will read. If the desire to do the right thing is insufficient motivation to make you avoid plagiarizing, keep in mind that teachers and editors can be remarkably adept at sniffing out possible plagiarism and that in the modern age of computer text-searching and the Internet, detecting plagiarism is easier than ever before. Why risk getting caught, when it is so simple not to plagiarize? In any case, what satisfaction can you have in claiming someone else's ideas as your own?

A first step in avoiding plagiarism is remembering always to use quotation marks to enclose words taken directly from other sources, even if you are quoting only one or two words. For example, if you were to write, without using quotes,

Roxy creates the possibility for David Wilson's ultimate triumph . . .

you would be guilty of plagiarism, since you would be using David L. Smith's distinct language without acknowledging him as your source. Instead, you should write:

Roxy "creates the possibility for David Wilson's ultimate triumph . . ." (Smith 9).

In this case, you clearly identify the borrowed phrase and properly credit it to Smith.

Summarizing the ideas of another author or changing or omitting a few words from a passage may free you from the need for quotations marks, but it does not free you from the obligation of citing your source. Although it is not necessary to document well-known facts that are considered common knowledge, any ideas or language that you take from someone else must be properly documented. Common knowledge generally includes such facts as birth and death dates of authors and other well-documented aspects of their lives. An often-cited rule of thumb is this: If you can find the information in three different sources, it is common knowledge. Despite this guideline, it is, admittedly, often difficult to know if the facts you uncover are common knowledge or not. Moreover, some misinformation is so frequently repeated that it becomes common knowledge, until someone comes along and proves that it is incorrect. When in doubt, document your source.

SAMPLE ESSAY

Kevin Bochynski

English 2A

Miss Ann Blatchford

December 10, 2007

THE TRUE TRAGEDY OF "THE TRAGEDY OF PUDD'NHEAD WILSON"

Mark Twain's 1894 novel *Pudd'nhead Wilson* traces several narrative threads, including the career of its title character, attorney David Wilson. When Wilson first arrives in the Missouri village of Dawson's Landing in 1830, he is regarded with suspicion because he is an outsider. He makes the mistake of uttering an odd remark about a dog and is instantly and permanently branded as "Pudd'nhead Wilson" (26). More than 20 years later, his brilliant defense of a murder suspect finally moves villagers to acknowledge his ability, retract the derogatory nickname they gave him, and reassign it to themselves. After long being regarded as a puddingheaded fool, Wilson is now a genius in their eyes. However, reasons remain to suspect he may actually be a fool, and if not a fool, at least the victim of a tragically wasted life of his own choosing.

Pudd'nhead Wilson is frequently published under the title *The Tragedy of Pudd'nhead Wilson*, but there are serious questions about whether Mark Twain himself intended that title for his book. Regardless of what he may have intended, however, the words "The Tragedy of . . ." do appear atop the title page of his book's first American edition (Rasmussen 372). Someone—either Mark Twain or an editor—clearly regarded the novel as a tragedy. Less clear is *what* that tragedy is.

In its classical literary sense, the term *tragedy* is usually applied to a serious drama that ends with the death of its hero (Burto, 111). That definition seems not to apply to *Pudd'nhead Wilson*, as the only character who dies toward its end is Judge York Driscoll, who is neither the story's hero nor even a major character. A stronger case might be made for Roxy, the slave woman whose decision to swap her infant son, Chambers, with the true Tom Driscoll, her master's son, drives the book's central narrative thread and eventually ends in tragic disaster. Roxy makes the switch so her natural son will grow up as a free man who can never be sold down the river (46). However, her scheme backfires, as her son is sold down the river at the end of the novel. Is Roxy's loss of her son the tragedy to which the novel's full title alludes? Probably not, *The Tragedy of Pudd'nhead Wilson* seems to refer to Wilson himself.

At first glance, Wilson scarcely seems a tragic figure. From his introduction in chapter 1 until he scores his spectacular success in a murder trial in chapter 21, his life appears quiet and free of trouble. Fellow villagers regard him as a puddingheaded fool because of his harmless eccentricities but nevertheless like him. Indeed, when he wins his first public renown for his role as a second in a duel, a committee of villagers invites him to run for mayor (177). After the duel is fought, Wilson becomes "a made man and his success assured" (198), and he later wins the election. Finally, his triumph in the murder trial elevates him to "a made man for good" (300).

Wilson's steady rise from village eccentric to a man of near-genius makes it difficult to find a tragedy in his story. However, if a tragedy cannot be found at the conclusion of his story, might it instead be found in the long, wasted years leading up to his success? Wilson is an example of one of Mark Twain's favorite themes: undiscovered genius—the notion that a person's greatness may never become known because he never has an opportunity to display his talent. For example, Mark Twain's *Extract from Captain Stormfield's Visit to Heaven* (1909) mentions men whom heaven recognizes as great who are unknown to human history because they never had opportunities to demonstrate their greatness (Rasmussen 60). Wilson is luckier. His genius is finally recognized at the end. However, during the two decades leading up to that moment, his neighbors not only fail to recognize his abilities, they also treat him as a fool. Through those years, he abandons his efforts to practice law in Dawson's Landing and lives a quiet, marginalized existence, doing odd surveying and bookkeeping jobs, while pursuing his hobby of collecting "finger marks" of villagers on glass slides—a pursuit that reinforces the villagers' opinion of him as a fool.

Is Wilson really a fool? Perhaps. An underlying question about him that the novel fails to answer is *why* he settles in Dawson's Landing in the first place. Chapter 1 describes him as a "college-bred" native New Yorker who "had finished a post-college course in an Eastern law school a couple of years before" and wandered into Dawson's Landing seeking his fortune (23). One of the "novel's greatest mysteries" is why an intelligent, professionally educated New Yorker would seek his fortune in a place like Dawson's Landing? (Smith 10)

After arriving in town, Wilson buys a house "on the extreme western verge of the town," rents a downtown office, and hangs a sign advertising his services as an attorney-at-law and surveyor (27). Unfortunately, "his deadly remark had ruined his chance—at least in the law. No clients came" (ibid.). He soon shuts down his law office and retreats to his house. Over the ensuing years he gets occasional surveying and bookkeeping jobs, but no law cases. Nevertheless, he keeps up his legal studies. Why does he bother? Moreover, why does he even stay in Dawson's Landing? His choice of living on the extreme edge of town and the fact he never marries suggest that he has no real interest in integrating himself into local society.

Among the reasons villagers consider Wilson eccentric are his odd interests, some of which reveal disturbing aspects of his personality. For example, he busies himself with hobbies such as writing enigmatic maxims, most of which are used as chapter headings credited to "Pudd'nhead Wilson's Calendar." Some of his maxims suggest that he might make an interesting case study for a psychiatrist. For example, the one heading chapter 9 reads, "Why is it that we rejoice at a birth and grieve at a funeral? It is because we are not the person involved" (111). Is that a cry for help? The maxim heading chapter 10 expresses a similar sentiment: "All say, 'How hard it is that we have to die'—a strange complaint to come from the mouths of people who have had to live" (121). That remark hints at Wilson's own personal unhappiness; could he be unconsciously lamenting his wasted life?

Wilson's other favorite hobby is collecting fingerprints. Soon after he arrives in Dawson's Landing, he begins collecting carefully labeled glass slides with villagers' prints. The use of fingerprints for identification was a late 19th-century development that would have been unknown during the period in which *Pudd'nhead Wilson* is set (Rasmussen 138–139). Thus, that hobby and some of Wilson's other pursuits, such as palmistry, merely add to his reputation as an eccentric. Modern readers sympathize with Wilson because they understand the value of fingerprints in ways that early 19th-century Missourians could not. However, exactly what Wilson does with his fingerprint collection remains a mystery for more than 20 years within the context of the novel, which says "He often studied his records, examining and poring over them with absorbing interest until far into the night; but what he found there—if he found anything—he revealed to no one" (29–30).

Wilson finally finds a practical use for his collection during Luigi Capello's murder trial, in which he uses fingerprint evidence to establish Capello's innocence and prove Tom Driscoll's guilt. He also uses fingerprints to prove that Tom and the slave Chambers were switched at birth. All these revelations make Wilson appear to be a genius and cement his new reputation as a "made man." Is he really brilliant, however, or merely lucky?

A curious aspect of Wilson's use of fingerprint evidence in Capello's trial is his failure to use it until the trial is well underway, even though the murder weapon, a bloody knife, is covered with prints he has carefully studied. Only after Tom Driscoll visits him and leaves his own prints on a drinking glass does it dawn on Wilson to compare Driscoll's prints with those on the knife. What he finds astonishes him: Not only do the knife's prints match Driscoll's, but Driscoll's prints match those of the infant slave baby Chambers—whom Wilson now recognizes is the true Tom Driscoll. Why does it take Wilson so long to make that connection? During the trial, he demonstrates his familiarity with his collection is so strong he can identify merely by sight prints made by men on a windowpane. His fingerprint collection contains carefully labeled and dated prints made by Chambers and Driscoll throughout their early years. What exactly is Wilson learning from all the time he spends examining his print collection? How could he not notice that Driscoll and Chambers's prints change after they are a few months old or that their early prints are mixed up?

Something about David Wilson is clearly wrong. Regardless of whether he is a fool or an eccentric genius, he is clearly a man who needs help. For reasons that *Pudd'nhead Wilson* never makes clear, Wilson wastes nearly half his life living on the outskirts of society, scratching for a living at jobs that do not use his professional training and talents, and indulging in hobbies with no evident practical value. His great chance to demonstrate his abilities finally comes when he is engaged to defend a murder suspect. He triumphs, but only after a chance incident moves him to make two sensational discoveries in the fingerprint collection he has spent more than 20 years assembling and studying. His success therefore appears to spring more from luck than from genius. The true "tragedy" of *Pudd'nhead Wilson* may be Wilson's wasted life, but the blame for the many years he has wasted may lie more on him than on the villagers who brand him a fool on the day he arrives in Dawson's Landing.

WORKS CITED

Burto, Barnet Berman. *A Dictionary of Literary, Dramatic, and Cinematic Terms*. 2d ed. Boston: Little, Brown, 1971.

Rasmussen, R. Kent. *Mark Twain A to Z*. New York: Facts On File, 1995.

Smith, David L. Afterword. *The Tragedy of Pudd'nhead Wilson and the Comedy Those Extraordinary Twins*. By Mark Twain. New York: Oxford UP, 1996. 1–17.

Twain, Mark. *The Tragedy of Pudd'nhead Wilson and the Comedy Those Extraordinary Twins*. New York: Oxford UP, 1996. Facsimile reprint; originally published 1894.

HOW TO WRITE ABOUT
MARK TWAIN

AN OVERVIEW

WHEN MARK Twain was working on his autobiography toward the end of his life, he commented on the impermanence of literary works: "In a century we have produced two hundred and twenty thousand books; not a bathtub-full of them are still alive and marketable." That observation is probably not far from the truth. Try to visualize what it means: The average 19th-century American book was about one inch thick; 220,000 such books would form a stack more than three miles high. How many of those books would fit in one bathtub? Now, a century after Mark Twain made that observation, more than 50,000 new books are published in the United States every year. How many of them will be alive and marketable a century from now?

The depressing fact is that most authors are forgotten soon after they pass from the Earth, if not sooner. This is not necessarily because the books they write lack merit; it is more a matter of the changing interests and tastes of readers. One need only look at a list of the best-selling books of 30 years ago to appreciate how quickly most authors are forgotten. Who still reads those books? How many people even recognize their authors' names? What interested readers 30 years ago may not interest readers today, and writing styles that were popular 30 years ago may no longer find favor. Moreover, with so many new books to read every year, who can keep up with all the good books from the past? Readers move on; most authors remain behind.

Given these discouraging statistics about the short life spans of most books, why is it that nearly 100 years after Mark Twain's death in 1910, his books remain very much alive and marketable? Most of them are still in print; some are available in dozens of editions. Clearly, many people still *want* to read Mark Twain, and not merely to satisfy classroom assignments. Indeed, Mark Twain is one of the few authors of the classics whose books may be read as much outside classrooms as within. The explanation for Mark Twain's enduring popularity lies in his timelessness: He is a writer whose books are likely to be read and enjoyed as long as literature endures. When future bathtubs are filled with the books that still live, many of his books will be in them.

A first question to consider about Mark Twain is what it means to say his books are timeless. The short answer is that modern readers enjoy his books now as much as readers did when they first came out during the 19th century. That statement may be true, but it explains nothing. *Why* do modern readers enjoy Mark Twain's books more than those of most other writers of his time? Mark Twain himself could probably not answer that question, as he was a notoriously poor judge of any author's writing, including his own. For example, he vastly overrated the work of his close friend W. D. Howells, the editor of the prestigious *Atlantic Monthly* and author of many respected novels. In an 1879 letter to Howells, he wrote:

> Possibly you will not be a fully accepted classic until you have been dead a hundred years,—it is the fate of the Shakespeares & of all genuine prophets,—but then your books will be as common as Bibles, I believe.

Mark Twain was wrong. In 2020, Howells will have been dead for 100 years, but he is already almost forgotten. In contrast, Howells's own estimation of Mark Twain's future reputation was much more accurate. In *My Mark Twain* (1910), which he wrote shortly after his friend died, Howells famously said:

> Emerson, Longfellow, Lowell, Holmes—I knew them all and all the rest of our sages, poets, seers, critics, humorists; they were like one another

and like other literary men; but Clemens [Mark Twain] was sole, incomparable, the Lincoln of our literature.

What makes that statement interesting is the way that Howells sets Mark Twain apart from other 19th-century literary giants, such as Ralph Waldo Emerson, Henry Wadsworth Longfellow, James Russell Lowell, and Oliver Wendell Holmes. He instead equates Mark Twain with President Abraham Lincoln, who even now is still considered one of the greatest presidents in American history. Like Lincoln, Mark Twain was unique—what Howells calls "sole" and "incomparable." Both men had qualities that distinguished them from the typical great figures in their fields. Moreover, many of the qualities that set Mark Twain apart as a writer are those that make his work endure: the vigor and authenticity of his language, the brilliance and originality of his humor, the power of his philosophical views, and the breadth of his interests. Let us consider this last point first.

There are many reasons why Mark Twain is considered relevant today. About a decade ago, when Professor Shelley Fisher Fishkin was editing the Oxford Mark Twain series (see Bibliography), she marveled at the fact that no matter how much time she invested in studying Mark Twain, she seemed never to grow bored with him. The reason, she gradually understood, was simple: Mark Twain connects with *everything*. There's much truth in that: Think of almost any subject, and the chances are you can find a Mark Twain connection. Not merely a weak, flimsy kind of a connection, but one that is strong and vigorous. Mark Twain had a long and active life. He worked at many different professions; he traveled widely within the United States and abroad; and he knew or corresponded with many of the leading literary figures, artists of all kinds, industrialists, scientists, and political leaders of his time. Even more important, his interests were almost boundless and his imagination even larger. There is scarcely a subject that he encountered that failed to attract his attention, and he wrote either essays or fiction on nearly everything that interested him.

Mark Twain was also exceptionally observant and had an almost unparalleled knack for putting what he saw into words, using well-turned phrases, comic exaggeration, and vivid imagery to bring even dry-as-dust subjects to life. Consider, for example, this simple passage describing a "jackass rabbit" (what we now call a jackrabbit):

> He is well named. He is just like any other rabbit, except that he is from one third to twice as large, has longer legs in proportion to his size, and has the most preposterous ears that ever were mounted on any creature but a jackass. When he is sitting quiet, thinking about his sins, or is absent-minded or unapprehensive of danger, his majestic ears project above him conspicuously; but the breaking of a twig will scare him nearly to death, and then he tilts his ears back gently and starts for home. All you can see, then, for the next minute, is his long gray form stretched out straight and "streaking it" through the low sage-brush, head erect, eyes right, and ears just canted a little to the rear, but showing you where the animal is, all the time, the same as if he carried a jib. Now and then he makes a marvelous spring with his long legs, high over the stunted sage-brush, and scores a leap that would make a horse envious. Presently he comes down to a long, graceful "lope," and shortly he mysteriously disappears (*Roughing It* chapter 3).

Can anyone who reads that passage fail to see the rabbit? In countless other passages Mark Twain conveys similarly rich images of everything interesting that passes before his sharp eyes: animals, landscapes, people, machines, buildings, works of art. Moreover, he does it with language so fresh and vigorous that his prose reads as well today as it did in his time. In contrast to most literary figures of his time, he was singularly free of the kind of affectations that color the prose of writers who strove to imitate genteel literary conventions.

Not only did Mark Twain have an observant eye, he was also an observant listener and a master at reproducing dialects and the natural rhythms of human speech. The naturalness of his prose is especially evident in dialogue and in vernacular narratives, such as that of Huck Finn. The very first sentence of *Huckleberry Finn* alerted 19th-century readers to expect something quite new that went against literary conventions: "You don't know about me, without you have read a book by the name of 'The Adventures of Tom Sawyer,' but that ain't no matter." The sentence may be ungrammatical, but it sounds like something a real boy might have said.

Mark Twain especially delighted in emphasizing contrasts between the vocabularies and idioms of people in different professions or from different regions. For example, *Roughing It* (1872) contains a conversation between Scotty Briggs, a western ruffian, and a refined eastern clergyman that is a comic masterpiece, built entirely around the characters' mutually unintelligible speech. Briggs simply wishes to ask the pastor to officiate at the funeral service of a friend, but the two men struggle mightily to understand each other:

> "Are you the duck that runs the gospel-mill next door?"
>
> "Am I the—pardon me, I believe I do not understand?"
>
> With another sigh and a half-sob, Scotty rejoined: "Why you see we are in a bit of trouble, and the boys thought maybe you would give us a lift, if we'd tackle you—that is, if I've got the rights of it and you are the head clerk of the doxology-works next door."
>
> "I am the shepherd in charge of the flock whose fold is next door."
>
> "The which?"
>
> "The spiritual adviser of the little company of believers whose sanctuary adjoins these premises."
>
> Scotty scratched his head, reflected a moment, and then said: "You ruther hold over me, pard. I reckon I can't call that hand. Ante and pass the buck."

Notice Mark Twain's use of card-game terms in that last line. It is typical of his tendency to use specialized jargon in unexpected places. He uses words from card games throughout his writings and is also fond of using the language of river navigation that he had learned as a pilot on the Mississippi before he went west. While Mark Twain is wonderful at describing the real world, he is also superb at creating imaginary worlds. In a few sentences, he can create characters so vivid that we immediately want to know more about them. This description of Huckleberry Finn's first appearance in *Tom Sawyer* is a fine example:

> Shortly Tom came upon the juvenile pariah of the village, Huckleberry Finn, son of the town drunkard. Huckleberry was cordially hated and dreaded by all the mothers of the town, because he was

idle, and lawless, and vulgar and bad—and because all their children admired him so, and delighted in his forbidden society, and wished they dared to be like him. . . .

Huckleberry was always dressed in the cast-off clothes of full-grown men, and they were in perennial bloom and fluttering with rags. His hat was a vast ruin with a wide crescent lopped out of its brim; his coat, when he wore one, hung nearly to his heels and had the rearward buttons far down the back; but one suspender supported his trousers; the seat of the trousers bagged low and contained nothing; the fringed legs dragged in the dirt when not rolled up.

Huckleberry came and went, at his own free will. He slept on doorsteps in fine weather and in empty hogsheads in wet; he did not have to go to school or to church, or call any being master or obey anybody; he could go fishing or swimming when and where he chose, and stay as long as it suited him; nobody forbade him to fight; he could sit up as late as he pleased; he was always the first boy that went barefoot in the spring and the last to resume leather in the fall; he never had to wash, nor put on clean clothes; he could swear wonderfully. In a word, everything that goes to make life precious, that boy had. So thought every harassed, hampered, respectable boy in St. Petersburg (*Tom Sawyer* chapter 6).

Any essential facts about Huck that those paragraphs fail to reveal we can guess at by reading between the lines. The passage also reveals a great deal about the attitudes of other St. Petersburg boys and provides strong hints of what is to come, as we can immediately see that Huck represents a chink in the social order, a potential catalyst for trouble. Why, exactly, do adults want their children to avoid him? Is it simply because he is poor and disreputable? Or, might it be because he is "lawless"—a free person who recognizes no master? Such questions are bound up in these brief paragraphs and make readers eager to learn more about Huck and what will become of him.

TOPICS AND STRATEGIES

The sections that follow suggest ideas for essay topics on Mark Twain. They are arranged under category headings indicating essay types:

"Themes," "Character," "Philosophy and Ideas," "Form and Genre," "Language, Symbols, and Imagery," and "Compare and Contrast Essays." The same headings are used throughout chapters 3–12, which cover selected individual works. These category headings are offered to guide your topic selections and help you focus on how to approach topics. Many of the suggestions could easily be listed under more than one category, so you should browse every category in the chapter on whatever work you are studying.

Topic suggestions in the present chapter are designed to help students writing papers that will discuss more than one of Mark Twain's works and to help students decide what types of papers to choose for their assignments on individual works. If you are lucky, you will find your ideal topic in one of these chapters. However, you should neither limit your choices to topics discussed in this book nor hesitate to combine two or more of them or to modify them to meet your own interests. The suggestions are offered to help you come up with your own ideas and get started writing, not to tell you on what to write or exactly what to say. In fact, throughout this book, you will be encouraged to approach everything with the same skepticism that you should apply to all opinions that you read. There is no mathematical certainty in literary interpretation; even the most distinguished authorities on Mark Twain can, and often do, disagree on how to interpret his works. Furthermore, there is no reason why their views are necessarily more valid than your own.

Another point stressed throughout this book is that the questions you raise about Mark Twain may not have definitive answers. For example, why did he write *Huckleberry Finn*'s "evasion" chapters as he did? No one knows for sure. What is the meaning of the cataclysmic ending of *A Connecticut Yankee in King Arthur's Court*? No one knows for sure. What is *Pudd'nhead Wilson*'s real message about race? No one knows for sure. The fact that even scholars cannot agree on answers to questions as basic as these should not discourage you from seeking answers. Indeed, that very fact should encourage you to try. At the same time, you should be careful to avoid the trap of searching for conclusive proofs that may not exist. Not all questions have pat answers.

Another trap to avoid is searching for more meaning in Mark Twain's texts than is actually there. Mark Twain is generally a very clear and straightforward author, and the meaning of much of what he wrote goes no deeper than what you see on the surface. For example, the frog in his jumping frog story, one of the short works covered in the present volume, is named "Dan'l Webster," and a dog in the same story is named "Andrew Jackson." One might naturally wonder why. Around the time in which the story is set, a man named Daniel Webster was the U.S. secretary of state; Andrew Jackson had been the president of the United States around two decades earlier. What connection could there possibly be between distinguished statesmen in Washington, D.C., and a frog and a dog in far-off California? Might the jumping frog story be some kind of subtle political allegory? Perhaps, but it may be more likely that Mark Twain assigned those names to animals simply because they sounded funny to him. Humor typically grows out of the unexpected; what can be more unexpected than a frog named "Dan'l Webster"? On the other hand, at least one distinguished scholar has suggested that Mark Twain used that particular name because he thought that the real Daniel Webster looked like a frog.

If you are free to choose the Mark Twain texts on which to write, there is another trap to avoid: selecting the wrong texts. If your assignment is to write only on *Huckleberry Finn,* your choice is already made. However, if you are to choose another book with which to compare *Huckleberry Finn,* or you are allowed to select from a large range of texts for another kind of essay, be careful to match your text selections with your topic choices. The jumping frog story is obviously a poor choice for an essay on Mark Twain's views on race, so it should never even occur to you to select it for such a topic. On the other hand, if you were to select the same story for an analysis of Mark Twain's use of irony, you might not find enough to say on that subject to build a complete essay until after you have spent a considerable amount of time struggling over it. You can avoid that kind of mistake by drafting a brief outline of what your essay will say before you make your selection final. If you have trouble fleshing out even a brief outline, look for a different text.

One final tip: Regardless of which Mark Twain work you choose to write about, take a few moments to skim through the essay suggestions in several chapters in this book. You may find that suggestions for other works give you ideas for topics on the work you are studying.

Themes

Essays on themes ask questions concerning what works are about. A book such as *Tom Sawyer*, for example, seems to be about a lot of different things, such as boyhood, showing off, violence and danger, quests for riches, and childish superstitions. An essay on the novel might take either of two approaches: It could focus on the question of whether the book has a single dominant theme and what that theme is or it could select any important theme in the book and attempt to show what role it plays in the novel. Whichever approach you take, you will need to determine what the book says about your selected theme.

Theme is a term that is often used broadly. Before selecting a theme, be sure to review the suggestions under other headings as some topics they discuss might also be considered themes. Pay particular attention to "History and Context," "Philosophy and Ideas," and "Compare and Contrast Essays."

Sample Topics:

1. **Central themes:** Identify the most important single theme in your selected work, explain what the work says about it, and how it works with other themes.

   This is an open-ended topic and may not be suitable for works without a central theme. To justify writing on this topic, you must not only identify your work's central theme, but also make a strong case why you think it is central, why Mark Twain may have made it so, and what the work has to say about that theme. For example, you might argue that the trials and tribulations of boyhood constitute the central theme of *Tom Sawyer*. You could attempt to prove that is true by discussing other themes in the novel—such as fear of violence, childish superstitions, and resistance to adult authority—that work together to support the central theme. Even without researching Mark Twain's life, you could argue that he chose to emphasize that theme because his prefatory remarks clearly express his nostalgic interest in recalling his own boyhood. Finally, you would need to sum up what *Tom Sawyer* says about boyhood by showing how the novel's plotlines, characters, and other literary features work together to develop the theme.

2. **Child v. adult worlds:** Examine how Mark Twain depicts conflicts between the world of children and that of adults.

This topic is suitable for both essays on single works, such as *Tom Sawyer* or *The Prince and the Pauper,* and those on selections of works. Conflicts between children and adults occur in some of Mark Twain's best-known fiction and also in lesser-known works, such as his early sketches and his historical novel *Joan of Arc* (1896). Perhaps the chief aspect of this theme to develop is how children and adults view the world differently. A particularly fruitful approach to take would be to compare the views of childhood expressed in *Tom Sawyer,* which is narrated by an adult, with those in *Huckleberry Finn,* which is narrated by a boy.

3. **Family:** What does Mark Twain's fiction say about the nature of families and relationships among their members?

This is another good topic for an essay on either a single work or a group of works, as family issues are central in much of Mark Twain's fiction. Particularly good titles to explore are *Tom Sawyer; Huckleberry Finn; The Gilded Age* (1874), which draws on Mark Twain's own family history; *The Prince and the Pauper*; and *Pudd'nhead Wilson.* Family issues are also central to some of his best short fiction, including "The $30,000 Bequest," about a couple who ruin their lives by placing all their hopes on a large inheritance, and a series of humorous stories about the McWilliamses—a fictional family modeled on Mark Twain's own family. A curious aspect of Mark Twain's long fiction is that most of the families are dysfunctional or not whole. For example, Tom Sawyer is an orphan, and Huck Finn has an abusive father and becomes an orphan. *Pudd'nhead Wilson* has the most complex family issues and ties these into issues of racial identity. Among the many questions to ask about these stories is why Mark Twain so rarely uses happy, functional families.

You might find it useful to do some reading on Mark Twain's life to gain some understanding of his own family experiences. He was one of seven children, only four of whom reached adulthood. Traces of all his family members can be found in his fiction. When he was 35, he married a woman to whom he remained devoted through the rest of his life. His relationships with his wife and daughters were not without serious problems, but the worst problems did not develop until after he had written most of his important fiction. If you look for parallels between his life and a fictional work, take into account during what period in his life he wrote it.

4. **Dualism and twins:** How does Mark Twain use dualism, twinning, switched identities, and other similar devices to drive his plots? Does his use of such devices suggest anything about his views on human identity?

Critics and scholars often make much of the fact that Samuel Clemens adopted as a pen name *Mark Twain,* a navigation term for a depth of two fathoms (12 feet). *Twain* is an Old English word for "two" that has survived in modern English mostly in usages relating to splitting things in half—which is exactly how Mark Twain himself typically uses the word in his prose. Critics see all this as bearing on one of the most pervasive themes in Mark Twain's writings: dualism—divided personalities, twins, identity switching, and other related subjects. Almost every novel he wrote has some kind of dualism theme or form of identity switching. Some of his short stories, such as "A Medieval Romance" (1870), involve male-female identity switches of such complexity as to defy description. In *The Prince and the Pauper* and *Pudd'nhead Wilson,* identity switching is a central theme, and mistaken identity drives the plot of *The American Claimant* (1892). Even *Huckleberry Finn* employs switched-identity themes. As that story unfolds, Huck himself pretends to be at least seven different people.

The true identities of the novel's so-called King and Duke are never revealed, and each of those characters often pretends to be yet another character. Whatever approach to this theme you undertake, your aim should be to assess what Mark Twain is trying to say about human identity. In *The Prince and the Pauper,* for example, could he be saying that the only real differences between a king and a commoner are the clothes they wear or their accidents of birth? Another kind of twinning theme to look for is the pairing of ostensible opposites, such as Tom Sawyer and his nemesis, Injun Joe, in *Tom Sawyer.* Can it be argued that Tom and the evil Joe represent opposite sides of the same person?

5. **Clothes make the man:** How do clothes help to define characters in Mark Twain's works? What does his emphasis on the importance of clothes say about the nature of human identity?

Closely related to dual-identity themes is another theme to which Mark Twain repeatedly returned: the importance of clothes to personal identity. In some passages, such as *Tom Sawyer's* description of Huck Finn's rags, this theme is expressed subtly. In other texts, the same theme is central. For example, in "The Czar's Soliloquy," a sketch attacking Russian totalitarianism published in 1905, Mark Twain has the czar muse on the true basis of his power. What is it that his subjects worship, he ponders? He then answers, "None knows better than I: it is my clothes. Without my clothes I should be as destitute of authority as any other naked person." Associations between clothes and identity are equally overt throughout such works as *A Connecticut Yankee* and *The American Claimant,* and the same theme even figures in *Huckleberry Finn,* in which clothes play a role in the novel's many identity switches and measurements of social status. This topic could be a fun one on which to write and would lend itself equally well to an analysis of one work or several.

Character

One clear advantage of choosing characters over themes for topics is that you should have no trouble retaining your handle on what your topic is about—tangible beings, not abstractions. Well-drawn characters can seem very much like real people. That makes us comfortable because we feel that we already know a great deal about real people. That statement may sound like an empty expression of the obvious, but it touches on a point central to any consideration of fictional character—namely, how *real* do those characters seem? Does Mark Twain tell us enough about them to make it worth our while to analyze their nature and behavior, as we would real people? Or are the characters so flat, so one-dimensional that they seem more like props in stories than full-blooded human beings? If you were to attempt to analyze a character such as Judge Thatcher, who appears in both *Tom Sawyer* and *Huckleberry Finn,* you might find that you have nothing to say about him, except that he is an example of a "type": an adult authority figure whose actions support social order in the community and whose presence in the stories serves as a counterpoint to the irresponsibility of the youthful protagonists. Nothing Judge Thatcher does surprises readers, partly because any other person in his place would probably act exactly the same way and partly because Mark Twain chooses not to call attention to him as a person. For these reasons, Judge Thatcher is probably more like a prop than a real character.

In judging whether one of Mark Twain's fictional creations is a real character or a type, be careful not to make the mistake of assuming that figures are not real characters simply because they appear only once, and briefly, in a story. Naturally, the more times a character appears, the more likely that that character will be fully rounded. However, Mark Twain occasionally invests real complexity in characters who appear only briefly. There are, for example, several fascinating characters in *Huckleberry Finn* who come and go within only a few pages but nevertheless reveal enough about themselves to provide plenty of grist for essay mills. One is Mrs. Loftus, the chatty and often surprising newcomer to St. Petersburg whom Huck encounters when he sneaks back into town disguised as a girl. She is the character who tests whether Huck is really a girl by asking him to thread a needle—one of the most famous small moments in the novel. Her one brief appearance tells enough about her to provide material for a paper longer than the passages in which she appears. A much different kind of character whose appearance is similarly brief is Colonel Sherburn, the prosperous Bricksville merchant who shoots down the drunken Boggs and later shames a lynch mob into timidly retreating from his home. Sherburn alone could easily be the focus of essays on southern class distinctions, southern concepts of honor, courage, and cowardice, and mob psychology—all themes explored in *Huckleberry Finn* and many of Mark Twain's other writings.

Sample Topics:

1. **Character development:** Track and analyze the changes that one or more characters display in one or more works.

   One of the most valuable ways to study character is by analyzing the development of a single major character throughout an entire narrative. Central questions to ask include how the characters change and why and what their changes reveal about them and about the narrative's themes. For example, a central theme in *Huckleberry Finn* is the breaking down of Huck's racist thinking as he learns to appreciate the slave Jim's innate humanity. If Huck did not change, the novel would not have much to say. If *Huckleberry Finn* were to end as the 1939 film *The Wizard of Oz* does, it might have a scene in which Huck relates his wondrous adventures and his friends ask him, "What have you learned, Huck?" It is doubtful that Huck would reply as Dorothy does: "If I ever go looking for my heart's desire again, I won't look any further than my own backyard." However, the important point should be clear: Both Dorothy and Huck learn from their experiences; their characters develop.

   Essays comparing character in two or more works can reveal important points that studies of the individual works might miss. However, you will probably find that an essay on a single character in one work will give you more than enough to discuss. Ideas for such essays are suggested in most of the chapters on individual novels in the present volume.

2. **Female characters:** Examine Mark Twain's use of female characters in one or more works and assess whether he treats them differently than he does male characters. Do his writings have a generally pro-male bias? What can be said about the views of women he expresses in his writings?

Some people see Mark Twain primarily as a writer for male readers. Is there any validity to that view? One possible reason people hold the view is the relative lack of important female characters in his works and the general weakness of the female characters—both child and adult—that he does use. For example, can it be argued that either Becky Thatcher or Aunt Polly is a strong character? In fact, is either of them even truly a *character,* rather than a type? Only a handful of strong female characters appear throughout Mark Twain's writings. Curiously, they tend to turn up in wholly different kinds of works, most notably in "A True Story" (1874), *Pudd'nhead Wilson* (1894), *Joan of Arc* (1896), and *A Horse's Tale* (1906). An essay on women characters should probably examine how they are used in several different works. If you prefer to concentrate on only one work, be sure to choose one with enough female characters to give you something to say. *Tom Sawyer* or *The Prince and the Pauper* would not serve well for this purpose, but *Huckleberry Finn* or *Pudd'nhead Wilson* would. *The Gilded Age* has some interesting women characters in it, but since Mark Twain coauthored that book, you would need to restrict your analysis to the chapters for which he was responsible, and that is a tricky thing to do.

3. **Boys:** What do Mark Twain's depictions of boy characters reveal about his views on childhood generally and boys specifically?

The flip side of Mark Twain's female characters is his male characters. Since he is best known for his novels with boy protagonists, they would make good subjects on which to focus. You might make a good essay out of a four-way comparison among Tom Sawyer, Huck Finn, and the title characters of *The Prince and the Pauper*—both of whom have interesting similarities to both Tom and Huck. Do those four characters have enough traits in common to generalize meaningfully about Mark Twain's views on the nature of boys? For additional ideas on Mark Twain's view of boyhood, read some of his earliest sketches, such as "The Story of a Bad Little Boy" (1865) and "The Story of a Good Little Boy" (1870). Are there traits in those stories' characters that anticipate the protagonists in his later novels? Another interesting approach to this subject would be to compare Mark Twain's boy protagonists with one or more of his adult protagonists. A particularly promising subject for this kind of study would be Hank Morgan, the title character of *A Connecticut Yankee.*

History and Context

All authors are products of their own times and places, but some transcend their origins to become true citizens of the world who live on through the ages. Mark Twain is arguably just such an author. He traveled widely, lived in every section of the United States, spent about 12 years of his life abroad, and had deep interests in the whole world, its history, and the nature of historical change. He was born and raised in Missouri, a southern state in which he lived amid a slaveholding society with parents who owned slaves themselves. He eventually settled in the North, came to see himself as a New England Yankee, and denounced the institution of slavery and what he regarded as the romantic claptrap of the South. After he died, his good friend W. D. Howells said of him that

> he was the most desouthernized Southerner I ever knew. No man more perfectly sensed and more entirely abhorred slavery, and no one has ever poured such scorn upon the second-hand, Walter-Scotticized, pseudo-chivalry of the Southern ideal. He held himself responsible for the wrong which the white race had done the black race in slavery . . . (Howells, *My Mark Twain* chapter 9).

Even if you know no more about Mark Twain's life than what you read here, the danger of judging him too quickly on the basis of his white southern origins and occasional charges that he was a racist should be evident. He was a complex man with a complex history of his own. To understand the full context of many of his writings you should read as much as you can about his life, particularly as it relates to the works you are studying. You can do this by reading one of the many fine biographies of him or by referring to a solid reference work, such as LeMaster and Wilson's *Mark Twain Encyclopedia* or Rasmussen's *Critical Companion to Mark Twain* or *Mark Twain A to Z*.

Sample Topics:

1. **19th-century America:** What views of America and its culture, people, and institutions does Mark Twain express in his writings?

   Quintessential is a rather pompous-sounding word, but it is a good word to apply to Mark Twain, who is sometimes called the "quintessential American," that is, a person who represents the most important things that make up America in their purest and most concentrated form. Despite his interest in the world as a whole, he was always first and foremost an American, and America's people, landscapes, values, egalitarianism, and institutions were always his favorite subjects. *The Innocents Abroad* (1869), *A Tramp Abroad* (1880), and *Following the Equator* (1897) describe his travels in other parts of the world, but none of them can go more than a few chapters without comparing American institutions and people favorably with what he observes abroad. However, he was no flag-waving chauvinist. In fact, he was ever ready to criticize American faults and suggest remedies. His narrator in *A Connecticut Yankee* (1889) expresses his own views on patriotism:

   > You see my kind of loyalty was loyalty to one's country, not to its institutions or its office-holders. The country is the real thing, the substantial thing, the eternal thing; it is the thing to watch over, and care for, and be loyal to; institutions are extraneous, they are its mere clothing, and clothing can wear out . . . (chapter 13).

   The sentiments expressed in that passage would make an excellent starting point for an exploration of Mark Twain's views on America. There is an abundance of texts on which to draw for material: Virtually all his travel books, most of his novels (*The Prince and the Pauper* and *Joan of Arc* would not be useful, but *A Connecticut Yankee* would be excellent), and scores of short stories, sketches, and essays. Choose a selection of different kinds of writings and from there summarize Mark Twain's observations on American traits. Which traits does he most and least admire? Which does he regard as superior to those of other parts of the world, particularly Europe? How does he support his judgments? What kinds of opinions does he tend to express explicitly, and what kinds does he express more subtly? *The Gilded Age* (1874), a novel that he cowrote with Charles Dudley Warner, is Mark Twain's most political novel and the book that is most critical of American institutions (particularly Congress). The views he expresses in that book are easy to identify and assess. A greater challenge would be to extract his views on America from works such as *Tom Sawyer* and *Huckleberry Finn*.

2. **The Mississippi River:** How does Mark Twain use the river in his fiction? How might his Mississippi writings differ if they were set elsewhere?

Every section of America claims Mark Twain as its own, but the region with which he is most closely identified is the Mississippi River basin, about which he writes so eloquently. The very first sentences of *Life on the Mississippi* (1883) sum up his feelings about the river: "The Mississippi is well worth reading about. It is not a commonplace river, but on the contrary is in all ways remarkable." Mark Twain grew up literally a stone's throw from the river and spent four years piloting steamboats on it between St. Louis and New Orleans. No writer could know the river better than he, and he uses it frequently in his fiction, mostly notably in *Tom Sawyer* and *Huckleberry Finn*. A good topic for an essay about the river would be a survey of Mark Twain's Mississippi fiction to assess how the river is used in each work. What characteristics of the Mississippi set it apart from other American rivers?

A comprehensive essay on this topic would cover *Tom Sawyer, Huckleberry Finn, The Gilded Age, Pudd'nhead Wilson,* and *Tom Sawyer, Detective* (1896). Strictly speaking, *Life on the Mississippi*'s piloting chapters are not fiction, but they have elements of fiction and they say so much about the river that they should not be overlooked. As a practical matter, covering only *Huckleberry Finn* and *Life on the Mississippi* would be enough to construct a strong essay.

3. **Slavery:** To what extent did Mark Twain attack or condone the institution of slavery in his writings?

Mark Twain is closely associated with attacks on slavery largely because of *Huckleberry Finn,* in which the slave Jim's attempt to flee from bondage is one of the engines that drives the novel's plot. However, Mark Twain's association with slavery goes much deeper than that one book. As has already been mentioned, he grew up within a slaveholding society and lived very close to slaves. His parents owned a few slaves, and he spent most of his summers on a uncle's farm where he mixed freely and intimately with slaves and a developed a life-long admiration for African Americans. Nevertheless, he has been criticized for failing to show sufficient sensitivity to the oppression of slaves in his writings. This may be due, in part, to his tendency to remember the conditions of slavery he had observed as a boy more nostalgically as he grew older. That tendency is most evident in his autobiographical writings.

An essay on this topic might survey the views of slavery that Mark Twain expresses in his fiction, mostly notably in *Tom Sawyer, Huckleberry Finn, The Gilded Age,* and *Pudd'nhead Wilson.* You should also look at *A Connecticut Yankee*; although that book is set in sixth-century England, it contains Mark Twain's most explicit attack on slavery. To put his views in context, you might also read some of his autobiographical writings on the subject, as well as Terrell Dempsey's *Searching for Jim: Slavery in Sam Clemens's World* (2003).

Philosophy and Ideas

This category is similar to the category on themes but deals with broader ideas and concepts. It is essential to have at least some notion of what is meant by *philosophy*. The word itself is used in many different ways, but its core meaning may be said to be.a coherent set of fundamental beliefs about the nature of reality that is derived more from speculative thinking and logical analysis than from empirical evidence. For this reason philosophical ideas generally deal with abstractions, such as that expressed in the French philosopher René Descartes's famous observation, "I think, therefore I am." Mark Twain is not generally regarded as a deep philosophical thinker, but he did develop a well-thought-out philosophy of his own, and traces of philosophical ideas can be found throughout his writings.

Sample Topics:

1. **Determinism:** Survey a selection of Mark Twain's later fiction to find evidence of his personal deterministic philosophy. Are the views that you find logical and consistent?

   A concept that began influencing Mark Twain's writings during the late 1870s and steadily took greater hold on his thinking was a determinist philosophy that he dubbed his personal "gospel." Having little or nothing to do with traditional Christian notions of determinism, predestation, or Providence, his ideas about determinism revolved around the concept that human beings are simply "machines" that operate automatically and are beyond individual human control. The main outside force that directs each person's behavior is training, which is generally dictated by the entrenched customs of society. Mark Twain summed up his philosophy in *What Is Man?*, a Socratic dialogue that he published anonymously in 1906. Meanwhile, traces of his philosophy found their way into many of his works, most notably perhaps in *A Connecticut Yankee* (1889) and *Pudd'nhead Wilson* (1894), both of which stress the power of training in each person's makeup and the ultimate futility of trying to act independently.

   To write an essay on this topic, you will need to read either *What Is Man?* (which is available in reprint editions) or a biography or article that addresses Mark Twain's views on determinism. The 1996 Oxford Mark Twain edition of *What Is Man?* contains substantial discussions of the book by Charles Johnson and Linda Wagner-Martin. You should also read several of Mark Twain's later fictional works to extract examples of his determinist thinking, such as Hank Morgan's tirade in chapter 18 of *A Connecticut Yankee* about Sandy, in which he says, "We have no thoughts of our own, no opinions of our own; they are transmitted to us, trained into us." Do the examples add up to a coherent and consistent philosophy? Or does Mark Twain sometimes apply his philosophy illogically or inconsistently? Alternatively, you could focus your entire essay on the arguments for determinism made in *What Is Man?* by applying the same questions to that dialogue.

2. **Freedom:** What ideas about freedom can be found in Mark Twain's writings and what forms do those ideas take?

If it can be said that a single thread runs throughout Mark Twain's writings, that thread may be his love of freedom in all its forms and his belief that all human beings should be free from oppression. More an instinctive impulse, perhaps, than an elaborate philosophy, these ideas show up in writings ranging from Mark Twain's simple tales about young boys struggling to free themselves from the shackles of school and adult authority to his mature polemics attacking repressive regimes in other nations. Among other enemies of freedom he takes on in his works are all forms of human slavery, the force of outmoded customs and traditions, oppressive religious dogmas, and corrupt governments.

An essay on this topic could survey the ideas of freedom that Mark Twain expresses in a selection of his works or in a single work. *Huckleberry Finn* would be a good work on which to focus because it revolves around two simultaneous quests for freedom: Jim's attempt to flee from slavery and Huck's attempt to flee from parental abuse, adult authority, and civilization in general. This essay should examine how concepts of freedom are expressed, the obstacles placed in the way of

the protagonists' achieving their goals, and possible contradictions on the nature of freedom that the book presents.

3. **Dreams v. reality:** What uses does Mark Twain make of dreams
   and confusion over the separation of dreams and reality in his
   writings?

Many of the long, unfinished manuscripts that Mark Twain
wrote during the last decade or so of his life concern characters unable to distinguish between dreams and reality. Eventually, they come to believe that their dream lives are their real
lives. Titles of some of these stories are suggestive: "Which Was
the Dream?," "Which Was It?," and "The Great Dark." Other
unfinished stories treating this theme include "The Chronicle
of Young Satan," "Three Thousand Years Among the Microbes,"
and "Refuge of the Derelicts." As he wrote these stories, Mark
Twain seems to have been headed toward an acceptance of a
form of solipsism, the belief that the only certain reality is one's
self and that everything else may exist only in one's imagination—or in one's dreams. That, in fact, is precisely the conclusion that his nearly finished story *No. 44, the Mysterious
Stranger* (written in 1902–08; published in 1969) reaches.

   An essay analyzing how Mark Twain's posthumously written
stories use dream themes could be a fascinating one. However,
the topic might also be approached from a different direction
by surveying Mark Twain's earlier, published works, many of
which have dream themes. For example, *The Prince and the
Pauper* might be examined as a story in which Tom Canty,
the pauper boy of the title, builds a dream life that becomes a
reality when an accident makes him king of England, leaving
him uncertain whether his new life is a dream or reality. Meanwhile, Prince Edward, whom Tom accidentally displaces, has
his own problems distinguishing between dreams and reality.
An essay could also focus entirely on *A Connecticut Yankee* by
posing this simple question: Is the Yankee's experience in sixth-
century England meant to be real or is it merely a dream? What
evidence is there for both conclusions? What does the Yankee

himself believe on that issue? Another novel in which confusion over dreams figures prominently is *Tom Sawyer.*

Form and Genre

Papers about the forms of works examine such issues as how they are constructed, the literary techniques they use to create effects, and how and why their structures succeed or fail. *Genre* is a term used in a variety of ways but is generally understood to refer to the categories in which literary works fit. The broadest categories are long fiction (novels), short fiction, drama, and poetry. Those categories are further divided into subgenres, which are also simply called genres. These may include coming-of-age stories, or bildungsroman; adventure stories; science fiction; fantasy; mystery stories; and autobiographical fiction. Applying genre terms to Mark Twain's writings can be difficult. He never thought consciously about genres and many of his writings might be labeled with many different terms simultaneously.

Why bother writing about these concepts when Mark Twain's works are notoriously difficult to categorize? The reason is that understanding the genre, form, and structure of a work can help you understand the work's meaning and purpose and thereby offer insights into what Mark Twain was trying to do. A good example of how such a study can help clarify what a work is about is the novel *A Connecticut Yankee in King Arthur's Court* (1889). That book's shocking ending has long puzzled people who read the book thinking it is a humorous satire. As another chapter in this volume shows, the book's purpose can only be appreciated if the book is understood to be something else. The same might even be said of a book such as *Tom Sawyer.* What is it supposed to be? A boy's adventure? A coming-of-age story? Autobiographical fiction? Or some combination of these genres or others?

Sample Topics:

1. **Narrative voices and points of view:** How do narrative voices and points of view vary among Mark Twain's works?

   One of the most important things you should pay attention to when you read anything by Mark Twain is its narrative voice and point of view, both of which can often be deceptive. In *Tom*

Sawyer, for example, the anonymous third-person narrator seems to shift back and forth between a detached observer and one who is opinionated and nostalgic, and the narrator's point of view seems to shift between that of an adult and that of a boy. In works that are ostensibly nonfiction, such as travel books, one cannot always be certain to whom the first-person narrative voice belongs—is it Mark Twain himself or does it belong to an invented persona? If so, why might he have invented that persona? Essays on these questions can take many different forms. For example, you might analyze how the narrative voice in any one travel book operates or compare the narrative voices in several different books. You could also compare how using a third-person narrator in *Tom Sawyer* and a first-person in *Huckleberry Finn* affect each book's point of view.

2. **Satire and irony:** How does Mark Twain use satire and irony in his writings, and what forms does it take?

   Mark Twain is often regarded as a great satirist, but is that judgment correct? To answer that question, you will need to define exactly what you mean by *satire.* Does its essence lie only in using literature to ridicule or scorn human folly and vices? Or is there more to it? Does any use of irony and sarcasm to attack folly and vice constitute satire? A work such as *Huckleberry Finn* seems clearly to use irony to expose racism and the injustices of slavery, but does that make the book a form of satire?

3. **Travel writings:** What common themes and writing techniques characterize Mark Twain's travel writings? How does his interest in travel writing show up in his fiction?

   Mark Twain was probably better known as a travel writer than as a novelist during his own time. Books such as *The Innocents Abroad* (1869) and *Roughing It* (1872) made him famous before he wrote his first novel. He eventually published five volumes that are regarded as travel books, and he also wrote many other essays and sketches that can be considered travel writing. All these writings are rich in themes and innovative techniques, any one of which could easily provide the basis for a strong essay. Among the many writing techniques you might explore is how Mark Twain exaggerated the youth and naïveté of his narrative personas in works such as *The Innocents Abroad, Roughing It,* the piloting chapters of *Life on the Mississippi* (1883), and *A Tramp Abroad* (1880). You could also look at how he used imaginary traveling companions, such as Harris in *A Tramp Abroad,* to make satirical observations that his narrators hesitate to express. Possible themes to explore include contrasts between New and Old World cultures and between eastern and western American cultures, the initiation of greenhorns in new environments, and the disillusionment often experienced by travelers. You could also look at Mark Twain's use of travel themes in his purely fictional works, such as *Huckleberry Finn, The Prince and the Pauper, A Connecticut Yankee,* and *Extracts from Captain Stormfield's Visit to Heaven* (1909)—all of whose protagonists go on long journeys.

4. **Humor:** What techniques and subject matter does Mark Twain use to make readers laugh?

Author, humorist, and radio personality Garrison Keillor has suggested that the main reason people enjoy reading Mark Twain is simply that "he is funny." Some of Mark Twain's humor may not work as well in the 21st century as it did during his time or even in the 20th century, but his writings can still make people smile or laugh. Why? That is a tall question, but it relates directly to many of the forms in which Mark Twain wrote—tall tales, satires, burlesques, hoaxes, parodies, and simple comic misadventures. He also frequently uses humor in works that are not so obviously intended to be funny.

The subject of humor in his writings is a vast one that has inspired numerous lengthy studies, so you should not have trouble finding an aspect of the subject to write about. However, you may find that humor is not as simple to explain as you expect. Indeed, reasons why people laugh are often inexplicable. You should probably begin by focusing on one or two of Mark Twain's books. Take notes on passages that you find humorous and categorize them according to their techniques, such as gross exaggeration, unexpected contrasts, outrageous anecdotes, and comic irony. Are there overall patterns in these techniques? Do some of them work better than others? Pay attention, too, to attempts at humor that do not work. Try to explain why they do not work—could the reason be that they use 19th-century references or assumptions that modern readers are unlikely to understand?

5. **Mystery and detective fiction:** To what extent do Mark Twain's detective stories conform to the conventions of the mystery genre? What use did he make of mystery and detective fiction conventions in other writings?

Mark Twain's writing career unfolded as the mystery and detective fiction genre was taking shape. He was well aware of the contributions being made by writers such as Edgar Allan Poe and Arthur Conan Doyle and enjoyed parodying them in stories such as "The Stolen White Elephant" (1878) and *A Double-Barrelled Detective Story* (1902). He wrote *Tom Sawyer, Detective* (1896), a more conventional mystery story, and *Pudd'nhead Wilson* (1894), a story that would now be classified as an "inverted mystery" because it shows the crime taking place. Mark Twain also often introduced mystery elements in other works. Consider, for example, the intriguing unresolved mysteries posed in *Huckleberry Finn:* a corpse found floating down a river, a dead body found in a mysterious floating house, men overheard planning a murder in a derelict steamboat, and the two men who upset the King and Duke's claim to be the Wilks brothers by making the same claim themselves, while lacking any proof of their identity—are they frauds too?

Essays on Mark Twain's use of mystery genre conventions could take many forms. You might survey all his detective stories and assess how closely they conform to the standard conventions of the genre or how he exploited the form to achieve satirical effects. You might also assess how he used elements of the genre in other fictional works, such as *Tom Sawyer* and *Huckleberry Finn*.

6. **Science fiction:** What science fiction elements does Mark Twain use in his writings? To what extent was he an innovator in that genre?

Scholar David Ketterer has suggested that if Mark Twain had finished more of the science fiction stories he started and published them during his lifetime, he might now be recognized, along with Jules Verne and H. G. Wells, as a pioneer of the genre. Unfortunately, he left the bulk of his science fiction stories unfinished, so his name is rarely associated with that genre. *A Connecticut Yankee in King Arthur's Court* (1889) is often seen as one of the first time-travel stories, but only a few other works he published during his lifetime have strong science fiction elements. On the other hand, his posthumously published writings include many stories with what would have been considered significant innovations at the time he wrote them. His imagination encompassed not only time travel but also interstellar travel, instantaneous communication, teleportation, alien beings, worlds shrunk to microscopic size, and other bold ideas.

This subject might be approached in a variety of ways. For example, you could survey all Mark Twain's science fiction works and look for common themes, such as far-traveling (both spatial and temporal). If you are interested in the history of science fiction, you could attempt to show which of Mark Twain's ideas were ahead of his time when he wrote about them. Or you could focus on a single work, such as *A Connecticut Yankee*, and analyze what kind of science fiction it is. Indeed, is it really a time-travel story or a fantasy? What is the difference? Is it sociological science fiction? Whatever approach you take to this topic, however, be careful to define your terms and to differentiate between science fiction and fantasy elements. Researching Mark Twain's science fiction should not be difficult, as his most important writings are collected in a well-annotated volume edited by David Ketterer.

Language, Symbols, and Imagery

This category of topics is an amorphous one that overlaps other categories. In general, it concerns the choices of words, symbols, and images that writers make when they actually put pen to paper. It may be said that writers make use of both literal and figurative language. Broadly speaking, the former conveys information and ideas in a straightforward manner in which words are intended to mean exactly what they appear to mean, leaving no ambiguity. By contrast, figurative language uses words to mean things other than their literal meanings. "The man is a coward" is a literal statement. "The man is a mouse" is a figurative statement expressing the same sentiment, but substituting for "coward" the word "mouse," which is generally understood to symbolize cowardliness. In this instance "mouse" is a metaphor for "coward." Symbols are a more subtle form of figurative language. They are generally words for recognizable objects, ideas, or even characters used to create moods or enhance atmosphere. Mark Twain's "The War Prayer," for example, makes heavy use of symbols to magnify the story's feeling of mounting war fever. Words such as "drums," "bands," "firecrackers," "flags," "uniforms," "mass-meetings," and "oratory" all symbolize fervent patriotism.

Sample Topics:

1. **Imagery:** What kinds of language does Mark Twain use to convey images in his writing?

Mark Twain was unusually adept at conveying visual, aural, olfactory, and even tactile sensations in his work, which is a primary reason why his writing seems so vigorous and his descriptions are so easy to visualize. He achieved this partly through accurate and detailed descriptions of sights, sounds, and smells and also through powerful imagery. Consider, for example, this description of a coyote (which he spelled "cayote"):

> The cayote is a long, slim, sick and sorry-looking skeleton, with a gray wolf-skin stretched over it, a tolerably bushy tail that

forever sags down with a despairing expression of forsakenness and misery, a furtive and evil eye, and a long, sharp face, with slightly lifted lip and exposed teeth. He has a general slinking expression all over. The cayote is a living, breathing allegory of Want. He is always hungry. He is always poor, out of luck and friendless (*Roughing It* chapter 5).

This one brief passage contains at least a dozen separate images of disreputable traits. Collectively, they create an unforgettable picture of the friendless coyote.

2. **Symbols:** What use does Mark Twain make of symbols in his fiction?

Mark Twain's writings generally do not make heavy use of symbolic language. Nevertheless, almost everything he wrote contains at least some recognizable symbols. Symbols are not necessarily subtle and profound. For example, in *Tom Sawyer*, Tom collects a great deal of loot from friends whom he tricks into paying him for the privilege of whitewashing a fence for him. Most of the items he collects are symbols of boyhood, as they are objects that no one other than a young boy would want, such as a dead rat, a useless key, a tin soldier, a one-eyed kitten, a brass doorknob, a dog collar, firecrackers, marbles, and tadpoles. Their symbolism takes on new meaning the next day at Sunday school, where Tom trades them for "tickets" he uses to claim a Bible prize and public acclaim. He swaps what might be seen as symbols of ill-gotten gain for a symbol of religious piety. His brass doorknob, one of the few objects he retains, later comes to symbolize his on-again off-again relationship with Becky Thatcher. Similar types of symbols can be found in other works. Select one or more texts, identify as many symbols as you can, explain what these symbols mean, and what they contribute to the texts.

Compare and Contrast Essays

A point stressed throughout this book is that a good thing about compare and contrast topics is that they allow you to be creative on two levels—first, in finding aspects of one or more works to compare; second, in finding significant points to make those comparisons. Your best chance to attain true originality—at least within the context of your class—may therefore lie in finding characters, plots, writing techniques, or other topics to compare that no one has previously considered. An essay comparing the characters Tom Sawyer and Huckleberry Finn could certainly offer some original observations, but the topic itself would scarcely be original. On other hand, if you were to compare Hank Morgan and David Wilson, the title characters of *A Connecticut Yankee in King Arthur's Court* (1889) and *Pudd'nhead Wilson* (1894), almost every point you make about them would be original because it is unlikely anybody else has addressed that subject. Moreover, such an essay could be more fun to write. Incidentally, a comparison between Morgan and Wilson may not be as far-fetched as you might think. Both characters are progressive, highly intelligent men with special talents who find themselves in alien and tradition-bound societies, living among people who distrust them because they are different. Some of those people even think they have supernatural powers.

Compare and contrast essays on Mark Twain need not be limited to the characters, settings, and other aspects of only one of his works or even to combinations of his closely related works, such as *Tom Sawyer* and *Huckleberry Finn*. Moreover, they need not even be limited to Mark Twain's own works. In fact, you might look upon a comparison between Mark Twain's writing and that of another writer as a kind of literary hybridization that will improve the stock. Comparisons among different works—perhaps especially those of different authors—often suggest ideas and interpretations that may not be apparent within only one work or within the work of only one author. For example, if you were to read *Life on the Mississippi*'s piloting chapters and wonder why Mark Twain exaggerates the youth and inexperience of his narrator's persona, reading the early chapters of *Roughing It* (1872), whose own narrative persona is similarly young and inexperienced, you would realize that exaggerating a narrator's youth, ignorance, and naïveté is not an accident; it is one of Mark Twain's favorite techniques for creating comic effects. Many of the humorous things that happen to his greenhorn narrators would not be nearly as funny if his narrators were older and more experienced.

If you choose to write a compare and contrast essay, stay alert to that form's special trap: failing to develop ideas as much as you should. Your preparation will almost certainly begin with the compilation of lists of similarities and differences between the subjects you are comparing. The danger in this approach is being satisfied with the lists themselves, as if they reveal anything. It would not be enough simply to outline points of comparison such as those mentioned about Hank Morgan's and David Wilson's traits above. You would need to answer such questions as why each character has the traits he has, what aspects of their backgrounds makes them similar or different, and how their differences affect the plots of the stories they are in. In short, why their similarities and differences matter. At the same time, you should also try to explain why Mark Twain might have created the characters as they are.

Sample Topics:

1. **Comparisons within single works:** Compare a combination of things within one work that allow you to forge arguments about what Mark Twain is trying to do.

   Mark Twain's individual works are generally rich in characters, themes, unusual writing techniques, and other facets. His novels offer particularly broad scope for finding things to compare. Obvious examples are pairs of characters, such as Tom Sawyer and Huck Finn, both of whom appear in *Tom Sawyer, Huckleberry Finn*, and several later stories, such as *Tom Sawyer Abroad* (1894). If you want to be more original, however, you should look for less obvious combinations that will give your greater scope for expressing fresh ideas. As in every compare and contrast essay topic, your aim should be to explain why similarities and differences are significant and what they reveal about the work you are analyzing.

2. **Comparisons across multiple works:** The basic approach to this type of essay is the same as that of an essay analyzing a single work, except that it involves two or more texts.

This type of essay is likely to require more time than an essay on a single work because it necessitates more reading. However, it offers some significant advantages, the chief of which is greater scope in finding interesting and original points of comparison. It also permits you to make broader observations about Mark Twain as a writer. For example, an essay comparing his depictions of African-American characters in *all* the works in which they appear should obviously say a great deal more on Mark Twain's views on race than what can be inferred from a single work. Of course, no student writing a school paper would be expected to read as many texts as that topic would require, so a different approach must be taken. You could either limit the number of texts you analyze or take on a broader range of texts and read parts of them selectively. The first approach is likely to produce better results. If you try the latter approach, you may miss important passages or misinterpret what you do read because you see it out of context.

3. **Comparisons between Mark Twain and other authors:** This type of essay is similar to making comparisons among multiple Mark Twain works, except that it entails reading at least one other author's work.

An essay making comparisons between aspects of Mark Twain's writings and those of one or more other authors offers the widest scope for finding interesting, original, and potentially significant topics. Most suggestions for topics in the present volume discuss issues only within the context of Mark Twain's writings. A multiauthor compare and contrast essay would place his work in a wider context that makes it easier to assess the quality of his writing and what, if anything, makes it unique.

Novelist Jane Smiley once savagely attacked *Huckleberry Finn*, charging not only that Mark Twain's book is a mediocre piece of literature but also that its treatment of slavery is less sensitive and authentic than that of Harriet Beecher Stowe's famous novel, *Uncle Tom's Cabin* (1851–52). Does she have a valid case? If you were to take up Smiley's challenge, obviously you would need to read both books and outline what each says about slavery. However, you would also have to look deeper—at how each author uses more subtle effects—such as sentimentalism and irony—to evoke emotional responses from readers. Moreover, you would need to take into account the different contexts in which each author wrote: Stowe published her book at a moment when the United States was beginning to tear itself apart over the issue of extending slavery into new territories. Mark Twain published his almost two decades after slavery had been abolished. How might the two books have differed if they had been written at the opposite times?

Infinite is a large word, but it may not be overstating things to say that the range of possible topics comparing Mark Twain with other authors is, in fact, infinite. Use your imagination. You might begin by looking for comparisons between the Mark Twain book you have most recently read (or are about to read) and a book by another author that you have recently read. What is each book about? What is its narrative point of view? What are its characters like? What uses does it make of irony, humor, and imagery?

Another way to approach this kind of essay would be to identify the feature or features in a Mark Twain work that most interests you and then find another author's work that offers significant points of comparison. For example, if you wanted to write on *Tom Sawyer*'s depiction of boyhood, Thomas Bailey Aldrich's *The Story of a Bad Boy* (1869) would provide an excellent text for comparison; you might even conclude that Aldrich's book helped to inspire *Tom Sawyer*. Teachers and reference librarians can help you find other texts to use.

Bibliography and Online Resources

This bibliography lists only a fraction of the many books written on Mark Twain and emphasizes recently published general studies likely to be helpful to students. More specialized bibliographies can be found at the end of each chapter in the present book. For additional titles, see the bibliographies by Jason Gary Horn and Thomas T. Tenney listed below. Other general reference sources with extensive bibliographical notes include LeMaster and Wilson's *The Mark Twain*

Encyclopedia and Rasmussen's *Critical Companion to Mark Twain.* This list omits many fine collections of essays, but many of them are described in the bibliography in Rasmussen's *Critical Companion.*

Books

Baldanza, Frank. *Mark Twain: An Introduction and Interpretation.* New York: Barnes & Noble, 1961. An old book but still one of the handiest and easiest-to-understand short guides to Mark Twain's writings.

Bloom, Harold, ed. *Mark Twain: Modern Critical Views.* New York: Chelsea House, 1986. Useful collection of a wide variety of previously published essays on Mark Twain.

Budd, Louis J., ed. *Mark Twain: The Contemporary Reviews.* New York: Cambridge UP, 1999. Nearly exhaustive collection of reviews of first editions of 43 of Mark Twain's books. Indispensable for understanding how Mark Twain's books were regarded during his lifetime.

Camfield, Gregg. *The Oxford Companion to Mark Twain.* New York: Oxford UP, 2003. Collection of about 300 thoughtful essays and miniessays on individual Mark Twain works, themes, subjects that interested him, and other topics. A handy source of stimulating ideas to help jump-start essay assignments.

Cox, James M. *Mark Twain: The Fate of Humor.* Princeton, NJ: Princeton UP, 1966. Stimulating analyses of most of the Mark Twain works covered in the present volume.

Dempsey, Terrell. *Searching for Jim: Slavery in Sam Clemens's World.* Columbia: U of Missouri P, 2003. Groundbreaking study revealing the harsh realities of the slave system under which Mark Twain grew up.

Emerson, Everett. *Mark Twain: A Literary Life.* Philadelphia: U of Pennsylvania P, 2000. Biography that emphasizes the development of Mark Twain's writing. Includes lengthy discussions of individual works. This is a revision of Emerson's *The Authentic Mark Twain* (1984).

Fishkin, Shelley Fisher. *Lighting Out for the Territory: Reflections on Mark Twain and American Culture.* New York: Oxford UP, 1997. Personal explorations of the complex interactions between Mark Twain's heritage and modern American culture that pay particular attention to African-American history in Hannibal.

Gerber, John C. *Mark Twain.* Boston: Twayne, 1988. Easy-to-understand analyses of Mark Twain's writings by a leading scholar in the field. Discusses most of the works covered in the present volume.

Horn, Jason Gary. *Mark Twain: A Descriptive Guide to Biographical Sources.* Lanham, MD: Scarecrow Press, 1999. Most of this bibliography's 285 substantially annotated entries are on biographical sources, but Horn also covers some works of literary criticism.

Howe, Lawrence. *Mark Twain and the Novel: The Double-Cross of Authority.* New York: Cambridge UP, 1998. Study of contradictory attitudes toward authority and social control in Mark Twain's major novels.

Howells, William Dean. *My Mark Twain: Reminiscences and Criticisms.* 1910. Reprint. Mineola, NY: Dover, 1997. Fascinating memoir by one of Mark Twain's closest friends and a major author in his own right. Includes reprints of Howells's reviews of *The Innocents Abroad, The Gilded Age, Tom Sawyer, A Tramp Abroad, Huckleberry Finn, A Connecticut Yankee,* and *Joan of Arc.* Useful for assessing 19th-century views of Mark Twain.

Ketterer, David, ed. *The Science Fiction of Mark Twain.* Hamden, CT: Archon, 1984. Collection of Mark Twain's best science fiction writings, including posthumously published works. Includes a general introduction and extensive notes. Reprinted as *Tales of Wonder* (Lincoln: University of Nebraska Press, 2003).

Knoper, Randall. *Acting Naturally: Mark Twain in the Culture of Performance.* Berkeley: U of California P, 1995. Examination of how Mark Twain uses performance in his writings in the context of 19th-century American culture.

LeMaster, J. R., and James D. Wilson, eds. *The Mark Twain Encyclopedia.* New York: Garland, 1993. Exceptionally useful general reference work covering Mark Twain's life and writings in depth. Especially helpful are its essays on themes and writing techniques. Individual articles include bibliographical notes.

Leonard, James S., ed. *Making Mark Twain Work in the Classroom.* Durham, NC: Duke UP, 1999. This teaching handbook is filled with articles by leading scholars addressing the kinds of issues about Mark Twain that are discussed in classrooms. Especially useful on *Huckleberry Finn.*

Magill, Frank N., ed. *Masterplots, Second Revised Edition.* 12 vols. Pasadena, CA: Salem Press, 1996. Collection of 1,800 articles with helpful summaries and analyses of classic literary works designed for students. Coverage includes *Adventures of Huckleberry Finn, The Adventures of Tom Sawyer, A Connecticut Yankee in King Arthur's Court, The Gilded Age, Life on the Mississippi, The Prince and the Pauper,* and *Roughing It.* Completely different essays on some of these same works, plus *Pudd'nhead Wilson,* can be found in Magill's

Masterplots II: Juvenile and Young Adult Fiction Series (1991) and its supplement (1997). All these Masterplots sets are also useful for other authors.

Messent, Peter. *Mark Twain.* New York: St. Martin's Press, 1997. Useful book by a leading British scholar of Mark Twain for a series on modern novelists. Includes chapters on "The Stolen White Elephant," *The Innocents Abroad, Roughing It, Tom Sawyer, Huckleberry Finn, Connecticut Yankee, Pudd'nhead Wilson,* and Mark Twain's later writings.

Messent, Peter, and Louis J. Budd, eds. *A Companion to Mark Twain.* Oxford, England: Blackwell, 2005. Collection of 35 original essays on a wide variety of subjects, including Mark Twain's most important individual works, themes in his writing, and stage and screen adaptations of his works.

Michelson, Bruce. *Mark Twain on the Loose: A Comic Writer and the American Self.* Amherst: U of Massachusetts P, 1995. Study of what Michelson calls the "outrageous and anarchic sides" of Mark Twain's writings.

Miller, Robert Keith. *Mark Twain.* New York: Frederick Ungar, 1983. Handy study that includes a substantial biography of Mark Twain and chapters on *Life on the Mississippi, Tom Sawyer, Huckleberry Finn, Connecticut Yankee, Pudd'nhead Wilson,* and selected short fiction.

Paine, Albert Bigelow. *Mark Twain, A Biography: The Personal and Literary Life of Samuel Langhorne Clemens.* 3 vols. New York: Harper & Bros., 1912. Not the most up-to-date biography of Mark Twain available but by far the fullest; written by his literary executor, who knew him well. Listed here because its electronic text is available free on Project Gutenberg.com. Project Gutenberg also has Paine's brief *The Boy's Life of Mark Twain* (1916).

Powers, Ron. *Mark Twain: A Life.* New York: Free Press, 2005. Up-to-date and masterful biography of Mark Twain by a Pulitzer Prize–winning author who grew up in Hannibal.

Quirk, Tom. *Mark Twain: A Study of the Short Fiction.* New York: Twayne Publishers, 1997. Contains useful descriptions and analyses of 50 important short works.

Railton, Stephen. *Mark Twain: A Short Introduction.* Malden, MA: Blackwell, 2004. Handy guide to some of Mark Twain's major writings by the scholar who maintains the *Mark Twain in His Times* Web site, discussed below.

———. *The Life & Work of Mark Twain.* Chantilly, VA: Teaching Company, 2002. Twenty-four lecture series in audio and video formats. In addition to stimulating lectures on aspects of Mark Twain's life, the series includes multiple lectures on *Huckleberry Finn, Tom Sawyer,* and *A Connecticut Yankee,* and single lectures on *Pudd'nhead Wilson, Roughing It,* and "Old Times on the Mississippi," the basis of *Life on the Mississippi*'s piloting chapters.

Rasmussen, R. Kent. *Critical Companion to Mark Twain: A Literary Reference to His Life and Work.* 2 vols. New York: Facts On File, 2007. Revised and significantly expanded edition of the author's *Mark Twain A to Z* (1995). New features of interest to students include extended analytical essays on major works, an expanded and fully annotated bibliography of books on Mark Twain, and a glossary explaining unusual words that Mark Twain used. Like *Mark Twain A to Z,* this work contains detailed plot synopses of most of Mark Twain's writings, along with entries on individual characters, places, and other subjects relating to those writings. It also has hundreds of entries relating to Mark Twain's life.

———, ed. *Cyclopedia of Literary Places.* 3 vols. Pasadena, CA: Salem Press, 2003. Collection of articles on more than 1,300 literary works analyzing the use of place as a literary device. Coverage includes *The Adventures of Tom Sawyer, Adventures of Huckleberry Finn, The Gilded Age, The Prince and the Pauper,* and *A Connecticut Yankee in King Arthur's Court.*

———, ed. *The Quotable Mark Twain: His Essential Aphorisms, Witticisms and Concise Opinions.* Chicago: Contemporary Press, 1997. Collections of Mark Twain quotations can be useful not only for finding pithy passages to quote in essays, but also to find ideas to get essays started. This collection is particularly helpful in this regard because it contains hundreds of brief summaries of Mark Twain's opinions on subjects that student essays often address. Other quote collections are available, but this one takes greater care than most in citing exact sources of quotes and in limiting quotes to verified Mark Twain texts. The book's alphabetical organization and thorough keyword index make it easy to use.

Skandera Trombley, Laura E., and Michael J. Kiskis, eds. *Constructing Mark Twain: New Directions in Scholarship.* Columbia: U of Missouri P, 2001. Collection of 13 entirely new essays on a variety of subjects, including ethnic caricaturing, race, and Mark Twain's black characters.

Sloane, David E. E. *Student Companion to Mark Twain.* Westport, CT: Greenwood Press, 2001. General guide to Mark Twain's writings in the context of his life; designed to meet students' classroom needs.

———, ed. *Mark Twain's Humor: Critical Essays.* New York: Garland, 1993. Large collection of essays on a much broader range of subjects than the book's title suggests.

Smiley, Jane. "Say It Ain't So, Huck: Second Thoughts on Mark Twain's 'Master-piece.'" *Harper's Magazine* (January 1996): 61f. Reasoned attack on *Huckleberry Finn* by a Pulitzer Prize–winning novelist. (Search on "say it ain't so, Huck" to find a PDF version of this article online.)

Smith, Henry Nash. *Mark Twain: The Development of a Writer.* Cambridge, MA: Belknap Press of Harvard UP, 1962. Still useful study of Mark Twain's work by an important Mark Twain scholar.

Tenney, Thomas Asa. *Mark Twain: A Reference Guide.* Boston: G. K. Hall, 1977. Most complete bibliography of writings on Mark Twain yet published; well indexed and easy to use to find annotated entries on books and articles on specific subjects. Updates to listings have been published in journals, and a new edition of the book is in the works.

Twain, Mark. *Collected Tales, Sketches, Speeches, & Essays, 1852–1890* and *Collected Tales, Sketches, Speeches, & Essays, 1891–1910,* edited by Louis J. Budd. New York: Library of America, 1992. These two volumes contain the most complete and authoritative collection of Mark Twain's short writings yet published. The first place to look for his short stories, sketches, and essays.

———. The Mark Twain Library. Edited by the Editors of the Mark Twain Project. 8 vols. Berkeley: U of California P, 1982–2001. Designed especially for students and general readers, these attractive and modestly priced hardback and paperback editions contain the most authoritative corrected texts yet published of *Tom Sawyer, Huckleberry Finn, The Prince and the Pauper, Connecticut Yankee, Roughing It,* and several other works. Each book also contains all the title's original illustrations, plus helpful explanatory notes. The University of California Press also publishes a companion series, Works of Mark Twain, much larger editions with the same corrected texts but also with much more information of interest to advanced scholars. Teachers selecting editions to assign to classes should consider Mark Twain Library books first. Among the best alternatives are the editions of the Modern Library and the Library of America that use corrected texts established by the Mark Twain Project.

———. The Oxford Mark Twain. Edited by Shelley Fisher Fishkin. 29 vols. New York: Oxford UP, 1996. Collection of reprints of the first American editions of all the books that Mark Twain published during his lifetime. Containing facsimile reproductions of original pages, with all their wonderful illustrations, these volumes allow you to read books that look like the books Mark

Twain himself handled. Better still, every volume has a substantial introduction by the editor, an original introduction by a noted author, and a new
afterword by a Mark Twain scholar—all features that can help you write
essays.

Wilson, James D. *A Reader's Guide to the Short Stories of Mark Twain.* Boston:
G. K. Hall, 1987. Useful reference work with 42 chapters analyzing individual stories.

Online Resources

These sites are among the most informative and trustworthy permanent Web
sites offering substantial information on Mark Twain. You can find other sites
by searching the Web, but be cautious about information you find there, as the
Web contains a great deal of misinformation about Mark Twain. Also, be especially cautious about information you get on Wikipedia.org. A growing online
encyclopedia, Wikipedia contains long, authoritative, and amazingly up-to-date
articles on thousands of subjects; however, anyone who visits the site can change
an article or add a new one. Wikipedia's administrators work to maintain high
standards, but they lack the resources and expertise needed to keep up with
everything posted. As a consequence, many Wikipedia articles contain errors
and distortions—mostly the products of well-meaning but nonexpert contribu-
tors. Cybervandalism is also a problem. It is wise to stick to printed and online
resources created and maintained by authorities known to be reliable.

Elmira College Center for Mark Twain Studies (www.elmira.edu/academics/
distinctive_programs/twain_center). The home of Mark Twain's in-laws,
Elmira, New York, was the place where Mark Twain spent most of his
summers and wrote most of his books during the 1870s and 1880s. Elmira
College's Center for Mark Twain Studies has a busy program of events and
lectures and makes downloadable podcasts of its lecture series available on
its Web site.

Mark Twain, edited by Jim Zwick (www.historyillustrated.com/twain). Large
and diverse Web site offering electronic texts, pictures, and original essays
on subjects ranging from Mark Twain's politics to collecting his books.
An expert on Mark Twain's views on imperialism, Zwick frequently adds
reviews of current books and new features to his site.

Mark Twain Boyhood Home and Museum (www.marktwainmuseum.org). Web
site for the museum organization that maintains the Hannibal, Missouri,

house in which Mark Twain passed most of his boyhood, as well as other buildings with Mark Twain connections and several museums. This Web site contains an illustrated tour of the buildings with Mark Twain connections and other information on Mark Twain. Another useful Hannibal Web site is maintained by the *Hannibal Courier* (www.hannibal.net/twain), the first newspaper for which Mark Twain worked as a printer when he was a boy. This site's Mark Twain information includes brief articles, electronic texts, video and audio clips, interactive maps of Hannibal, and educational games.

Mark Twain Forum (www.twainweb.net). Web site for an online discussion group, maintained through a listserver, in which members share information and thoughts about Mark Twain and seek answers to questions. Most of the forum's more than 400 members are scholars and teachers, but students and others are welcome. The forum's Web site contains a searchable archive of past postings, a large collection of perceptive book reviews by Mark Twain authorities, photographs, links to other Mark Twain sites, and other features.

Mark Twain House, The (www.marktwainhouse.org). Official Web site of Mark Twain's Hartford, Connecticut, house in which he lived for nearly 20 years. The house is now a public museum; its Web site contains pictures and descriptions of the house, news on museum events, and special features on Mark Twain for teachers and students.

Mark Twain in His Times (etext.virginia.edu/railton/index2.html). Constructed and maintained by Stephen Railton, this extremely helpful Web site has special sections on Mark Twain's major works that include facsimile pages from first editions, complete and searchable texts of the books, early advertisements and promotions for the books, contemporary reviews, and special sections on topics such as slavery. For other Web sites offering downloadable texts, see Project Gutenberg below.

Mark Twain Project (www.lib.berkeley.edu/banc/mtp). Web site of the document-editing project at the University of California in Berkeley that houses most of Mark Twain's surviving papers. The site offers descriptions of the project's collections, news about its work and publications, and other features.

Project Gutenberg (www.gutenberg.org). Online collection of the complete texts of thousands of literary works in the public domain (meaning that they are out of copyright) that can easily be downloaded. Contains almost all the books and stories that Mark Twain published during his lifetime, as well as some of his posthumously published works. Also has Albert Bigelow Paine's monumental 1913 biography of Mark Twain.

TwainQuotes.com (www.twainquotes.com). This Web site maintained by research expert Barbara Schmidt includes a large and searchable directory of Mark Twain quotes; full texts of early newspaper articles by and about Mark Twain; hundreds of book illustrations and photographs, many of which are not published elsewhere; and many articles on subjects of interest to Mark Twain scholars and admirers.

THE ADVENTURES
OF TOM SAWYER

READING TO WRITE

A MONG THE many reasons Mark Twain's books give pleasure to so many readers is their wide range of subjects and themes. *The Adventures of Tom Sawyer* is a good example of a story that has much greater depth than may at first appear. Ostensibly a simple tale, it is set in a relatively confined space—a village and its surroundings—in a relatively short time, only a few months. In contrast to *The Prince and the Pauper* (1881)—set in England during the time of King Henry VIII—*Tom Sawyer* concerns no epochal events and none of its characters has rank or distinction. It is merely a story about an obscure village boy who stumbles onto thrilling adventures. For young readers, that makes for pleasurable reading. However, is there more to the novel than that?

The Adventures of Tom Sawyer is the Mark Twain story most widely read by children. However, that does not mean it is necessarily a children's novel. Indeed, one critic has dubbed it a "nightmare vision of America," scarcely the kind of description one expects of a beloved children's classic. The fact is that people of all ages read and enjoy *Tom Sawyer*, and many people read it repeatedly throughout their lives. As we approach the novel, among the first questions to ask are: For whom did Mark Twain write the book, and what was he trying to do with it? When he finished writing it, he regarded it as a novel for adults and tried to get it serialized in the *Atlantic Monthly,* a distinguished literary magazine published in Boston. The magazine's editor, his good friend W. D. Howells, read his manuscript and thought it marvelous but told Mark Twain it was better suited for children. In fact, he called it the best boys' novel ever written.

When Mark Twain finally published *Tom Sawyer* in 1876, he was still uncertain about its proper audience. The brief preface he wrote for the book is revealing. Readers often skip over introductions and prefaces, but *Tom Sawyer*'s preface repays a close reading. This extract from it provides a useful starting point for assessing the novel:

> Although my book is intended mainly for the entertainment of boys and girls, I hope it will not be shunned by men and women on that account, for part of my plan has been to try to pleasantly remind adults of what they once were themselves, and of how they felt and thought and talked, and what queer enterprises they sometimes engaged in.

Mark Twain clearly states that *Tom Sawyer*'s primary purpose is to entertain children; however, he also expresses his desire for adults to look at childhood from their perspective. Are these two goals compatible? And is Mark Twain being entirely honest? You might do well to start your own reading of the novel by asking whether the book is better suited for children or adults. That may sound like a simple challenge, but it might prove difficult. However, it is an issue that demands an answer because it relates to almost every theme or subject on which you are likely to write an essay.

In his introduction to the Oxford Mark Twain edition of *Tom Sawyer*, novelist E. L. Doctorow points out the sharp distinctions in the story between the separate cultures of children and adults. He adds that each of Tom's adventures arises from disparities between those two cultures. Indeed, the novel opens with Tom defying the authority of his aunt Polly, who wants to punish him for an unspecified offense and finds him fleeing from a closet where he has been stealing jam. She seizes him, but he escapes and then plays hooky from school. Thus, in the first few pages of the book, Tom defies both parental and school authorities, setting the tone for the more serious transgressions to follow. Something to watch for as you read the book is whether Tom's attitude toward adult authority changes.

A more dramatic example of the disparities that exist between the worlds of children and adults occurs when Tom shares his first major adventure with Huck. In chapter 9, the two boys go to a graveyard at midnight to perform a wart-removing ritual over a fresh grave. When they arrive, they find three men digging up the grave. Their boyish enterprise is interrupted by a deadly serious adult enterprise: grave-robbing. The boys are horrified when an argument among the grave robbers becomes violent and the doctor is killed. The murderer, the fearsome Injun Joe, then convinces his drunken partner, Muff Potter, that he, Muff, killed the other man in his drunken stupor. Tom and Huck sneak away and then perform another boyish ritual by swearing a blood oath never to reveal what they have just seen. An adventure that starts as boyish play thus becomes a deadly serious affair involving a murderous adult. Through the ensuing chapters, Tom is haunted by his fear of Injun Joe, while feeling consumed with guilt for remaining silent about Potter's innocence. He is thus torn between the obligation he incurs by swearing the oath and what he recognizes as his mature obligation to speak up in the cause of justice. His struggles to resolve his conflicting loyalties and overcome his fear suggest a number of possible essay topics.

Tom shares his second major adventure with Huck and Joe Harper. Feeling unloved and misunderstood, he leads his friends on a raft trip to Jackson's Island, where they set up a pirate community. Can it be argued that Tom is consciously choosing to reject the adult world by creating a world ruled by boys? Is there a message behind the fact that the boys soon become homesick and return to accept adult authority? Adults might react to the conclusion of that episode with a knowing smile; however, Tom transforms the boys' defeat into a triumph by suddenly appearing with his friends at their own funeral service. That dramatic moment makes for immensely satisfying reading, but does it also say something about the possibility of children being able to live out their fantasies?

Closely related to the question of who constitutes *Tom Sawyer*'s proper audience is the question of whether the book should even be read by younger readers. Many episodes—such as the one in which Tom tricks his friends into whitewashing a fence—delight young readers. However, the novel also contains episodes that are horrifying. Indeed, some people argue that the book is inappropriate for young readers because it contains passages too intense for children. This charge raises the question of whether Mark Twain's uncertainty about his intended audience influenced *how* he wrote *Tom Sawyer*. Was he, perhaps, consciously writing for children in some passages and for adults in others? Or was he simply being careless?

TOPICS AND STRATEGIES

Here we shall discuss possible topics for essays on *Tom Sawyer* and general approaches to those topics. Keep in mind that these paragraphs are intended merely to help you develop your own ideas, not to outline what you should write. The keys to successful essays are originality of thought and clearness and force of argument. Many questions, such as those suggested below, have no right or wrong answers. The strength of an essay comes not from the conclusions it reaches, but from the power and clarity of the arguments it advances. In choosing a subject, try to avoid the example of Tom Sawyer, who, when he had to select Bible verses to memorize, went for the simplest. Instead, consider going for the most complex subjects, as these will be the ones that most simulate your thinking and help you come up with original ideas.

Themes

As discussed at the start of this chapter, Mark Twain wrote *Tom Sawyer* at least partly for adults, with the professed goal of reminding them what it was like being a child. Although children are his book's main characters, they are seen primarily through the eyes of adults. Some critics have described the book as having a "dual" narrative: At some moments it seems to be written from a child's perspective; at others, from an adult's. Ironically, the adult point of view is particularly evident at the conclusion of chapter 2's fence-painting episode, in which Tom not only persuades his friends to whitewash a fence for him but also gets them to *pay* him for that privilege. One of the most famous episodes in the book, Tom's whitewashing triumph delights young readers, who rarely fail to appreciate its irony. However, the chapter's summation of the episode is clearly aimed at the book's adult readers: As you look for themes on which to write, keep in mind the novel's basic division between child and adult points of view.

Sample Topics:

1. **"Hymn to boyhood" or "nightmare vision"?:** Mark Twain once described *Tom Sawyer* as a "hymn to boyhood." Is that description accurate? In what ways does the book celebrate childhood—particularly boyhood? Conversely, how does it express the terrors of childhood?

   You might begin an essay on this subject by compiling two lists: one listing moments in the novel that reflect the joys of being a child, the other listing horrific moments. Compare the two lists to see if they balance and use your findings to argue whether Tom's village is a "paradise for boys" or a "nightmare vision of boyhood." Examine the adult characters. What kind of role models do they present? What do they represent that might make children look forward to growing up?

2. **Boyhood v. girlhood:** How do girls figure into *Tom Sawyer*? Does any part of the novel's view of boyhood also apply to girlhood?

   Discussions of the novel tend to use the concepts of childhood and boyhood almost interchangeably. Is that a valid way to look at *Tom Sawyer*? To consider the extent to which the novel's depiction of boyhood also applies to girls, identify the activities that involve both boys and girls, the narrator's observations that apply equally to both sexes, and moments when actions initiated by girls help to drive the plot. What would the novel lose if there were no girls in it? Keep in mind that 19th-century Americans had very different ideas about the proper roles and activities of girls.

3. **Violence:** A theme closely allied to that of boyhood vision is the use of violence in the novel. How does the novel use violence, and the threat of violence, to move the story along, and how does it regard violence? How does violence relate to the intersection of child and adult worlds?

Disparities between child and adult worlds are reflected in the novel's treatment of violence. The obvious beginning point for an essay on this subject is to catalog incidents of violence—both real and in play—as well as episodes in which the threat of violence looms. Between fights with other boys, mock battles, and pirate and Robin Hood games, Tom is involved in a great deal of ostensibly violent behavior. How is his play violence reflected in the real violence of the adult world? Does the intersection of play and real violence change his attitude?

4. **Thirst for glory:** In an autobiographical dictation that he recorded three decades after publishing *Tom Sawyer*, Mark Twain said "celebrity is what a boy or a youth longs for more than for any other thing. . . . it is the same with every grown-up person." (*Mark Twain in Eruption* 233). To what extent does that statement apply to Tom Sawyer? Does it apply to other characters in the novel?

   Tom Sawyer provides a fertile field for explorations of this subject. You might begin by examining Tom's thoughts and his behavior around other people. Tom clearly savors the idea of winning glory, but how consciously is he aware of his thirst for attention? Are there contradictions between his desires and his actions? Look for indications of other characters seeking attention and glory, such as the Sunday-school superintendent and librarian in chapter 4.

5. **Folklore and superstitions:** As we have seen, one of Mark Twain's goals for his book was to "remind adults of what they once were themselves, and of how they felt and thought and talked, and what queer enterprises they sometimes engaged in." Among the things he wished to remind adults of were the "odd superstitions . . . prevalent among children and slaves in the West at the period of this story . . ." To what superstitions does he allude and how do they help drive the story?

This theme is closely tied to the separation of the child and adult worlds in the novel. To develop an essay on this subject, begin by identifying the scenes in which Tom or other boys attempt to invoke charms and incantations, swear blood oaths, or otherwise express their faith in superstitions. A list of such moments might grow quite long. Does anything ever happen to give the boys reason to believe in the efficacy of their superstitions? How do the boys explain the apparent failings of their incantations? Do they invoke reason or do they look for alternative explanations? Consider also how the scenes involving superstitions lead into collisions between the child and adult worlds. The most obvious example occurs in chapter 9, when Tom and Huck go to the village graveyard to perform a ritual with a dead cat but instead happen on the murder of Dr. Robinson. Any discussion of encounters between child and adult beliefs should also consider examples of adult attitudes toward what they regard as childish superstitions, as in chapter 23, when Tom testifies at Muff Potter's murder trial and explains why he was in the graveyard at midnight. You could also consider examples of adult superstitions. Would it be fair to regard Aunt Polly's faith in patent medicines (see chapter 12) as a form of superstition?

A related theme easily worthy of a fascinating essay is the role of religion in the novel. However, in the context of superstition and folklore, it would probably be wise to restrict that subject to the role of religion as it is perceived by a village boy. To Tom, religion revolves around the distasteful burden of having to attend Sunday school and his vague ideas about a remote God who dispenses retributive justice on the good and the wicked. In this latter regard, Tom's ideas about God tie into his general superstitions and fears and can therefore be discussed in the same context.

Character

Questions about characters and their development in *Tom Sawyer* offer another rich field for topics. One might, for example, look at how Tom changes throughout the novel or make comparisons between pairs of characters, such as Tom and Huck. If your writing assignment lets you extend your enquiries beyond the bounds of this one book, you will find an even wider scope for Tom-and-Huck comparisons. You might ask, for example, whether the Tom of *Tom Sawyer* is the same character as the Tom of *Huckleberry Finn*? Even broader comparisons might take in characters from books by other authors. For example, Tom is clearly one of the literary ancestors of J. K. Rowling's Harry Potter and much might be said about the traces of Tom to be found in Harry.

A general question to consider while reading any novel is the extent to which its characters are, in fact, *characters,* and not merely one- or two-dimensional figures inserted as little more than props to move the story along. True characters are complex and three-dimensional (or "fully rounded") people, about whom readers learn enough not to expect them always to behave predictably. One way to test a character's complexity is to ask whether that character is capable of surprising you. Tom Sawyer is full of surprises, but can the same be said of Huckleberry Finn, Aunt Polly, or Becky Thatcher in this novel?

You can observe characters in *Tom Sawyer* at least three different ways: through the descriptions provided by the novel's anonymous observer, through the words and thoughts of the characters themselves, and through their actions. There is naturally some overlap among these methods of observation, as everything we know about the characters comes through the words of the narrator. This actually raises a question about the reliability of narrators: Should readers trust everything that they report? Anonymous, third-person narrators are generally reliable, but the same is not always true of first-person narrators, such as Huck Finn in *Huckleberry Finn.* In any case, as you study the characters in *Tom Sawyer,* pay attention to whether information comes to you through the narrator's own assessments, through the revealed thoughts or words of the characters themselves, or through the actions of the characters. Allow for the possibility there may be contradictions between what characters say or think and what they actually do. Such contradictions may in themselves reveal something about the characters. An example occurs in chapter 20, in which Tom waits, expecting the schoolmaster to bully Becky into confessing she tore his book. He privately gloats at the thought of the punishment Becky will receive, but at the last second—with no warning to the reader—he springs up and shouts, "I done it!" Where does that impulse come from? And what does it tell us about Tom?

Sample Topics:

1. **Tom's character development:** What can be said about what kind of person Tom is? What are his values? What motivates him to act? How does he change throughout the novel?

   One of the most persistent criticisms of *Tom Sawyer* is its inconsistent depictions of Tom. If you read the novel closely for physical descriptions of Tom, you will probably be surprised to find none. How old is he? How tall is he? What color is his hair? We can only guess. Questions about Tom's age have particularly perplexed readers. In the early chapters, he seems to be about nine years old. As the novel progresses, however, he seems to become older. By the end of the novel, he appears to be a young adolescent. Meanwhile, his sweetheart, Becky Thatcher, seems to remain about nine years old.

   To write an essay on Tom's character development, you will need to look closely at the novel's descriptions of his behavior and thought processes. What do his thoughts and actions reveal about his maturity and his attitude toward conventional values? What evidence can you find to support the conclusion that he matures as the novel unfolds? For example, does his interest in purely boyish pursuits decline? Is he ever, at heart, a rebel against social conventions? Or are his condemnations of conventional values and misbehavior merely the transitory expressions of restlessness of a purely conventional boy? Do changes in his behavior indicate he is moving from the world of children into the world of adults? Is his behavior always consistent with each stage of its development?

2. **Huckleberry Finn:** What kind of character is Huck? What motivates him? What are his values? Does he change within the novel?

Many questions about Tom Sawyer might apply equally to Huck Finn; however, their answers might differ greatly. Differences between Tom and Huck are discussed in the section on Compare and Contrast Essays that follows; here you should consider Huck on his own terms. When Huck is first introduced in chapter 6, he is described as the village's "juvenile pariah"—a boy hated by the town's mothers but admired and envied by all the "respectable" boys. In his first appearance, Huck seems to be more of a "type" than a character. Indeed, the contrast between him and Tom is so sharp that one wonders if Mark Twain created him to serve mainly as a foil for Tom. Is that possibility supported by the text?

A comparison between the Huck of *Tom Sawyer* and the Huck of *Huckleberry Finn* would make a good topic for an essay; however, if you choose to focus on *Tom Sawyer*'s Huck, you should probably put *Huckleberry Finn* out of your mind. Mark Twain was not giving much thought to a sequel when he wrote *Tom Sawyer*, so what *Huckleberry Finn* reveals about Huck is irrelevant to a discussion of *Tom Sawyer*.

3. **Injun Joe:** What is his role in the novel?

Injun Joe may be the most fearsome character that Mark Twain ever created. A vicious murderer, unprincipled thief, and shameless liar, he seems to represent pure evil, for he has no apparent redeeming qualities. He even betrays his own criminal partners. If his role in the novel is simply to frighten the daylights out of Tom and Huck, he certainly succeeds. However, might it be argued he has a deeper role? Consider the possibility he is a kind of evil double, or dark mirror image, of Tom. While Tom plays his pirate games, talks gaily of the "nobility" of robbers, and plans to organize a robber gang, kill people, and hold prisoners for ransom, Injun Joe is the real thing. How does Joe's record of crime compare to Tom's boyish notions about criminals? Might Mark Twain have created Joe for ironic effect, to point up the foolishness of boyhood fantasies?

History and Context

Among other reasons for *Tom Sawyer*'s enduring popularity is the book's value as a document of small-town life on the edge of the American frontier during the mid-19th century. It is generally agreed that Mark Twain modeled St. Petersburg on Hannibal, Missouri, the Mississippi riverfront town in which he grew up during the 1840s and early 1850s. Does this mean that *Tom Sawyer* is set in Missouri? Probably. However, if you study the novel's geographical clues carefully, you might be surprised at how little reference to Missouri can be found. That fact suggests a first question to consider: Does it matter exactly where and when the novel is set? Could the same basic story work in another region or in a more recent time period? What aspects of mid-19th-century life on the edge of the frontier give the story meaning that it might lack in other settings? As you read the novel, pay particular attention to the subtle conditions of life that differ from those of our own time. These might include such day-to-day matters as the perils of epidemics, folk superstitions, primitive schools, limited communication with the outside world, and conformity to small-town values.

Sample Topics:

1. **"America's Hometown":** Modern Hannibal, Missouri, identifies itself so closely with Mark Twain and with the St. Petersburg of *Tom Sawyer* that it likes to call itself "America's Hometown." That nickname seems to celebrate the small-town values of Tom Sawyer's hometown, but exactly what values does St. Petersburg represent?

   An essay on this subject could either restrict itself to what you find in *Tom Sawyer* or incorporate research on the development of the American frontier during the early 19th century, when Missouri was considered the threshold to the western territories. Whichever approach you take, you will need to read *Tom Sawyer* closely to draw out all the information it contains on schools, churches, local businesses, industries, commerce, and people in Tom's village. What kinds of enterprises does St. Petersburg have? What kind of entertainments does it offer its residents? What are the town's positive and negative features? And, finally, what, if anything, about it makes it worthy of being held up as a model of American communities? If you wish to expand your research, you could build a fascinating essay around comparisons between the fictional St. Petersburg and Mark Twain's real-life Hannibal. Such an essay should also try to explain why Mark Twain may have made St. Petersburg differ from Hannibal.

2. **Slavery:** Does slavery play any role in *Tom Sawyer*?

Mark Twain's birthplace and boyhood home, Missouri, was a slave state, and Mark Twain grew up around slavery. Indeed, his own parents owned slaves, one of whom, a young boy named Sandy, is generally regarded as the model for the carefree Jim, "the small colored boy" of the first two chapters of *Tom Sawyer.* (Note that this character is not related to the Jim of *Huckleberry Finn.*) Apart from Jim's presence in the novel, what evidence is there of slavery in Tom Sawyer's world? Does its presence or absence reflect on the realism of the novel as a document of 19th-century American life?

This subject is closely tied to that of the first sample topic. Indeed, one of the criticisms of modern Hannibal's efforts to capitalize on its ties to *Tom Sawyer* is its tendency (which is being corrected) to ignore its own history of slavery. To write a strong essay on slavery in *Tom Sawyer,* you should go beyond the novel, either by researching slavery in Hannibal or Missouri, or by comparing *Tom Sawyer* with *Huckleberry Finn.* The latter novel opens in the St. Petersburg of *Tom Sawyer* but evidence of slavery and slave trading quickly becomes more apparent. *Huckleberry Finn* considers many questions about slavery that are not addressed in *Tom Sawyer* and thus offers a fertile field for comparison.

3. **The Mississippi River:** How does the river figure in *Tom Sawyer*? Does the novel's depiction of it differ from that of Mark Twain's other Mississippi writings in any significant ways?

Set along the banks of America's most majestic river, *Tom Saw-yer* is generally regarded as a central work in Mark Twain's various Mississippi writings, which also include *Huckleberry Finn, Life on the Mississippi* (1881), and *Pudd'nhead Wilson* (1894)— all of which are discussed in other chapters in this volume.

An essay on this subject would benefit from your having some familiarity with Mark Twain's other Mississippi writings, but it should be possible to write a good essay on the river drawing only on *Tom Sawyer*. Examine the novel's references to the river and pay special attention to the river's symbolic meanings. A question connected to the first topic in this section is how the river relates to the life of the town. Apart from the boys' use of the river for play, is there any indication in the novel that the river has any importance to St. Petersburg?

Philosophy and Ideas

Another way to look at *Tom Sawyer* is to explore the broad philosophical ideas that the novel expresses. This approach is related to the study of themes described above, but it operates at a more general level.

Sample Topics:

1. **Dreams v. reality:** The novel frequently alludes to its characters' dreams, particularly Tom's. What role do dreams play within the novel?

During his last years, Mark Twain wrote many long stories in which characters so confuse their dreams with reality that they become uncertain about which is which. Tom experiences a similar confusion early in chapter 27, in which he begins to think the adventure he and Huck experienced in the Haunted House was only a dream. An essay about dreams in *Tom Sawyer* might offer an interesting key to the later development of Mark Twain's thinking. Look for passages in which dreams figure prominently and ask yourself what role they play in advancing the plot or developing the characters. What would the novel lose if it were to contain no allusions to dreams?

A closely related idea that might be tied into dreams is Tom's recurrent death wishes. Note the passage in chapter 8 in which Tom envies his recently deceased friend, Jimmy Hodges, and imagines how peaceful it would be "to lie and slumber and dream forever and ever . . . and nothing to bother and grieve about, ever any more." Are Tom's fantasies about being dead a form of dreaming?

2. **Community values:** *Tom Sawyer* is often seen as an archetypal example of a "bad-boy" story. The novel's very first chapter states explicitly that Tom is "not the Model Boy of the village." Is he, however, a "bad" boy? What distinguishes the two? Does his frequent defiance of adult authority expression his rebellion against community values?

This is another subject for which the novel provides a rich field for exploration. You might begin by examining the first chapter's definition of a "Model Boy" and then compare it to what Tom becomes by the end of the novel. The novel opens with Tom stealing jam, defying Aunt Polly's authority, and getting into a fight with the town's new boy, and examples of his misbehavior and defiance of authority abound. However, is Tom truly a bad boy? Compiling lists of his good and bad deeds would help you develop an essay on this subject, but you need to go deeper than cataloging Tom's transgressions. What evidence can you find to reveal his true attitude toward the conventional values of his community? Who are the adult authority figures he defies? Which, if any, of them merits respect? In his acts of defiance, how does Tom differentiate among adults? Is he really a rebel? Or is he at heart a highly conventional boy who simply has a lively imagination, a taste for adventure, and disrespect for those who do not merit respect? In this regard, what does Mark Twain—as the self-described "great and wise philosopher" who wrote the book (see chapter 2)—have to say about the respect that adult authority figures merit? Who among the adult figures is *not* a hypocrite?

You might carry your discussion of nonconformity v. conventional values further by comparing Tom with Huck Finn. Huck is described far more fully in *Tom Sawyer*'s sequel, *Adventures of Huckleberry Finn* (1884); however, *Tom Sawyer* reveals enough about his nature to enable rewarding comparisons between his and Tom's attitudes toward society.

Form and Genre

Essays about a novel's form examine issues such as how the novel is constructed, the literary techniques it uses to create effects, and how and why its structure succeeds or fails. *Tom Sawyer*'s basic form is a third-person narrative related by an anonymous adult. In this respect, it differs greatly from its sequel, *Huckleberry Finn*, which is narrated by its young protagonist, Huck. A comparison of how these two novels differ in form would be an excellent subject for an essay, but much can be said about *Tom Sawyer*'s form without reference to other books. For example, what is the narrator's point of view, and how does it shift throughout the novel?

Genre is generally understood to refer to the categories in which literary works fit. Sometimes, a single work can be assigned to more than one genre. For example, *Tom Sawyer* might be considered a coming-of-age story, an adventure story, a children's novel, or autobiographical fiction. If you choose to write on which genre terms you think *Tom Sawyer* is, your essay must address the question of why classification matters. Keep in mind it is unlikely that Mark Twain himself gave a moment's thought to genre categories. Most writers do not, but Mark Twain wrote books that are unusually difficult to categorize.

Sample Topics:

1. **Bildungsroman:** Should *Tom Sawyer* be regarded as a coming-of-age novel?

   A classic coming-of-age story, or bildungsroman, traces the maturation of a protagonist from callow youth to a person on the threshold of possessing adult wisdom. A major aspect of this genre is the protagonist's growing self-awareness and acceptance of responsibility. There can be little disagreement on the question of whether Tom Sawyer is callow and heedless at the beginning of *Tom Sawyer*. Is he, however, wiser and more mature by the end of the novel? It should be possible to write a strong essay arguing either answer to that question. Whichever side you choose, keep in mind the opposite side's arguments.

Much of what you will need to do if you write an essay on this topic is define your terms clearly and provide examples of their application. Explain what you mean by "maturing," "wisdom," "heedlessness," "self-awareness," and any other terms you use to make your points. This is necessary not merely to impress your instructor with your own wisdom and maturity, but to help clarify in your mind exactly what you are trying to say. An essay on this topic that fails to explain its own terminology could easily become a mess. Meanwhile, you can develop your arguments by citing examples of Tom's behavior and thought processes and showing how and why they change over the course of the novel. Allow for the possibility that his growth may not always be in one direction.

Another aspect of Tom's development to consider is the question of Tom's actual biological age. Mark Twain seems to have left that matter deliberately vague. (Can you think of a reason why he may have done that?) The entire narrative unfolds within a matter of months, so Tom cannot age much from beginning to end. Does he, however, seem to remain at about the same age throughout? For an interesting comparison, apply the same questions to Becky Thatcher.

2. ***Tom Sawyer* as autobiography:** What does the novel reveal about Mark Twain himself?

Many critics regard *Tom Sawyer* as at least partly autobiographical. Many of its characters, incidents, and places come out of Mark Twain's own boyhood in Missouri. For example, like Tom Sawyer, Mark Twain joined an organization called the Cadets of Temperance and relished the idea of marching in grand processions. Moreover, like Tom, he eventually grew weary of waiting for an occasion that would prompt a procession and quit the organization.

An essay on this subject demands some research into Mark Twain's early life, so you can assess its relationship with his novel. There are many good biographies to choose from, and his autobiographical writings (published in a variety of editions) are especially revealing about his youth. After you have done some reading on Mark Twain's boyhood, try to determine which parts of his novel have their origins in his youth and which are wholly invented. Are there patterns in the types of characters and events that fall into each group? Why might he have chosen to use the childhood memories that he did use and omit others?

Compare and Contrast Essays

Compare and contrast papers offer a vast scope for developing original ideas, but they also make it easy to fall into the trap of doing exactly the opposite. Preparation for any compare and contrast essay usually begins with the compilation of lists of similarities and differences—between characters, plots, points of view, and so on. The danger in this approach is allowing yourself to be satisfied with the lists themselves. It is not enough to say that Tom Sawyer seeks public attention while Huck Finn shuns it. You must try to explain why the characters differ in this regard, how this difference affects each boy's behavior, and how it relates to other aspects of each boy's personality.

An attractive feature of compare and contrast essays is that they allow you to be creative on two levels: first, in finding aspects of one or more works to compare; second, in finding significant points to make about the similarities and differences you observe. True originality is often difficult to achieve, but one of your best chances of attaining it lies in innovative compare and contrast essays. Comparing Tom and Huck would give you a wide scope for interesting analyses, but the only chance for originality that approach would offer would be in the comparisons you draw, not in the basic question. On the other hand, if you were to compare and contrast a less obvious pair of characters, such as the schoolmaster Dobbins and the Sunday school superintendent Walters, you would certainly be on to something original.

Sample Topics:

1. **Comparing Tom and Huck:** What are the most striking similarities and differences between these two boys? How do they interact?

   Images of Tom Sawyer and Huckleberry Finn are inextricably linked in modern American culture. To many people, the characters are virtually interchangeable, carefree, and fun-loving rascals. Are they? To write an essay on this subject, you'll need to look closely for clues as to what motivates each boy. For example, do the boys share the same values and goals? Are their temperaments similar? Is Tom always a leader and Huck always a follower? How can you account for their differences?

   A clue to the fundamental differences between the boys can be found in Mark Twain's own words. In July 1875, after he finished writing *Tom Sawyer,* he wrote to his friend W. D. Howells to ask him to read the manuscript of his novel and mentioned that he was thinking about writing another book about a boy:

   > By & by I shall take a boy of twelve & and run him on through life (in the first person) but not Tom Sawyer—he would not be a good character for it. (*Mark Twain—Howells Letters* 92)

   The book to which he was alluding was *Adventures of Huckleberry Finn,* a story narrated by Huck himself. In view of the fact that Mark Twain wrote his letter to Howells well before he even started writing *Huckleberry Finn,* he probably knew less about that novel than you do, even if you have not yet read it. His judgment about the unsuitability of Tom Sawyer as the central character of his unwritten book was therefore based on what he knew about Tom from *The Adventures of Tom Sawyer.* Why might he have concluded that Tom would be an unsuitable narrator in another story? And why do you suppose that he eventually chose Huck Finn to be that story's narrator? You can address these questions in one of two ways: You can either limit your discussion to what you know about Tom and Huck from

Tom Sawyer, or, if your assignment allows you to compare that novel to *Huckleberry Finn,* you can consider the type of character that Huck becomes in his own novel to the type of character that Tom is in *Tom Sawyer.*

2. **Comparing *Tom Sawyer* and *Huckleberry Finn:*** These two novels share many characters and settings, but are they the same kinds of books? In what important ways do they differ?

This subject lends itself to some of the most interesting questions you might address. Just as Tom and Huck are closely linked in the public mind, so too are the two novels in which they are central characters. In fact, Mark Twain began *Huckleberry Finn* as such a close sequel to *Tom Sawyer* that its opening chapters are almost a seamless continuation of the earlier novel. Nevertheless, most people familiar with both books regard them as very different novels. The most obvious structural difference between them is that *Tom Sawyer* is told by an omniscient narrator, evidently an adult looking back about 30 years in the future, while *Huckleberry Finn* is narrated by a young boy, Huck himself, immediately after the events that he describes. The two books differ in many important ways but perhaps the most profound difference lies in their narrative structures. To write a comparative essay on these books, you will need to pay close attention to how their narrative voices differ and what impact those differences have on the overall novels. How might *Tom Sawyer* differ if it were narrated by Tom himself (or Huck)? Conversely, how might *Huckleberry Finn* differ if it had the same kind of narrator *Tom Sawyer* has?

Bibliography for *Tom Sawyer*

Blair, Walter. "On the Structure of *Tom Sawyer.*" *Mark Twain's Humor: Critical Essays.* Ed. David E. E. Sloane. New York: Garland, 1993. 137–64.

De Koster, Katie, ed. *Readings on "The Adventures of Tom Sawyer."* San Diego, CA: Greenhaven Press, 1999.

Doctorow, E. L. Introduction. *The Adventures of Tom Sawyer.* By Mark Twain. New York: Oxford UP, 1996. xxxi–xxxviii.

————. "Sam Clemens's Two Boys." *Creationists: Selected Essays, 1993–2006.* New York: Random House, 2006.

Evans, John D. *A "Tom Sawyer" Companion: An Autobiographical Guided Tour with Mark Twain.* Lanham, MD: UP of America, 1993.

Hirsch, Tim. "Banned by Neglect: *Tom Sawyer*—Teaching the Conflicts." *Censored Books I: Critical Viewpoints, 1985–2000.* Lanham, MD: Scarecrow Press, 2002. 1–9.

Hutchinson, Stuart, ed. *Mark Twain's "Tom Sawyer" and "Huckleberry Finn."* New York: Columbia UP, 1999.

Messent, Peter. *Mark Twain.* New York: St. Martin's Press, 1997.

————. "Discipline and Punishment in *The Adventures of Tom Sawyer.*" *Journal of American Studies* 32, no. 2 (1998): 219–35.

Molson, Francis. "Mark Twain's *The Adventures of Tom Sawyer:* More Than a Warm Up." *Touchstones: Reflections on the Best in Children's Literature.* Ed. Perry Nodelman. West Lafayette, IN: Children's Literature Association, 1985. 262–69.

Morris, Linda A. "*The Adventures of Tom Sawyer* and *The Prince and the Pauper* as Juvenile Literature." *A Companion to Mark Twain.* Ed. Peter Messent and Louis J. Budd. Oxford: Blackwell, 2005. 371–86.

————. *Gender Play in Mark Twain: Cross-Dressing and Transgression.* Columbia: U of Missouri P, 2007.

Norton, Charles A. *Writing "Tom Sawyer": The Adventures of a Classic.* Jefferson, NC: MacFarland, 1983.

Project Gutenberg. Complete text of *Tom Sawyer* online at www.gutenberg. org/etext/74.

Railton, Stephen. *The Life & Work of Mark Twain.* Chantilly, VA: Teaching Company, 2002 (Includes two lectures on *Tom Sawyer*; available in audio and video formats).

————. *Mark Twain in His Times.* etext.virginia.edu/railton/index2.html (Includes full text of *Tom Sawyer* and numerous study aids).

Rasmussen, R. Kent. "*The Adventures of Tom Sawyer.*" *Cyclopedia of Literary Places.* Ed. R. Kent Rasmussen. Pasadena, CA: Salem Press, 2003. 1: 14–15.

————. *Mark Twain for Kids.* Chicago: Chicago Review Press, 2004.

————. "*Tom Sawyer, The Adventures of.*" In *Critical Companion to Mark Twain.* New York: Facts On File, 2007. I: 477–507.

Scharnhorst, Gary, ed. *Critical Essays on "The Adventures of Tom Sawyer."* New York: G. K. Hall, 1993.

Sloane, David E. E. *Student Companion to Mark Twain.* Westport, CT: Greenwood Press, 2001.

Smith, Henry Nash, and William M. Gibson, eds. *Mark Twain-Howells Letters: The Correspondence of Samuel L. Clemens and William D. Howells, 1872–1910.* 2 vols. Cambridge, MA: Belknap Press, 1960.

Stone, Albert E. Afterword and For Further Reading. *The Adventures of Tom Sawyer.* By Mark Twain. New York: Oxford UP, 1996. 1–19. (Back matter has separate pagination.)

Twain, Mark. *Mark Twain in Eruption: Hitherto Unpublished Pages About Men and Events.* Ed. Bernard DeVoto. New York: Capricorn Books, 1968.

———. *The Adventures of Tom Sawyer.* Mark Twain Library edition. Berkeley: U of California P, 1981.

———. *The Adventures of Tom Sawyer.* Ed. Lucy Rollin. Orchard Park, NY: Broadview Press, 2006.

ADVENTURES OF HUCKLEBERRY FINN

READING TO WRITE

BECAUSE OF its reputation as one of the greatest and one of the most studied American novels, Mark Twain's *Adventures of Huckleberry Finn* may seem an intimidating book on which to write an essay. With scores of books and hundreds of articles already written about it, if it has not inspired more analysis and criticism than all Mark Twain's other writings combined, the amount by which it trails cannot be great. It would be natural for you to fear you cannot possibly say anything new about the book. Try to put that thought out of your head and approach the novel as you would a gold mine waiting for you to come and scoop up its riches. Essentially the story of a boy and a man drifting down the Mississippi River on a raft, *Huckleberry Finn* is not a particularly complex novel. However, it offers an abundance of colorful characters, exciting episodes, humorous incidents, and challenging ideas. Although scholars and critics have worked on the novel for more than a century, they keep finding things in it that no one seems to have noticed before. New ideas do not simply jump off the book's pages. You have to work at finding them, and one way to do that is constantly to ask yourself questions about the book as you read it.

Perhaps the first question to ask is what it is about *Huckleberry Finn* that attracts so much attention and so much praise. It may seem an obvious question, but you should nevertheless keep it in mind as you read the novel. There are many reasons why the book is considered important, but those reasons are not all compatible, and not everyone agrees on what makes *Huckleberry Finn* great. In fact, in 1996 the Pulitzer Prize–winning novelist Jane Smiley published an article in *Harper's Magazine* arguing that *Huckleberry Finn* is vastly overrated and actually a very poor novel—and one that should not be inflicted on students. A reasoned response to Smiley's article would make a good essay topic.

What matters most in your topic choice is that you have your own views on the importance of *Huckleberry Finn* and you can support those views with concrete evidence and reasoned arguments. As you form your own views, consider some of the broad qualities possessed by any novel that is regarded as worthy of praise: powerful prose, a compelling narrative, believable characters, and challenging ideas. Critics and readers generally—though not universally—agree that *Huckleberry Finn* possesses all these qualities. Indeed, in 1884 when the novel was first published, it was regarded as a major turning point in American literature.

In *The Green Hills of Africa* (1935), the great American novelist Ernest Hemingway (1899–1961), who would later receive a Nobel Prize in Literature, made a comment about *Huckleberry Finn* that has been frequently quoted and analyzed but never fully explained:

> All modern American literature comes from one book by Mark Twain called *Huckleberry Finn*. . . . it's the best book we've had. All American writing comes from that. There was nothing before. There has been nothing as good since.

What Hemingway may have meant by that extravagant praise would provide the basis for a challenging and possibly exceptionally strong essay. However, regardless of your topic, as you read *Huckleberry Finn,* you would do well to ask yourself what it was about the novel that moved Hemingway to say what he did about it. Was it the power of the novel's story? The development of its characters? The naturalness of Huck's vernacular narration? A combination of all these qualities, or possibly something else?

Although many people regard *Huckleberry Finn* as one of the great American novels, others, including Jane Smiley, think it a poor book and have campaigned to remove it from schools—an issue that is, incidentally, the subject of Nat Hentoff's young adult novel *The Day They Came* to *Arrest the Book* (1982). The outcry against the novel began shortly after its original publication, when Louisa May Alcott—the author of *Little Women* (1868)—persuaded the Concord, Massachusetts, Public Library to ban *Huckleberry Finn*. The library's committee issued a public notice to explain its decision:

> One member of the committee says that, while he does not wish to call it [*Huckleberry Finn*] immoral, he thinks it contains but little humor, and that of a very coarse type. He regards it as the veriest trash. The librarian and the other members of the committee entertain similar views, characterizing it as rough, coarse and inelegant, dealing with a series of experiences not elevating, the whole book being more suited to the slums than to intelligent, respectable people.

Modern readers may have trouble understanding some of *Huckleberry Finn*'s vernacular dialogue, but few would share the Concord library committee's objections to the book. Nevertheless, the book is probably more controversial now than it was in the 19th century. Twentieth-century attacks on *Huckleberry Finn* shifted to a different objection—the book's alleged racism. African-American readers in particular have been troubled by its frequent use of the word *nigger*, particularly in reference to the escaping slave Jim. Is the book racist? That is a very serious question and one that demands an answer. However, before you try to judge whether the book is racist, you must define your terms. What do you mean by *racist*? If the mere use of the word *nigger* makes a person racist, does that mean that most modern African-American comics and rap artists are racists? If not, why not? Defenders of *Huckleberry Finn* argue that Huck's use of the word as the book's narrator (which is not the same thing as Mark Twain's using the word) was natural for a southern boy of his time and background. It should be clear you must look deeply into what Huck is saying and how he behaves. If the word *nigger* were replaced by some unobjectionable word, would the book still appear to be racist? If so, why?

A primary reason why modern readers regard *Huckleberry Finn* as racist may be that they fail to see the powerful ironies that permeate the book. For example, consider this simple exchange in chapter 32, in which Huck invents a story for Aunt Sally Phelps, who, unbeknownst to him, thinks that he is her nephew Tom Sawyer and wants to know why the steamboat on which he arrived was grounded:

> I didn't rightly know what to say, because I didn't know whether the boat would be coming up the river or down. But I go a good deal on instinct; and my instinct said she would be coming up—from down towards Orleans. That didn't help me much, though; for I didn't know the names of bars down that way. I see I'd got to invent a bar, or forget the name of the one we got aground on—or—Now I struck an idea, and fetched it out:
>
> "It warn't the grounding—that didn't keep us back but a little. We blowed out a cylinder-head."
>
> "Good gracious! anybody hurt?"
>
> "No'm. Killed a nigger."
>
> "Well, it's lucky; because sometimes people do get hurt. . . ."

As Aunt Sally soon demonstrates, she is a loving, gentle, and generous person who would never do an unkindness to anyone, including black people. Indeed, she goes out of her way to make sure that Jim is comfortable and has plenty to eat when he is held captive on her property. Nevertheless, because of her training in a white-ruled slave culture, it does not occur to her that a black person's being killed in a steamboat accident is as tragic as the death of white person. Should not the quoted passage be read as an example of Mark Twain's use of irony to expose the racist underpinnings of southern culture? It is also a very humorous passage, as the contradiction between "killed a nigger" and "it's lucky because sometimes people do get hurt" makes modern readers want to shout to Sally, "Aren't you listening?" Well, the same remark might be leveled at readers of *Huckleberry Finn:* We need to listen carefully as we read, before drawing conclusions.

Other examples of powerful irony can be found throughout *Huckleberry Finn.* In order to read those passages correctly, you need to keep your mind open to the nature of irony—using language to express ideas that appear to contradict the literal meaning of what is said. A particularly apt example occurs in chapter 6, in which the drunken Pap Finn rants about a black college professor from Ohio whom he once encountered. By Pap's own words, the man was the very model of an ideal citizen—intelligent, highly educated, impeccably clean, well dressed, and evidently well mannered (the exact opposite of Pap himself). Pap goes on:

> "And that ain't the wust. They said he could vote, when he was at home. Well, that let me out. Thinks I, what is the country a-coming to? It was 'lection day, and I was just about to go and vote, myself, if I warn't too drunk to get there; but when they told me there was a State in this country where they'd let that nigger vote, I drawed out. I says I'll never vote agin. Them's the very words I said; they all heard me; and the country may rot for all me—I'll never vote agin as long as I live."

To determine whether it is fair to call *Huckleberry Finn* a racist book, you will need to work out the meaning of passages such as that.

TOPICS AND STRATEGIES

This section discusses both general and specific ideas for possible essay topics. You need not limit your essay choice to the topics discussed here. If you allow your imagination to roam freely, you may find that your ideal topic combines ideas from two or more of the suggestions discussed here or that these suggestions help you come up with original ideas. Keep in mind that the broad categories under which topics are discussed are designed merely to help you find the subjects that interest you most and help focus your thinking. Some topics might fit under other headings. It is the topics, not the categories, that matter.

These suggestions are not intended to serve as outlines for what you yourself should write. In fact, it is a good idea to approach every suggestion by questioning whether the ideas it expresses are valid and worth developing. Literature is not an exact science. Different authorities can, and often do, disagree on issues, and *Huckleberry Finn* is a virtual battlefield for disagreement. You should also remember that questions raised here, or that you raise, do not necessarily have right or wrong answers. Avoid the trap of searching for conclusive proofs that may not exist. The strength of your essay will come not merely from the decisiveness of your conclusions, but from the power and clarity of the arguments you advance to reach them. Whatever topics you choose to write about, use your imagination and try to consider all possible sides of every question.

Themes

Although *Huckleberry Finn* is a comparatively simple narrative, it touches on so many different themes that it has kept critics, scholars, and students busy making fresh discoveries through several generations. On one level, for example, it is a coming-of-age story about a young boy who seeks to escape from the burdens that society places on him, only to accept the greater burden of responsibility for someone else. The story is thus also about the interdependence of human beings, the nature of friendship, and the meaning of family.

Sample Topics:

1. **Imposture and identity:** What do the frequent names changes and false identities of major characters contribute to the plot?

   One of the most amusing things about *Huckleberry Finn* is the frequency with which its major characters pretend to be people other than who they really are. Huck becomes proficient at changing his identity and quickly contriving cover stories. At various times, he calls himself "Sara Mary Williams," "George Peters," "George Jackson," "Charles William Allbright," "Aleck James Hopkins," "Adolphus," and even "Tom Sawyer." Toward the end of the book, when the real Tom Sawyer reappears, he calls himself "William Thompson," then claims to be his own brother, Sid Sawyer. Meanwhile, the real names of the scoundrels who call themselves the Duke of Bridgewater and the King of France are never revealed, and both those characters assume other identities at various times. Indeed, it seems that most of the time no major character is really who he claims to be. Are there discernible patterns in all these name and identity changes? How do they affect Huck's relationships with other people? What purpose might Mark Twain have had in putting his characters through so many changes?

2. **Parental child abuse:** What does *Huckleberry Finn* say about the nature of child abuse and its effects on an abused child?

So much attention is paid to *Huckleberry Finn*'s treatment of subjects such as slavery and race relations that its theme of child abuse is generally overlooked. It is a surprising oversight, in view of the fact that the novel's central character is a young boy running away from an alcoholic father's physical abuse; however, the fact that this theme has been neglected opens the field for you to discover fresh perspectives on the subject. If you opt to write on this topic, begin by paying close attention to everything Huck says about his father—not merely in the early chapters in which Pap Finn makes his only appearances, but throughout the novel. Note the ways in which Pap mistreats and frightens Huck and also see if you can detect indications of Pap's influence on Huck's personality and behavior. For example, can you detect any signs of how having an abusive father affects Huck's attitudes toward other adults or his relationships with substitute-parent figures, such as the Widow Douglas and Miss Watson, Jim, the Grangerfords, and the Phelpses? Also, do not overlook the King and the Duke, who may be more like Pap Finn than any other characters in the novel and who also become something like father figures to Huck. If you wish to carry this topic even further, read Jon Clinch's *Finn* (2007), a powerful novel that explores Pap Finn and attempts to show what makes him the kind of man he is. If you wish to make this a compare and contrast essay, look at Tom Canty's relationship with his abusive father in *The Prince and the Pauper* (1881).

3. **Dysfunctional families:** Does *Huckleberry Finn* express any views about the possibility of families being whole and functional?

Closely related to the subject of child abuse is the subject of dysfunctional families, another pervasive theme throughout Mark Twain's writings. Indeed, it is difficult to find completely whole and healthy family units in any of his fiction. Almost all his fictional families are either missing one or more natural parents or have flaws that prevent them from functioning properly. For example, Tom Sawyer is an orphan being raised by his aunt; Huck Finn's mother is dead and his father is an abusive and absent alcoholic. As *Huckleberry Finn* unfolds, Huck goes through a series of surrogate family units—first with the Widow Douglas and her sister, until his father takes him away; with Jim—and later with Jim, the King, and the Duke—on the raft; with the Grangerfords; with the King, the Duke, and the Wilks sisters; and, finally, with the Phelpses. Are any of these units successful? If so, in what ways? What do all these experiences teach Huck about family? Is it disdain for being "sivilized" or distaste for family life that impels him to want "to light out for the Territory" at the end of the novel?

4. **Vice on the river:** What does Huck's narrative say about greed, corruption, and depravity on the river?

A powerful undercurrent running through *Huckleberry Finn* is Huck's generally deadpan descriptions of the many forms of vice that he observes as he goes down the river. He encounters gamblers, murderers, robbers, con men, and charlatans and gets caught in the middle of a murderous and utterly pointless feud. Although he is constantly struggling with his conscience over the morality of helping a slave to escape, he rarely expresses any judgments on the corruption and wrongdoing that he observes. Why is that? Does he simply accept vice as part of the natural order of things? Or does he see himself as unfit to pass judgment on others? What does his behavior say about his natural instincts? To get at answers to these questions, pay special attention to Huck's introspective moments, when he reflects on his own sins and speculates about what he may become, as in chapter 13, when he thinks that "there ain't no telling but I might come to be a murderer myself . . ." Note also another remark that Huck makes in that chapter, when he reflects on what the Widow Douglas might think, if she knew about his efforts to save the murderers on the wrecked steamboat *Walter Scott* from drowning: "I judged she would be proud of me for helping these rapscallions, because rapscallions and dead beats is the kind the widow and good people takes the most interest in." Is it possible that Huck's limited religious training has conditioned him to go overboard in his empathy for criminals?

Character

Huckleberry Finn has so many fascinating and well-developed characters that it may offer the widest range of topics on character of any of Mark Twain's books. Dozens of different kinds of essays might be written on Huck alone. You could, for example, examine how he matures throughout the novel, how he battles with his conscience, how he develops into a first-rate liar, or how he overcomes his training as a white southerner to bond with the slave Jim. To come up with fresh topics of your own, try this experiment: Identify an episode in the novel in which Huck's behavior is particularly interesting and ask yourself if that behavior reveals something about Huck's nature. For example, the way in which Huck fakes his own murder and escapes from his father's control in chapter 7 demonstrates more intelligence and initiative than we might expect from Huck. Is he merely imitating what he imagines Tom Sawyer would do in the same situation? Or he is drawing on a reservoir of intelligence and creativity that shows up in other episodes in the novel?

Other characters on whom essays might focus include Jim, Pap Finn, the King, the Duke, the Grangerford family, Colonel Sherburn, Silas and Sally Phelps, the Widow Douglas and Miss Watson, and Tom Sawyer. If your assignment lets you extend your enquiries beyond this one book, you might find it interesting to compare the Huck of this novel with the Huck of *Tom Sawyer* or the Huck of one or more of the later sequels, such as *Tom Sawyer Abroad* (1894) and *Tom Sawyer, Detective* (1896). Comparisons among sets of different characters can also be rewarding; some of these are discussed in the section on Compare and Contrast essays below.

An important matter to consider in *Huckleberry Finn* or any other novel is the extent to which its characters are, in fact, *characters*, and not merely one- or two-dimensional figures who serve as props who move the story along. True characters are complex and three-dimensional, or fully rounded, people, about whom readers learn enough not to expect them to behave exactly the same in every similar situation. You can test a character's complexity by asking whether he can surprise you. You might start with Huck and Jim; do they always behave predictably?

Sample Topics:

1. **Huck's development:** What signs of growth and maturity does Huck show throughout *Huckleberry Finn*? At the end of his narrative, in what important ways does he differ from the character he is at its beginning?

   One way to read *Huckleberry Finn* is as a coming-of-age novel by paying close attention to signs of Huck's increasing maturity as the story progresses. His diverse and often horrendous experiences would seem certain to change any young boy, but how does Huck's narrative reveal his changes? The most obvious place to look is at Huck's changing attitude toward Jim, whom he evidently comes to see as a fellow human being rather than a slave or an object of property. Do Huck's attitudes toward slavery and other African Americans show similar changes? Does he show increasing initiative and independence as the story advances? What other changes does he display? Finally, are there signs of regression in his maturity in the final chapters, in which he acquiesces to Tom Sawyer's elaborate "evasion" plans for Huck's escape? If you wish to carry this topic further, you might consider comparing *Huckleberry Finn* and *Tom Sawyer* as coming-of-age novels.

2. **Huck as a liar:** Is Huck a natural liar, or is he forced into lying by circumstances?

   Mark Twain had a lifelong interest in distinctions between truth and lies and wrote a great deal on both. Since he often tried to be ironic or facetious—in remarks such as "Never tell the truth to people who are not worthy of it"—it is not always easy to know when he was being serious. Nevertheless, it should be possible to understand why he makes Huck Finn lie. Throughout *Huckleberry Finn,* Huck repeatedly gets into difficult situations from which he tries to extricate himself by lying. Notable examples include his pretending to be a girl when he meets Mrs. Loftus in chapter 11, his making the slave-catchers he confronts in chapter 16 believe there are smallpox victims on his raft, and his allowing Aunt Sally Phelps to think he is Tom Sawyer when he meets her in chapter 32. His lies often trip him up and force him to invent other lies. Does he tend to lie only out of necessity? Are some of his lies more complicated than they need to be? Are there patterns to his lying and do those patterns change as his narrative progresses? Another aspect of the subject to consider is the elements of irony connected with Huck's lying, such as the moment in chapter 29 when Levi Bell tells Huck, "I reckon you ain't used to lying, it don't seem to come handy; what you want is practice."

This should a fun topic on which to write. You will need to begin by reading *Huckleberry Finn* carefully to identify all the episodes in which Huck lies. Try to classify these episodes by the types of lies that Huck tells, by the circumstances in which he lies, and by the consequences of his lying. When you complete your cataloguing of Huck's lies, you should be able to discern patterns that will allow you to answer the questions discussed here. It may help you to read some of Mark Twain's remarks about truth and lies in his other writings, and you will find many such remarks in published collections of quotes, such as R. Kent Rasmussen's *The Quotable Mark Twain.*

3. **Jim:** How fully rounded and convincing is Jim as a character?

In some ways, Jim may be the most compelling character in *Huckleberry Finn,* but we do not know nearly as much about him as we do Huck because we must rely on what Huck chooses to tell us, and Huck naturally says more about himself. The novel even has several long sections in which Jim disappears from Huck's narrative (most notably chapters 25–27). Within the context of *Huckleberry Finn,* Jim is a slave, a commodity whose legal ownership is often at issue. Jim's treatment in discussions of the novel is often not much different; at times he seems to be regarded more as a commodity than as a character in the book. What does the novel really tell us about him? Is its portrait of him fully rounded and consistent? Does it show him changing and maturing as it does Huck?

This topic is a rather open-ended one. Whatever approach you take, you should aim at constructing a full portrait of Jim that encompasses his background, his family ties, his religious and superstitious beliefs, his intelligence, his honesty, his loyalty to friends, his ignorance and naivete, and anything else you see as important. Read everything Huck says about Jim, but do not be too quick to accept Huck's own judgments. Look instead at what Jim's words and actions tell you.

4. **The rapscallions:** How does Huck really feel about the King and the Duke?

Almost immediately after the scoundrels who call themselves the King of France and the Duke of Bridgewater enter the story in chapter 19, they take control of the raft and put Huck and Jim through a series of mostly unpleasant experiences that push them ever farther from their goal, the Ohio River and freedom. They force Huck to assist in their criminal schemes, they threaten him with violence, and eventually the King sells Jim back into slavery for 40 dollars, only to blow the entire sum on whiskey and gambling. Huck knows all along that the scoundrels are "low-down humbugs and frauds," but despite all that they do to him and Jim, he feels sorry for them when they finally receive their just desserts by being tarred and feathered in chapter 33 and regrets not being able to save them. Do his feelings merely reflect his good heart and general empathy toward all human beings? Or, does he have ambivalent feelings toward the scoundrels that show up elsewhere in his narrative? Does he look upon them as father figures?

To write an essay on this topic, carefully examine everything that Huck says about the King and the Duke. Look for indications that he empathizes with them or appreciates things they do. Does he seem to relish the excitement they add to his life? Are his feelings toward them similar to his feelings toward his abusive father, Pap Finn?

5. **Tom Sawyer:** Would *Huckleberry Finn* be the same kind of book if Tom Sawyer were its protagonist instead of Huck?

Mark Twain started planning *Huckleberry Finn* shortly after finishing *Tom Sawyer.* That novel was a big success, but he quickly decided that Tom Sawyer was unsuitable for the kind of protagonist he wanted for his new book. Why might he have come to that conclusion? Had he decided to use Tom, instead of Huck, perhaps he could have given Tom an equally good reason for running away, so he could end up on the raft with Jim. After all, *Tom Sawyer* says nothing about Tom's father; like Huck, Tom could have had a good-for-nothing father turn up in town to claim his share of the treasure, just as Pap Finn does. Assume, however, that Mark Twain did use Tom as his protagonist. How differently might the book's events have played out? How different might Tom's narrative voice have been?

It is possible that no one has ever developed an essay on this topic, so it should give you latitude to be original. To pull it off, however, you will need to read both *Tom Sawyer* and *Huckleberry Finn,* as Mark Twain based his opinion of Tom on the character he created for that earlier novel. The Tom Sawyer of *Huckleberry Finn* may or may not be the same kind of character as the Tom of *Tom Sawyer,* but that question is irrelevant. You will need to assess the Tom of *Tom Sawyer* and imagine him taking Huck's place in *Huckleberry Finn.* What fundamental characteristics do you find that would make Tom a poor substitute for Huck? It may help to know that it was important to Mark Twain that his protagonist have a good heart.

History and Context

The title page of *Huckleberry Finn*'s first American edition identifies the story's setting with some precision:

SCENE: THE MISSISSIPPI VALLEY
TIME: FORTY TO FIFTY YEARS AGO

Since Mark Twain published the book in the United States in 1885 (the year after it came out in England), it appears that he intended its setting to be between about 1835 and 1845—the very period in which he had grown up in Missouri. However, neither the story's precise time nor its precise location greatly matters. In fact, the geography of *Huckleberry Finn* seems almost deliberately vague. While it mentions the names of real states and rivers and a number of real towns, such as St. Louis, Missouri, Cairo, Illinois, and New Orleans, all the places that Huck actually visits are fictional and we cannot even be sure where they are. What *is* important is that Huck's story is set somewhere in the slaveholding South at a time well before slavery became a divisive national issue in the United States. Few white people then questioned the legality or morality of slavery, and their general acceptance of it is an important premise of *Huckleberry Finn.* Indeed, Huck never questions whether slavery is right or wrong. So far as he is concerned, it is part of the natural order of things, and he goes through the entire novel believing that by helping Jim escape, he is committing a sin.

Sample Topics:

1. **Slavery:** How is slavery depicted throughout *Huckleberry Finn*?

   Huckleberry Finn deals with slavery in the pre–Civil War American South, but slavery is far from being the book's central subject. A main character, Jim, is an escaping slave, but we see little of his life before he flees St. Petersburg. In fact, apart from glimpses of working slaves belonging to the Grangerfords, Wilkses, and Phelpses, Huck's narrative does not delve into the day-to-day conditions of slaves. Nevertheless, it says a great deal about slavery as an institution. How does it achieve that and what views about slavery does it express? Does it condemn the institution directly or indirectly? Does it condone it? Or does it seem to have no point of view on the subject? Does Mark Twain use irony to attack slavery?

This is a large subject for a school essay, with an immense amount of material, so you should try to narrow your focus. You might, for example, limit your topic to how *Huckleberry Finn* uses irony to attack slavery or you might look at the book's treatment of slavery in the context of Mark Twain's outspoken views against the institution. Although he grew up in a slave-owning family whose members never thought to question the morality of slavery, Mark Twain eventually came to regard slavery as "a bald, grotesque, an unwarrantable usurpation" for which "it would not be possible for a humane and intelligent person to invent a rational excuse . . ." Can you find any echoes of those sentiments in *Huckleberry Finn*?

A good place to begin research on Mark Twain's views on slavery is Terrell Dempsey's *Searching for Jim: Slavery in Sam Clemens's World* (2003). You might also read the discussions of slavery in this book's chapter on *Pudd'nhead Wilson* (1894), a novel that treats the subject much more directly than *Huckleberry Finn* does.

2. **Abolitionism:** What use does *Huckleberry Finn* make of southern white fear of abolitionists?

Closely related to slavery is the subject of abolitionism—the organized movement to abolish slavery in the United States during the early 19th century. Huck alludes to abolitionists several times in his narrative, but uses the term in a slightly different sense, to describe people—usually northerners from free states—who tried to liberate individual slaves. Such people were not only despised and feared within white slaveholding communities, they also violated federal laws against taking slaves into other states against the wishes of their legal owners. In Huck's mind, abolitionists are about the most "low-down" form of human beings imaginable, and he repeatedly expresses his contempt for himself for doing what abolitionists do. In addition to revealing Huck's struggles with his conscience over his abolitionist behavior, *Huckleberry Finn* has Tom Sawyer exploit white fear of abolitionists to stir up excitement around the Phelpses' farm the night that he and Huck finally spring Jim free from his captivity.

As the basic outlines of what *Huckleberry Finn* says about abolitionists are readily evident, an essay on this topic needs to probe more deeply into what the novel says about white fear of abolitionism. Part of your goal should be to assess how realistically the novel treats the subject. This will necessitate your doing a background read on the era of slavery, the nature of the abolitionist movement, and the fear that it aroused within slaveholding communities. To that end, there is no better place to start than with Terrell Dempsey's *Searching for Jim: Slavery in Sam Clemens's World*. For a much different take on the novel, read John Seelye's revision, *The True Adventures of Huckleberry Finn* (1970 and 1987), which removes Tom Sawyer from the end of the narrative and shows that southern white attitudes toward abolitionists were no laughing matter.

Philosophy and Ideas

Another way to consider *Huckleberry Finn* is to explore the broad philosophical ideas it expressed, such as the meaning of freedom, the nature of racism, and the essence of truth. This approach is related to the study of themes described above, but it works at a more general level.

Sample Topics:

1. **Freedom:** What does *Huckleberry Finn* say about the meaning of freedom?

One of the most pervasive themes throughout Mark Twain's many writings is the quest for freedom. It is easy to say that *Huckleberry Finn* is about Huck and Jim's quests for freedom, but what kind of freedom do they really seek? Jim begins the novel as a slave; by law, he is the property of another person, Miss Watson. He naturally seeks to be free from the legal confines of chattel slavery and particularly from the peril of being sold down the river and forever separated from his wife and children. However, as a legally free black man living amid a white racist society, what kind of freedom can he and his family hope to enjoy?

As a legally free white boy, Huck seeks a different kind of freedom—escape from both the abuse of his father and the civilizing influences of the Widow Douglas and her sister. The novel ends with Huck and Jim apparently triumphing, but is either truly free? Conversely, is it possible that they have been free all along without fully realizing it? The best way to get answers to these questions is to read *Huckleberry Finn* attentively and look for every indication of what kind of freedom Huck and Jim seek, clues that they may already be enjoying such freedom, and signs of what the future may hold for them.

2. **Conscience:** What does *Huckleberry Finn* say about how a person's conscience dictates his actions?

When Huck witnesses the tar and feathering of the King and the Duke in chapter 33, he goes home feeling that somehow he is to blame, even though he had nothing to do with the awful event. "But that's always the way," he reflects, "it don't make no difference whether you do right or wrong, a person's conscience ain't got no sense, and just goes for him anyway." Throughout his entire narrative, Huck struggles with his conscience, particularly in the matter of his helping Jim to escape from slavery. As a white southerner, Huck is conditioned to accept slavery as a legal and morally justified institution and to regard abolitionists as the most "low-down" form of human scum. Does his perseverance in helping Jim escape from slavery thus represent a significant triumph over his conscience? Does the novel provide any clues as to why Huck's conscience is formed as it is? Are there any indications that matters of conscience trouble any other characters in the book? In trying to answer these questions, you should pay particular attention to Huck's introspective remarks about his conscience in chapters 16 and 31.

Mark Twain wrote a great deal about the nature of conscience and what he called the "moral sense." For a helpful discussion of this subject, see the article by Earl F. Briden listed in the Bibliography below. You might also find it helpful to read Mark Twain's story "The Facts Concerning the Recent Carnival of Crime in Connecticut" (1876), a compelling monologue in which an unnamed author describes his lethal confrontation with his conscience.

3. **Civilization:** What does *civilization* mean to Huck?

Among the most famous passages in *Huckleberry Finn* is Huck's final paragraph, in which he says he must "light out for the Territory ahead of the rest, because Aunt Sally she's going to adopt me and sivilize me and I can't stand it. I been there before." That passage makes a nice bookend to the novel, whose first chapter opens with Huck complaining about the Widow Douglas's efforts to "sivilize" him. Huck thus expresses exactly the same attitude toward civilization at the end of his narrative that he expresses at its beginning. He seems to resist the idea of civilization throughout the novel, but what can that idea possibly mean to him? So far as we know, at the beginning of *Huckleberry Finn,* Huck is nearly illiterate and knows almost nothing of the world outside St. Petersburg. By the end of the novel, however, he has had some formal schooling, has learned to read, has lived in the homes of at least four respectable families (the Widow Douglas, the Grangerfords, the Wilkses, and the Phelpses), and has traveled more than 1,000 miles. Nevertheless, his attitude toward civilization remains the same. Why?

To write on this topic, you will need to keep an open mind on what *civilization* means to Huck, as you will find that he uses the word *sivilize* only three times in the entire book (chapters 1, 6, and unnumbered last). Your goal should be to discover what the word means to Huck and why he ultimately rejects being civilized. Pay particular attention to chapters 17 and 18, in which Huck lives with the Grangerfords. There, apparently for the first time, he seems to become reconciled to the idea of living in a fine home and being regarded as civilized. However, could what happens to that family affect his ideas about civilization?

4. **Racism:** Is *Huckleberry Finn* a racist book?

This book opens with a prologue about how scholar Shelley Fisher Fishkin first encountered *Huckleberry Finn* when she was a high school junior in 1965. As she recalls, she was expecting the novel to be a humorous adventure story, similar to *Tom Sawyer,* and was stunned by the essay topic that her English teacher assigned: "How Mark Twain used irony to attack racism in *Huckleberry Finn.*" That challenge is as valid now as it was when Fishkin's teacher posed it more than four decades ago. Is the novel racist, as many critics have charged? How much of the criticism directed at the book has to do with the book's frequent use of the racially charged word *nigger*? To answer these questions, you will need to define what makes a book racist. You will need to assess how Mark Twain uses irony to depict 19th-century views on race. You can start by reading this book's first chapter. You would also do well to read discussions of *Huckleberry Finn* by African Americans, such as scholars Jocelyn Chadwick and David L. Smith and Nobel Laureate Toni Morrison (see Bibliography below). Morrison wrote a new introduction to *Huckleberry Finn* for the Oxford Mark Twain edition—which was edited by Shelley Fisher Fishkin, who has also written several important books on race in Mark Twain's writings. Fishkin might never have written her books on Mark Twain or edited the Oxford edition had she not received the essay assignment she was given in high school.

Form and Genre

An essay about *Huckleberry Finn*'s form would examine aspects of how the novel is constructed, what literary techniques Mark Twain uses, and how and why the novel's structure succeeds or fails. The novel's basic form is a first-person narrative related by its youthful protagonist, Huck, who, as we learn in the novel's last paragraph, has written down his story as a book. In this regard, it is similar to *A Connecticut Yankee in King Arthur's Court* (1889), another first-person narrative that is supposed to be handwritten. An important question to ask as you read *Huckleberry Finn* is how it might differ if it were told in a different form, such as a third-person narrative similar to *The Adventures of Tom Sawyer.*

The term *genre* is used in a variety of ways, but basically refers to the category into which a work fits. A single work might properly be assigned to several different genres, and that is true of *Huckleberry Finn.* Among the genre terms applied to it are coming-of-age novel, or bildungsroman, and picaresque. It might also be classified as historical fiction or regional fiction, as Mark Twain set it in the American South during the era of slavery, about three or four decades before the time he published it. However, what might qualify it as a historical novel or a regional novel is not merely the fact that it is set in the South of the past, but that its story and themes would not work anywhere else or in any later time period. Finally, the book's strong comic elements might justify classifying it as a humorous novel. The appropriateness of applying any of these terms to *Huckleberry Finn* would make a good subject for an essay, as long as your essay addresses the question of why the issue matters in the first place.

Sample Topics:

1. **Huck as an author:** Does Huck really write a book that tells his story?

   In the very last paragraph of *Huckleberry Finn*, Huck says, "there ain't nothing more to write about, and I am rotten glad of it, because if I'd a knowed what a trouble it was to make a book I wouldn't a tackled it . . ." If we read that passage as the literal truth (within the context of the novel), must we conclude that Huck actually *wrote* a book and did not merely narrate his story orally? Are there reasons why it matters whether he wrote the book or not?

   This topic could be fun, as some clever detective work will be needed to answer the question of whether Huck wrote a book. If well handled, the topic could provide the basis for a strong essay. However, it might not be an easy essay to write. The important issues are not whether Huck actually wrote down his story in his own hand, but why that question matters and what *Huckleberry Finn* has to say about books generally. You will therefore need to approach this topic at two levels. The first is the fun part—searching Huck's narrative for evidence that he is capable of writing a book. Look for clues relating to his literacy and understanding of language and pay particularly close attention to the first and last paragraphs of his narrative. If you conclude that he did write the book, determine *when* he wrote it—relative to the time of the story—and why that question matters. On the second level, you will need to examine what Huck says about books and reading throughout his narrative. Among Huck's numerous allusions to books, the very first may be the most important—his discussion of *The Adventures of Tom Sawyer* in the first two paragraphs of chapter 1. Huck twits Mark Twain himself for not always telling the truth in his book; is he also hinting that his own book will be more truthful? Other books that Huck mentions include Bibles and testaments, schoolbooks, books looted from the wrecked *Walter Scott* (note the name of the steamboat!), books in the Grangerford house, and Joanna Wilks's dictionary. Pay particular attention to Huck's many references to books read by Tom Sawyer. Do all Huck's allusions to books add up to a coherent attitude toward literature or books or suggest reasons why he would or would not want to write a book himself?

2. **Huck Finn as a picaro:** Should *Huckleberry Finn* be classified as a picaresque novel?

Picaresque novels are typically satiric narratives that follow the adventures of amiable rogues, who are usually the narrators. The term comes from the Spanish word for "rogue," *pícaro.* Picaresque tales tend to be episodic, with their heroes traveling from place to place, having encounters with the lowest members of society and triumphing over the middle-class people with whom they clash along the way. Picaresque elements can be found in many of Mark Twain's books, and perhaps most notably in *Huckleberry Finn.* Is it accurate to classify the book as picaresque?

If you write an essay on this topic, you should begin by spelling out what you mean by "picaresque" and "picaro." To do that, you will need to do some background reading on picaresque fiction in a literature textbook or a general literary reference work. The classic picaresque tale is Miguel de Cervantes's *Don Quixote* (1605). Reading that novel merely for background information would be a tall order, but you can find synopses in publications such as Frank N. Magill's *Masterplots* (1996), which can be found in many libraries.

3. **The "evasion" chapters:** What do the final chapters of *Huckleberry Finn* contribute to the book?

From a literary viewpoint, one of *Huckleberry Finn*'s most controversial aspects is the sharp, perhaps even jarring, contrast between the last 10 or so chapters and the rest of the book. Huck and Jim's river voyage ends in chapter 31. Huck is finally free from the King and the Duke, but the two scoundrels have sold Jim to Silas Phelps, who holds him prisoner, expecting to receive a reward from the man whom he believes to be Jim's rightful owner in New Orleans. After Huck finds Phelps's farm, he determines to set Jim free, but the novel changes radically in chapter 33 when Tom Sawyer reappears (he is Phelps's nephew) and offers to help free Jim. Huck sensibly suggests simply stealing the key to the hut confining Jim, but Tom instead concocts an elaborate and time-consuming scheme to liberate Jim in "style." The chapters that follow are commonly known as the "evasion" episode, after Tom's statement that "when a prisoner of style escapes, it's called an evasion." Aside from young readers who enjoy the humorous excesses of Tom's ludicrously complicated scheme, few readers admire the evasion chapters. When Ernest Hemingway wrote the lavish praise of the novel discussed at the beginning of this chapter, he advised readers to stop at the point where Jim is stolen from Huck, saying "That is the real end. The rest is just cheating." John Seelye took Hemingway's advice several steps further when he rewrote Mark Twain's novel as *The True Adventures of Huckleberry Finn.* In Seelye's version, Tom Sawyer never reappears, and the story ends abruptly with Jim being killed by slave catchers. It is a shocking conclusion but one that Seelye believes is more realistic than Mark Twain's.

An essay on this topic should address three interrelated questions: In what important ways do the evasion chapters differ from the rest of the book? Do they strengthen or weaken the novel? And, finally, why might Mark Twain have written them as he did? To answer the first two of those questions, you should pay special attention to what happens to Huck and Jim's character development in those chapters. Does Huck continue to mature? Or does he show signs of regression? Is Jim's comparatively passive behavior consistent with what the earlier chapters say about him? How does what happens in the final chapters conform with Huck and Jim's quests for freedom? The third question is the most difficult and one that has yet to find an explanation that satisfies all critics and scholars. To get ideas on how to deal with that question, look at one or two of the many analytical works listed in the Bibliography below. Of particular relevance are Shelley Fisher Fishkin's *Lighting Out for the Territory* and James S. Leonard, Thomas A. Tenney, and Thadious M. Davis's *Satire or Evasion? Black Perspectives on "Huckleberry Finn."* Reading Seelye's *The True Adventures of Huckleberry Finn* should also give you some helpful ideas.

Language, Symbols, and Imagery

Among the many reasons *Huckleberry Finn* ranks as an important work is its role in freeing American literature from the confines of the genteel literary tradition associated with such writers as James Fenimore Cooper, Nathaniel Hawthorne, and Ralph Waldo Emerson. That tradition strove for high literary standards, which were measured, in part, by polite language and faultless grammar. The vernacular narrative voice of *Huckleberry Finn* is something much different; it is often far from being polite and its grammar is almost never faultless. It is, however, always energetic and natural—characteristics that make the book seem as fresh and real today as it did when Mark Twain wrote it. The same cannot be said for many works of the genteel tradition. Indeed, *Huckleberry Finn*'s language may be a primary reason why Ernest Hemingway said that "All modern American literature comes from . . . *Huckleberry Finn*."

Sample Topics:

1. **Huck's language:** What does the novel's vernacular language contribute to the book?

   What makes *Huckleberry Finn*'s language so strikingly different from that of other novels of its time is that the book's narrative voice is that of a young, uneducated boy from the edge of the western frontier who is too ignorant and naive to recognize the imperfections of the language he speaks. It is so filled with errors and crudeness that members of the Concord, Massachusetts, Public Library committee denounced the book as "the veriest trash" and called it "rough, coarse and inelegant . . ." Is it? If so, is that necessarily a bad thing?

   You might also wish to write on the topic of Huck's frequent use of the word *nigger.* Is it a necessary part of the narrative? Would the book be as powerful without that word? This topic touches on such an emotionally charged issue that before you undertake it, you should probably discuss it with your instructor.

2. **Symbols of southern decadence:** What kind of picture of southern culture does *Huckleberry Finn* offer?

   In addition to its being an attack on slavery and racism, *Huckleberry Finn* is also often seen as an attack on the moral and cultural decay of the American South, a phenomenon that Mark Twain blamed on the debilitating effects of slavery on slaveholders and the South's antiquated ideas about chivalry, the nobility of royalty, and other "romantic juvenilities." His most focused attack on the South can be found in chapters 40 to 47 of *Life on the Mississippi* (1883), which describe his return to New Orleans in 1882. In that book, he even goes so far as to hold the Scottish writer Sir Walter Scott (1771–1832) partly responsible for the

U.S. Civil War because his novels encouraged white southerners to hang on to outmoded romantic ideals and thereby resist the kinds of progressive changes that would have allowed the South to keep up with the North's development. All these ideas were on Mark Twain's mind when he was writing *Huckleberry Finn,* and traces of them can be found in his novel. What an essay on southern decadence should try to do is show what kind of a picture of the South the novel builds.

As you read *Huckleberry Finn,* you will not find explicit condemnations of the South. To write on this topic, you will need to look for symbols of romanticism and decadence and the use of ironic language. An example of an obvious symbol is the wrecked steamboat in chapter 13 in which Huck stumbles upon two criminals who are about to murder a partner. The image of a wrecked steamboat containing no one but murderers is powerful in itself; it is made even more powerful by the boat's name—the *Walter Scott.* An example of powerful irony is the Grangerford family (chapters 17–18). To Huck's naive eyes, the Grangerfords represent the very pinnacle of southern culture. However, that same family destroys itself in an utterly pointless feud with the Shepherdsons in which the only thing that seems to matter is honor. Might the Grangerfords' feud be seen as a symbol of the self-destructive tendency of the South? For more subtle examples of symbols, consider how the scoundrels whom Huck meets in chapter 19 claim to be the King of France and the Duke of Bridgewater and demand to be treated as royalty. Pay attention also to Huck and Jim's discussion of kings in chapter 23.

3. **The majestic Mississippi:** How does the river function as a symbol in *Huckleberry Finn*?

Mark Twain wrote about the Mississippi River in many different works but perhaps nowhere more poignantly than in *Huckleberry Finn.* An essay should find much to say about the river's use as symbol in the novel. For example, when Huck and Jim's raft trip begins, the river acts as a highway to freedom.

However, when they accidently pass the Mississippi's confluence with the Ohio River, the Mississippi becomes something different as it then carries Huck and Jim further from their goal and deeper into the heart of slavery, the last place they wish to go. If you write on this topic, look for the river's other symbolic meanings, such as its role as a cleanser of sin and a provider of bounty. Pay special attention to what Huck says about the river itself and note the distinctions between things that happen on the river and things that happen on land.

For additional ideas on Mark Twain's feelings toward the Mississippi, consider dipping into his *Life on the Mississippi*, the first part of which is discussed in another chapter in this book. You will find more ideas on Mark Twain's use of place in *Huckleberry Finn* and other works in R. Kent Rasmussen's *Cyclopedia of Literary Places*, which is listed in the Bibliography below.

4. **Ironic language:** How does Mark Twain use irony to create comic effects and to convey more serious points in *Huckleberry Finn*?

Huckleberry Finn is a book rich in ironies, both large and small. Other sections of this chapter discuss some of Mark Twain's uses of ironical language in relation to specific thematic issues. Regardless of the topic on which you write, you should stay alert to the use of irony. Indeed, Mark Twain's use of irony would make a fine essay topic. If you decide to write this, begin by identifying passages that use irony. A good example is the King and Duke's putting $415 of their own money into Peter Wilks's sack of gold coins to "make up the deffisit" (chapter 25), only to lose everything because they are too greedy to get away with what they have already stolen. That minor incident might be seen as a use of irony that achieves a comic effect while also making a serious point about the consequences of greed. A broader use of irony is Huck's constantly thinking that he is doing the wrong thing by helping Jim escape, when he is actually doing the right thing.

After collecting examples of ironies in the book, separate them into categories, such as comic, serious, or both, and look for patterns as to how and where each type of irony is used. Be sure to define what you mean by irony and explain how some of the examples you discuss work. Your goal should be to show what the different kinds of irony contribute to the book. You should also consider the question of whether some of Mark Twain's irony might be so subtle or obscure that readers overlook it and misunderstand what the book is trying to say. For further ideas on this point, read the discussion of racism in the section on Philosophy and Ideas.

Compare and Contrast Essays

Writing a compare and contrast essay allows you to be creative on at least two levels: first, in finding aspects of one or more works to compare; then in finding significant points to make about the similarities and differences you observe. Writing this type of essay may offer your best chance of doing something original. An essay comparing Huck Finn with Tom Sawyer could be a very strong one, but its subject would not be original. On the other hand, comparisons of Aunt Polly with her sister Sally Phelps or of Pap Finn with the King or the Duke would be more original topics.

Compare and contrast topics offer considerable scope for developing original ideas, but they also present a trap to avoid, namely, failing to develop your essay fully. You are likely to begin a comparison essay by compiling lists of similarities and differences between pairs of characters, types of plots, different points of view, or other aspects of *Huckleberry Finn.* That is certainly a sensible way to start. However, do not assume that inventories of comparisons mean anything by themselves. It would not be enough simply to list Tom and Huck's similarities and differences. You would also need to say something about *why* the two boys are similar or different, how their similar and different traits relate to other aspects of their personalities, and how those traits affect their behavior and help to drive the novel's story lines. (For a discussion of Tom-and-Huck comparisons, see the Compare and Contrast section of this book's chapter on *Tom Sawyer.*)

The sample topics that follow represent only a fraction of possible compare and contrast topics. You will find additional ideas relating to

Huckleberry Finn in other chapters, but you should be able to come up with original ideas of your own.

Sample Topics:

1. ***Huckleberry Finn* v. *Tom Sawyer:*** Are these two novels similar or very different kinds of books?

As you know, *Huckleberry Finn* is a direct sequel to *Tom Sawyer.* In fact, the beginning of its story line is so closely connected to the end of *Tom Sawyer* that if its first few chapters were changed from a first-person to a third-person narrative and added to *Tom Sawyer,* readers would scarcely notice the transition. After those first few chapters, however, *Huckleberry Finn* starts to change and becomes a very different kind of book. It has some of the same characters and settings as *Tom Sawyer,* but is it the same kind of novel? Many scholars and critics argue that the books are fundamentally different. An essay comparing the books that builds a convincing case for considering them very different could be a strong one. However, it would need to go beyond superficial differences between the books and probe for essentials, such as what the books are about, how they are structured and narrated, how they use humor and irony, and emphasize what makes *Huckleberry Finn* the greater book.

While *Huckleberry Finn* and *Tom Sawyer* may truly be very different books, you should not overlook their similarities. Indeed, some readers argue that *Huckleberry Finn* is more than a mere sequel to *Tom Sawyer*—that in many ways it is a reworking of the *same* story. Before dismissing that idea out of hand, consider some of the parallels between the two books: The protagonists are both young boys who attempt to run away from civilization and who respond successfully to unusual challenges and reach higher levels of maturity. Both boys are terrorized by loathsome adults, face crises of conscience, and make difficult choices requiring self-sacrifice. You should find other examples of parallels between the two books.

2. **The King v. the Duke:** Are the novel's two scoundrels essentially the same or different types of characters?

The scoundrels who call themselves the King of France and the Duke of Bridgewater are among Mark Twain's most entertaining comic inventions. Sometimes hilariously outrageous and at other times loathsome, these rapscallions who take control of Huck and Jim's raft in chapter 19 make an intriguing pair of characters to discuss in a compare and contrast essay. Both are greedy con men, but how similar are they otherwise? Are they equally unprincipled and ruthless? Or do they operate under different ethical principles? How do their similarities and differences affect their ability to work together and their interactions with other characters? Does one of them play a more dominant role? Do they exhibit elements of modern comedy teams made up of straight men and stooges? If so, which of them is the straight man and which is the stooge? There are clearly many points on which the scoundrels can be compared.

To write on this topic, study everything that Huck says about the King and Duke in chapters 19 through 33. Pay close attention to their own words and actions. If you conclude the King and the Duke are significantly different types of characters, look for evidence to explain what makes them different. Could Mark Twain have created them to symbolize different forms of depravity along the Mississippi River? (See also the discussion of Huck's attitude toward the King and the Duke in the Character section above.)

3. **The novel v. films:** What do the difficulties of adapting *Huckleberry Finn* to the screen reveal about the novel itself?

Since 1920, about a dozen attempts have been made to adapt *Huckleberry Finn* to the screen, in both feature films and television dramas. None of these efforts has been recognized as a complete success, and most are regarded as failures. Why the greatest novel by one of America's greatest writers has not fared better on the screen raises interesting questions about the problems of adapting literary works to other media. It also raises interesting questions about the nature of *Huckleberry Finn* as a novel. Is there something about the book's structure, plotlines, or subject matter that helps to explain why it has yet to be adapted to the screen successfully? A partial answer to that question may lie in a comparison of the novel with one of its screen adaptations.

The easiest way to undertake an essay on this topic would be to watch a film version of *Huckleberry Finn* on a machine you can pause, reverse, and replay so that you can study individual scenes carefully. However, you should avoid watching any film version until you have read the novel completely. Before seeing the film, write out a checklist of what you regard as the most important points that the novel makes. Examples might include Huck's flight from "civilization," Huck's growing awareness of Jim's humanity and his and Jim's developing relationship, and the insanity of the Grangerford-Shepherdson feud. Your checklist might also include brief notes on the novel's characters, particularly Huck and Jim's. Leave room on your list to add comments as you watch the film. Then, while you are watching the film, keep an eye on your checklist and note the ways in which the film lives up to, or departs from, the novel.

Keep in mind that prose and film are different media that do not and cannot tell stories in the same ways. Even the best film adaptations of literary works omit characters and episodes and make other changes. What your essay should discuss, then, is not such details as whether a film includes every episode in *Huckleberry Finn* (and no film does), but whether the film is true to the novel's fundamental spirit and whether its characters are faithful representations of those in the novel. If you conclude that the film fails to meet those standards, can you find difficulties—such as Huck's narrative voice—within the novel that may account for the problems?

A good film to use for this exercise is the 1993 Disney feature, *The Adventures of Huck Finn,* which stars Elijah Wood as Huck, as copies of it should be readily available. That film also makes a particularly good case study because it departs from Mark Twain's novel in many interesting ways. A primary question to ask of that film is whether its Huck is the same character as the novel's Huck. You should also consider how the film's comparatively heavy-handed treatment of slavery compares to the more subtle points made in the novel.

Bibliography for *Huckleberry Finn*

Arac, Jonathan. "Revisiting Huck Finn: Idol and Target." *Mark Twain Annual* 3 (2005): 9–12.

Beaver, Harold. *Huckleberry Finn.* London: Unwin Hyman, 1988.

Blair, Walter. *Mark Twain and Huck Finn.* Berkeley: U of California P, 1960.

Briden, Earl F. "Conscience." *The Mark Twain Encyclopedia.* Ed. J. R. LeMaster and James D. Wilson. New York: Garland, 1993. 179–81.

Budd, Louis J., ed. *New Essays on "Adventures of Huckleberry Finn."* Cambridge: Cambridge UP, 1985.

Chadwick, Jocelyn. "Huck Finn: Icon or Idol—Yet a Necessary Read." *Mark Twain Annual* 3 (2005): 37–42.

Chadwick-Joshua, Jocelyn. *The Jim Dilemma: Reading Race in "Huckleberry Finn."* Jackson: UP of Mississippi, 1998.

Champion, Laurie, ed. *The Critical Response to Mark Twain's "Huckleberry Finn."* Westport, CT: Greenwood Press, 1991.

Clinch, Jon. *Finn.* New York: Random House, 2007.

Cox, James M. "Southwestern Vernacular." *Mark Twain: The Fate of Humor.* 2d ed. Columbia: U of Missouri P, 2002. 156–84.

De Koster, Katie, ed. *Readings on "The Adventures of Huckleberry Finn."* San Diego, CA: Greenhaven Press, 1998.

Dempsey, Terrell. *Searching for Jim: Slavery in Sam Clemens's World.* Columbia: U of Missouri P, 2003.

Donoghue, Denis. *"Adventures of Huckleberry Finn." The American Classics: A Personal Essay.* New Haven, CT: Yale UP, 2005. 217–50.

Doyno, Victor A. "Huck's and Jim's Dynamic Interactions: Dialogues, Ethics, Empathy, Respect." *Mark Twain Annual* 1 (2003): 19–30.

———. Afterword and For Further Reading. *Adventures of Huckleberry Finn.* By Mark Twain. New York: Oxford UP, 1996. 1–28. (Back matter has separate pagination.)

———. "Presentations of Violence in *Adventures of Huckleberry Finn.*" *Mark Twain Annual* 2 (2004): 75–93.

———. *Writing "Huck Finn": Mark Twain's Creative Process.* Philadelphia: U of Pennsylvania P, 1991.

Fishkin, Shelley Fisher. *Lighting Out for the Territory: Reflections on Mark Twain and American Culture.* New York: Oxford UP, 1997.

———. *Was Huck Black? Mark Twain and African-American Voices.* New York: Oxford UP, 1993.

———, et al. "Looking over Mark Twain's Shoulder as He Writes: Stanford Students Read the *Huck Finn* Manuscript." *Mark Twain Annual* 2 (2004): 107–39.

Graff, Gerald, and James Phelan, eds. *"Adventures of Huckleberry Finn": A Case Study in Critical Controversy.* Boston and New York: Bedford Books of St. Martin's Press, 1995.

Haupt, Clyde V. *"Huckleberry Finn" on Film: Film and Television Adaptations of Mark Twain's Novel, 1920–1993.* Jefferson, NC: MacFarland, 1994.

Hearn, Michael Patrick, ed. *The Annotated Huckleberry Finn.* New York: W. W. Norton, 2001.

Hentoff, Nat. *The Day They Came to Arrest the Book.* New York: Delacorte Press, 1982.

Hutchinson, Stuart, ed. *Mark Twain's "Tom Sawyer" and "Huckleberry Finn."* New York: Columbia UP, 1999.

Inge, M. Thomas, ed. *Huck Finn Among the Critics: A Centennial Selection.* Frederick, MD: UP of America, 1985.

Kiskis, Michael J. *"Adventures of Huckleberry Finn* (Again!): Teaching for Social Justice or Sam Clemens' Children's Crusade." *Mark Twain Annual* 1 (2003): 63–78.

———. "Critical Humbug: Samuel Clemens' *Adventures of Huckleberry Finn.*" *Mark Twain Annual* 3 (2005): 13–22.

Leonard, James S., ed. *Making Mark Twain Work in the Classroom.* Durham, NC: Duke UP, 1999. (Contains 13 chapters on *Huckleberry Finn* that should be useful to essay writers.)

———, Thomas A. Tenney, and Thadious M. Davis. *Satire or Evasion? Black Perspectives on "Huckleberry Finn."* Durham, NC: Duke UP, 1992.

Mensh, Elaine, and Harry Mensh. *Black, White and "Huckleberry Finn": Re-Imagining the American Dream.* Tuscaloosa: U of Alabama P, 2000.

Messent, Peter. "Racial Politics in *Huckleberry Finn.*" *Mark Twain.* New York: St. Martin's Press, 1997. 86–109.

Morrison, Toni. Introduction. *Adventures of Huckleberry Finn.* By Mark Twain. New York: Oxford UP, 1996. xxxi–xli.

Pitofsky, Alex. "Pap Finn's Overture: Fatherhood, Identity, and Southwestern Culture in *Adventures of Huckleberry Finn.*" *Mark Twain Annual* 4 (2006): 55–70.

Quirk, Tom. *Coming to Grips with "Huckleberry Finn": Essays on a Book, a Boy and a Man.* Columbia: U of Missouri P, 1993.

Railton, Stephen. *The Life & Work of Mark Twain.* Chantilly, VA: Teaching Company, 2002. Includes four lectures on *Huckleberry Finn*; available in audio and video formats.)

———. *Mark Twain in His Times.* etext.virginia.edu/railton/index2.html (includes full text of *Huckleberry Finn* and numerous study aids).

———. "Running Away: *Adventures of Huckleberry Finn.*" *Mark Twain: A Short Introduction.* Malden, MA: Blackwell, 2004. 50–74.

Rasmussen, R. Kent. "*Adventures of Huckleberry Finn.*" *Cyclopedia of Literary Places.* Ed. R. Kent Rasmussen. Pasadena, CA: Salem Press, 2003. 1:10–11.

———. "*Huckleberry Finn, Adventures of.*" In *Critical Companion to Mark Twain.* New York: Facts On File, 2007. 179–241.

Sattelmeyer, Robert, and J. Donald Crowley, eds. *One Hundred Years of "Huckleberry Finn": The Boy, His Book and American Culture—Centennial Essays.* Columbia: U Missouri P, 1985.

Seelye, John. *The True Adventures of Huckleberry Finn.* 2d ed. Urbana: U of Illinois P, 1987.

Sloane, David E. E. *Student Companion to Mark Twain.* Westport, CT: Greenwood Press, 2001.

Smiley, Jane. "Say It Ain't So, Huck: Second Thoughts on Mark Twain's 'Masterpiece.'" *Harper's* January 1996: 61f. (Search on "say it ain't so, Huck" to find a PDF version of this article online.)

Smith, David L. "Humor, Sentimentality, and Mark Twain's Black Characters." *Constructing Mark Twain: New Directions in Scholarship.* Eds. Laura E. Skandera Trombley and Michael J. Kiskis. Columbia: U of Missouri P, 2001. 151–68.

Twain, Mark. *Adventures of Huckleberry Finn.* Eds. Victor Fischer and Lin Salamo. Berkeley: U of California P, 2001 (supersedes the Mark Twain Project's 1985 edition).

————. *Adventures of Huckleberry Finn.* 3d ed. Ed. Thomas Cooley. New York: W. W. Norton, 1999.

————. "The Facts Concerning the Recent Carnival of Crime in Connecticut." *Collected Tales, Sketches, Speeches, & Essays, 1852–1890.* Ed. Louis J. Budd. New York: Library of America, 1992. 644–60.

Wieck, Carl. *Refiguring "Huckleberry Finn."* Athens: U of Georgia P, 2000.

THE PRINCE
AND THE PAUPER

READING TO WRITE

FIRST PUBLISHED in 1881, *The Prince and the Pauper* occupies a peculiar place in Mark Twain's writings. Although it has attained the status of a classic and remains one of his most popular books among modern readers, it is generally regarded as unrepresentative of Mark Twain's work—in both subject matter and style. Many critics and admirers of Mark Twain go so far as to say the book is unworthy of its author, and some may even wish that he had never written it. If these seem like odd things to say about a book that has been in print continuously for more than a century, that has given great pleasure to many thousands of readers, and that has inspired at least a half-dozen films, it should not be difficult to formulate the first questions to bring to your reading of *The Prince and the Pauper*: On what are those criticisms based? Do they have any validity? What are the chief merits of the novel?

A central criticism of *The Prince and the Pauper* is that when Mark Twain wrote the book, he stepped too far outside his natural genius as a writer of authentic vernacular works on 19th-century America. Instead of sticking to an idiom with which he was intimately familiar and writing about subjects he knew at first hand, he delved into the remote and unfamiliar world of 16th-century England. Moreover, he was evidently trying to be serious, when his greatest strength as a writer lay in his humor. Indeed, the greatest failing of the book, according to critic James M. Cox, is that it fails to be humorous. Is that true? Does it matter?

As a writer, Mark Twain is most closely associated with the Mississippi River and the American West, which he wrote about in such works as *The Adventures of Tom Sawyer* (1876), *Adventures of Huckleberry Finn* (1884), *Life on the Mississippi* (1883), *Pudd'nhead Wilson* (1894), and *Roughing It* (1872). With its mid-16th century English setting, *The Prince and the Pauper* obviously differs greatly from those other books. To appreciate the gulf that separates it from them, compare this exchange of dialogue between Prince Edward and Tom Canty (the pauper) with the passage from *Huckleberry Finn* that follows. This extract comes from chapter 3, in which the prince asks Tom about his life outside the palace:

> "What is thy name, lad?"
>> "Tom Canty, an it please thee, sir."
>> "Tis an odd one. Where dost live?"
>> "In the city, please thee, sir. Offal Court, out of Pudding Lane."
>> "Offal Court! Truly, 'tis another odd one. Hast parents?"
>> "Parents have I, sir, and a grandam likewise that is but indifferently
> precious to me, God forgive me if it be offense to say it—also twin sisters,
> Nan and Bet."
>> "Then is thy grandam not overkind to thee, I take it."
>> "Neither to any other is she, so please your worship. She hath a wicked
> heart, and worketh evil all her days."

This attempt to reproduce genteel 16th-century English has a strained and artificial quality that gets in the way of the dialogue. Its quaintness has certain charms, but does it convey any feeling of authenticity? When you read it, do you feel you are listening to real people talking or to characters reciting scripted dialogue in a play? Note the contrasts between that exchange and this excerpt from chapter 14 of *Huckleberry Finn*, in which Huck and the fleeing slave Jim discuss the French language:

> "Why, Huck, doan' de French people talk de same way we does?"
>> "No, Jim; you couldn't understand a word they said—not a single
> word."

"Well, now, I be ding-busted! How do dat come?"

"I don't know; but it's so. I got some of their jabber out of a book. Spose a man was to come to you and say 'Polly-voo-franzy'—what would you think?"

"I wouldn't think nuff'n; I'd take en bust him over de head. Dat is, if he warn't white. I wouldn't 'low no nigger to call me dat."

Despite the radical differences in language and tone between these passages from *The Prince and the Pauper* and *Huckleberry Finn*, *The Prince and the Pauper* may not be as great a departure from Mark Twain's main works as one might expect. Although Mark Twain is certainly best known for his vernacular works, he actually launched his career as an author of books with *The Innocents Abroad* (1869), a massive travel book that explores and satirizes Old World culture and has a great deal to say about earlier periods of European history. He returned to the subject of European culture and history in *A Tramp Abroad* (1880), another travel book that he published only a year before *The Prince and the Pauper*. He also later wrote two other historical novels set in Europe: *A Connecticut Yankee in King Arthur's Court* (1889), set in sixth-century England, and *Personal Recollections of Joan of Arc* (1896), set in 15th-century France. Is it fair, then, to dismiss *The Prince and the Pauper* as being outside Mark Twain's proper sphere of interests?

One might make a strong case that *The Prince and the Pauper*, far from being unrepresentative of Mark Twain's work, is a kind of key to his later more important books, as it illustrates many themes and techniques that he later explored. An obvious example is the novel's switched-identity theme, which anticipates Mark Twain's later fascination with twins and dualism—a theme central to *Pudd'nhead Wilson* and many other works. In his Afterword to the Signet edition of *The Prince and the Pauper*, scholar Kenneth S. Lynn develops this argument and points out the crucial role of coincidences in the novel, whose very premise is the unlikely coincidence of Tom and Edward's being physically—and apparently temperamentally—identical. As you read the novel, note how many times coincidences bring characters together to push the plot along. Coincidences also play major roles in such other works as *Huckleberry Finn* and *Pudd'nhead Wilson*.

The Prince and the Pauper is often regarded as essentially a children's book and, for this reason too, it does not receive the same scholarly attention that his other books receive. Is it fair to consider it merely a children's book? As you read it, you will find that it actually deals with very serious subjects—the nature of political power, slavery, government oppression of the poor, cruel punishments, religious intolerance, and the grinding misery of poverty and disfranchisement. Are these the types of subjects that one expects to find in a book written for children? The fact is that Mark Twain probably was uncertain who he was writing for, just as with *Tom Sawyer*. While he certainly had young readers in mind when he was constructing *The Prince and the Pauper*, he was also thinking about his adult readers. For that reason, he affixed this subtitle to the book: "A Tale for Young People of All Ages."

This may not be an easy question to answer if your knowledge of Mark Twain's life and other writings is limited, but as you read *The Prince and the Pauper*, try to give some thought to the question of why he wrote the book. You should be able to find enough in this novel alone to get at least a sense of what he trying to do. Some scholars have suggested that he wrote the book to improve his literary reputation. The theory is that through his early writing career, he became so sensitive to charges that he was merely a crude humorist, that he wrote *The Prince and the Pauper* to prove that he could produce respectable literature. (Some people argue that he especially wanted to win his respectable wife's approval. In that, he succeeded.) His novel was warmly received as respectable literature, and therein lies another criticism of the book: Many authors were capable of writing similar works, but none could write the kind of work at which Mark Twain was best. It is, perhaps, largely for this reason that *The Prince and the Pauper* is criticized. Whether or not it is a good book, it is not as a good a book as Mark Twain was capable of writing.

TOPICS AND STRATEGIES

The general and specific ideas for essay topics on *The Prince and the Pauper* discussed below are designed merely to help you develop your own ideas. Do not treat them as outlines of what you should write and do not limit your choice of subjects to those discussed here. You would do well to always question whether the ideas expressed here are valid. Literature is not an exact science. Different authorities often disagree on the same issues; their opinions are not necessarily any more valid than your own. As always, the keys to successful essay writing are originality of thought and clearness and force of argument.

The questions raised below do not necessarily have any right or wrong answers. The strength of your essay will come not merely from the conclusions you reach, but from the power and clarity of the arguments you advance to reach those conclusions. Whichever topics you choose to write about, use your imagination and try to consider all possible sides of every question. A good way to stimulate your imagination is to outline arguments that take different sides on the same issues. For example, if you wish to argue that *The Prince and the Pauper* is an attack on monarchical government, you may find it helpful to outline all the reasons for arguing that the novel endorses monarchy.

Themes

As in Mark Twain's other books, many themes can be found in *The Prince and the Pauper*. Perhaps not surprisingly, the themes that stand out most clearly are those that Mark Twain explored in many of his other writings. Moreover, these themes are closely related: dualism and switched identities, unrecognized claimants, and the relationship between identity and clothes. Other themes can be found as well. For example, in her introduction to the Oxford edition of *The Prince and the Pauper*, Judith Martin—who is better known as the syndicated columnist "Miss Manners"—points out the importance of manners in the behavior of the novel's characters and finds unexpected similarities between Edward and Tom Canty.

Sample Topics:

1. **Unrecognized claimants:** What does the novel say about the nature of birthright and inherited privilege?

   The most obvious theme in *The Prince and the Pauper* is one that fascinated Mark Twain throughout his life: people who cannot get anyone else to recognize that they are who they claim to be. Both Edward Tudor and Tom Canty are examples of such claimants. From the moment that Edward is expelled from the palace until he interrupts the coronation ceremony that is about to make Tom king, he convinces no one of his true identity—apart from two young girls and a madman. Meanwhile, after Tom accidentally finds himself in Edward's rightful place, he can convince no one of his true identity. Even Miles Hendon fails to be accepted for who he really is when he finally returns to his home after many years.

Claimants are, by their nature, closely related to impostors, and both can be found throughout Mark Twain's fiction. Indeed, Mark Twain even devoted an entire book to the subject: *The American Claimant* (1892), a short novel about a flamboyant American who claims to be the rightful heir to an English viscountcy. That character's claims may be valid. However, in *Adventures of Huckleberry Finn* (1884), the two scoundrels who take control of Huck and Jim's raft are clearly impostors. One claims to be an English duke, the other the rightful king of France. They contrast with the claimants in *The Prince and the Pauper*, who really are who they say they are.

Perhaps the first question an essay on this subject should address is how the theme of claimants helps to drive the novel's plot. As you read the novel, examine every aspect of how each character presses his claims, why others do not believe him, and how his interactions with the doubters affect his own actions. It might be illuminating to consider what the effect on the narrative would be if some of the doubters were to believe the claimants. For example, could the narrative proceed as it does if Miles Hendon were to accept Edward as the true king? (This actually happens in several film adaptations of the novel; the result is, unavoidably, a much different kind of story.)

Of greater importance, perhaps, is what the novel says about the nature of birthright. During his brief time on the throne, Tom Canty proves himself a fine ruler, and he might even make a better king than Edward. However, both law and society recognize Edward's claim to the throne because of

his birth: As the son of King Henry VIII, Edward is universally recognized as the rightful heir. Do you find anything in
the novel to challenge that view? Or does the novel tend to
support the idea of inherited monarchy? For a different perspective from Mark Twain on monarchy, read *A Connecticut
Yankee* (1889) and compare that novel's ideas about birthright and inherited privilege with those of *The Prince and
the Pauper.*

2. **Do clothes make the man?:** What does the novel say about the
importance of clothes to identity?

All the major characters in *The Prince and the Pauper* are
defined by their clothes. When Tom is in his natural element, he wears rags. The first time he sees Prince Edward at
the royal palace, he instantly recognizes Edward is a prince
because of his splendid royal garments. Miles Hendon, on
his first appearance, is described as a "sort of Don Caesar
de Bazan in dress" (a comparison with a flamboyant opera
character). The clothes that these and other characters wear
are frequently mentioned throughout the novel, whose narrative begins in earnest when Tom and Edward exchange their
clothes on a lark.

   After Tom and Edward swap outfits, they find that no
change seems to have been made: They look like each other.
From that moment, everyone who sees Tom believes him to be
the prince, and everyone who sees Edward thinks he is merely
a ragged pauper boy. Is the novel saying that the only difference between commoners and kings is the clothes they wear?
That is an idea that Mark Twain explores in other writings,
such as "The Czar's Soliloquy," in which the ruler of Russia
privately thinks,

> Without my clothes I should be as destitute of authority as any
> other naked person. Nobody could tell me from the parson,
> a barber, a dude. Then who is the real Emperor of Russia? My
> clothes. There is no other.

In *A Connecticut Yankee in King Arthur's Court,* the Yankee finds a man who has been imprisoned for expressing the very same thought. It is clear that Mark Twain regarded the idea as heretical in societies ruled by monarchies. He does not seem to make that point explicitly in *The Prince and the Pauper,* but does his book express the idea implicitly? To write on this subject, pay close attention to everything that the novel says about clothes. List the passages that support the idea that the identities and status of people are connected to the clothes they wear. Pay particular attention to moments when characters change their attire.

3. **Violence:** How is violence depicted in the novel and how essential is it to advancing the narrative?

Like Mark Twain's other historical novels, *The Prince and the Pauper* contains much more violence than his other fiction. In addition to descriptions of beatings by abusive parents, attacks on individuals by mobs, fights among criminals, a murder and a would-be murder, whippings, and cruel executions, the novel also presents backstories of characters who were earlier victims or perpetrators of violence. Is the purpose of all the novel's violence simply to demonstrate that 16th-century England was a harsh place in which to live? If so, to what extent does the novel make that intent explicit? If you write on this subject, pay particular attention to the attitudes of Tom Canty and Edward Tudor toward violence, cruelty, and injustice. Each boy appears to have a gentle nature that abhors cruelty (though Edward occasionally threatens death to those who offend him). What reasons does the novel offer to explain the boys' humanitarian impulses? Does the boys' gentleness detract from the book's realism?

Character

The Prince and the Pauper revolves around three characters—Tom Canty, Edward Tudor, and Miles Hendon. At least one of them is at the center of virtually every scene. Many other figures also populate the novel, but an important question is whether any of them can be considered characters in the same sense as Tom, Edward, and Miles. This question relates to another issue that one should always consider when reading any novel: the extent to which its characters are, in fact, *characters*, and not merely one- or two-dimensional figures inserted as props to advance the story. (This question, in turn, relates to melodrama, which is discussed in the Form and Genre section below.) True characters are complex and three-dimensional, or fully rounded. They grow and develop throughout a novel, and readers cannot always expect them to behave predictably. Indeed, one might ask whether any of the characters in *The Prince and the Pauper* is truly three-dimensional. If you choose to write an essay on character, it would be equally valid to concentrate on one character or discuss several characters together.

Sample Topics:

1. **Prince Edward:** How does Mark Twain's fictional Edward relate to the historical Edward and how does Edward's character develop in the novel?

As discussed below in the History and Context section, Mark Twain originally intended to set *The Prince and the Pauper* in his own time and use the future King Edward VII as his protagonist. Instead, however, he hit on the happy idea of using the 16th-century's Edward VI (1537–53), the son of Henry VIII who became king while still a boy. To make Edward fit his story, Mark Twain made him several years older at the time of his accession to the kingship and physically more robust than the real Edward may have been. Why were these changes necessary? A more important question to consider is the validity of Mark Twain's description of Edward's short reign as "singularly merciful . . . for those harsh times." Is there any truth in that assessment? Since you are probably writing for a literature class, not for a history class, it is not so much the historical facts that matter as it is Mark Twain's literary use of history. One of the conceits of his novel, as expressed in the book's brief preface, is that the story *"could* have happened." In other words, the "singularly merciful" nature of Edward VI's reign might be attributed to the lessons that he learned about injustice in England during his involuntary exile from the confines of the royal place. An essay on Edward should therefore do at least two things: Examine his character development in the context of the novel, and compare the fictional Edward with the historical Edward. To do that, you will need to do a little reading on English history.

2. **Tom Canty:** Is Tom a realistic character, and how does he change throughout the novel?

Tom Canty has many of the same appealing traits as Tom Sawyer—a lively imagination and a keen sense of justice. Both boys are avid readers of romantic literature and dream of rising to lofty eminence. Where Tom Canty differs from Tom Sawyer is in actually realizing his dream by becoming the king of England. If we set aside the matter of the unlikely accident that places Tom on the throne, there remain a number of interesting questions that we can ask about him. The first, perhaps, is how is it possible he can make anyone believe that he is the true heir to the throne (especially when his greatest desire is to escape from the palace). How could an uneducated boy from the slums of London speak and behave like the true Edward? Tom not only sustains this deception for several weeks, but when the true Edward reappears, Tom has trouble convincing anyone that he himself is *not* Edward. Moreover, during his brief period on the throne, he displays distinctly modern sensibilities in matters such as publicly doubting the powers of an accused witch. Is there anything in his makeup to indicate why he express such skepticism? In what ways is Tom believable as a character? What might Mark Twain have done to make his behavior and his successful imposture as king more plausible?

Set aside, for the moment, the matter of Tom's believability and consider his development as a character. Does he change? If so, how and why? Is his behavior consistent, or does his position of power begin to corrupt him? At the end of the novel,

Tom could easily have the true Edward cast out of Westminster Abbey and become king permanently. However, he does the right thing by proving to the skeptical court officials Edward's true identity, even though he may be risking his life in doing so. Is this behavior consistent with the changes through which he has gone? Or, is it dictated by the needs of the plot, according to the conventions of melodrama? (See the Form and Genre section below.)

3. **Miles Hendon:** Is he a rounded character or merely a plot device?

Among children who read *The Prince and the Pauper*, Miles Hendon is probably a favorite character. He is brave, dashing, flamboyant, loyal, and repeatedly heroic. Indeed, when Mark Twain's own children staged dramatic productions of the story, Mark Twain insisted on playing Hendon himself. Admirable though Hendon is, is he anything more than a cardboard saint designed to push the story along and help Edward regain his throne?

To write on this subject, begin by surveying Hendon's actions to assess his character. We first meet him in London, when he rescues Edward from an angry mob that has grown impatient with the boy's protestations that he is the Prince of Wales. The idea that a stranger might risk his life to save a boy—even a ragged beggar, as Edward appears to be—is certainly plausible. Why, however, does Hendon become so devoted to Edward that he not only puts up with the boy's tiresome insistence that he is the prince but also quietly acquiesces to Edward's unreasonable orders and tiresome royal pretensions? Is there anything in descriptions of Hendon or his behavior to suggest that he has more than a single dimension? If you find it difficult to say enough about Hendon to write an entire essay, look at the discussions of melodrama and the picaresque in the Form and Genre section below to help broaden your discussion.

History and Context

The first of the two historical novels that Mark Twain set in England, *The Prince and the Pauper* resembles *A Connecticut Yankee in King Arthur's Court* in some ways—such as its treatment of monarchy and slavery. However, it differs greatly in being set during a real historical era with real historical personages, in contrast to *Connecticut Yankee*'s setting in semimythical Arthurian times.

The novel opens shortly before King Henry VIII dies in early 1547. The prince of its title is Henry's real son, Edward Tudor, who became King Edward VI on Henry's death. The preface is interesting and presents the story as a tradition handed down from father to son and adds, "It may be history, it may be only legend, a tradition. It may have happened, it may not have happened: but it *could* have happened." The story did *not* happen, of course, but by suspending their disbelief and imagining that the story might have happened, the readers' pleasure is enhanced. However, for the purpose of writing an essay on the history and context of the novel, the first questions you need to consider are these: How do the events of the novel relate to what is known about real history? Do discrepancies between the novel and known history (such as Prince Edward's age at the time of his father's death) matter? Finally, what serious purpose, if any, was Mark Twain striving for in setting his novel in 16th-century England?

Sample Topics:

1. **Edward VII v. Edward VI:** Does Edward VI work better as the novel's prince than Edward VII might have?

When Mark Twain began planning *The Prince and the Pauper*, he considered setting the story in the 19th century and making the then-future king Edward VII (who was almost his exact contemporary) his novel's prince. He soon decided, however, that that approach would not work and switched the setting to the time of King Henry VIII's death in the mid-16th century. That change allowed him to use Edward VI as his prince, who was still a boy when he became king. In what important ways would the story have differed if it had been set in the 19th century? What, if anything, about the 16th century makes it a better setting for the novel?

To write on this subject, you will need to do a little research on both Edward VI and Edward VII and their times. Also, it would be a good idea to read a biography of Mark Twain that discusses his writing of *The Prince and the Pauper*. As you collect your notes (be sure to keep track of page references), consider such issues as the circumstances of each prince's boyhood, his relationship with his regal parent, his accession to the kingship, and the nature of his rule. Before beginning the essay, list the advantages and disadvantages of using each prince in the novel. You can have some real fun with this essay by suggesting how Mark Twain might have plotted the novel differently had he used Edward VII.

2. **16th-century England:** What serious historical issues does the novel address?

This topic is closely related to the subject of why Mark Twain chose to write about Edward VI, instead of Edward VII. You might discuss that matter briefly within this essay topic, but the essay's main focus should be on the broader issues that the novel treats, such as monarchy, inherited rank and privilege, slavery, and social injustice.

This is such a large topic that an essay could take any number of directions. For example, you might try to assemble a sweeping overview of the novel's issues, discussing each of them briefly. Or, you might focus on one or two issues and treat them in depth. The first thing to do is to read the novel carefully and take brief notes on every point relating to what appears to be a major historical issue. After completing those notes, select the issues that strike you as most important— either in their true historical context or within the framework of the novel. Then, do enough research on each of those subjects to determine the accuracy of the novel's treatment of them.

You might start your research by looking at King Henry's order to execute the Duke of Norfolk, which was followed by Tom Canty's ordering Norfolk's release the moment he is proclaimed king. Was there really a Duke of Norfolk? Did Henry order his execution (and why)? What became of the duke? Did Edward VI have anything to do with the matter? Does any of this really matter within the context of *The Prince and the Pauper*? If episodes such as this are merely fictions, what purpose do they serve in the novel?

The Norfolk episode, though significant in the novel, is a narrow issue. Perhaps more important are broad issues such as unjust laws, oppression of the poor, and other forms of social injustice. Is the real purpose of *The Prince and the Pauper* to condemn the harsh injustices of early England? Or might Mark Twain have used the novel to attack a target nearer at hand, such as social injustice in the United States, which had only recently abolished slavery when he wrote the book? Can the novel be read as an indictment of social injustice in all its forms and wherever it exists?

Philosophy and Ideas

It may be that the core of *The Prince and the Pauper* lies in the broad philosophy and ideas that the book contains. Many of them—such as inherited privilege and critiques of monarchy—are discussed in other sections of this chapter. However, this is a good place to bring some of those ideas into sharper focus. Keep in mind that the purpose of these sections is not to dictate how you should categorize your own essay but merely to guide you. It does not matter at all which sections supply your ideas.

Sample Topics:

1. **Is training everything?:** What, if anything, does the novel say about the roles of birth, environment, and training in the makeup of its characters?

An issue that concerned Mark Twain increasingly as he grew older was the role of training in the formation of character. Indeed, it is a central theme in *Pudd'nhead Wilson*, in which a slave woman switches her baby son with the infant son of her master, to ensure that her son will grow up a free man. The result of this identity switch is that the baby who was born free grows up with all the character traits of a slave, while the slave baby grows up with those of a master. The point that the novel tries to make is that such traits are not inborn but are instead the result of training, which is everything. In *The Prince and the Pauper*, a similar switch occurs, with Tom Canty, one of the lowest-born English subjects imaginable, taking the place of Prince Edward, the highest-born person in England and heir to the throne. If training is, in fact, everything, would not one expect Tom Canty to fail miserably in the role of king? However, he does not. In fact, his brief reign as king is exemplary. Is this, then, a refutation of Mark Twain's later thinking about birth and training? Or is there something else going on in the novel that actually supports his idea? To find answers to these and other related questions, you will need to sift the novel carefully to find every allusion to the importance of birth and training and their effects on the characters. Do not limit your enquiries to the major characters, but look also at minor characters, such as officials at the royal court, members of the Ruffler's gang, and others.

2. **The nature of power:** What does the novel say about the nature of political power, its limitations, and the difficulties involved in exercising it?

As *The Prince and the Pauper* is essentially a novel about kingship, it is natural that the book expresses ideas about the nature of political power and its exercise. This is a topic that should lend itself well to developing original ideas, as the subject of power pervades the novel but is largely implicit. In other words, the supreme power of the monarchy is always present but is rarely discussed openly. To assess what the novel says on this subject, you will need to read between the lines. You might begin by considering who the main holders of political power in the novel are and what use they make of their power.

Early in the novel, King Henry wants badly to have Norfolk executed, but despite his supremacy, even he cannot get his order carried out unless it is stamped with the Great Seal, which no one can find. By contrast, when Tom Canty finds himself in possession of the throne, he is so uncertain of his own power that he hesitates to scratch his own nose. Meanwhile, the rightful king, Edward, wanders the land issuing royal commands, but can find no one who will obey him because he lacks the visible symbols of power. (The one exception is Miles Hendon, who obeys Edward only because he thinks the boy mad and wishes to humor him.) Do all these observations and other examples in the novel add up to a coherent depiction of the nature of power?

Form and Genre

Despite the many forms of criticism that have been leveled at *The Prince and the Pauper,* the book is generally regarded as one of Mark Twain's best-constructed novels. It begins with a clear and logical (though perhaps far-fetched) premise; it moves smoothly toward its conclusion, with few of the distractions and derailments that characterize Mark Twain's other books; and it reaches a satisfactory conclusion that leaves no plot points unresolved and forgets about no characters along the way (with the possible exception of John Canty). An unusual feature of the novel is its dual narrative, which shifts back and forth between pauper Tom Canty in the royal palace and the displaced Prince Edward, whose struggle to get back into the palace draws him from one perilous adventure to another, on a long journey that has many picaresque qualities. (In the original novel, illustrations of the two boys' separate adventures were drawn by different artists.) An essay might be written on the question of whether the dual narrative works satisfactorily.

Sample Topics:

1. **A democratic fable?:** What elements of a classical fable does *The Prince and the Pauper* have?

   In *Mark Twain: The Fate of Humor* (1966 & 2002), James M. Cox argues that *The Prince and the Pauper* should be seen as a "democratic fable," not a mere adventure story or comedy. To support that argument, he points out that events in the novel are driven, not by character, but by tricks and gimmicks in the plot designed to drive the story toward a moralistic conclusion, as in a classical fable. Borrowing a term coined by an earlier scholar, he calls the book a "democratic fable" because the story's moral is that there is no essential difference between a commoner and a king. Does that view have any validity?

To construct an essay on this subject, begin by reviewing what is meant by a *fable*. After you define it, identity the elements of *The Prince and the Pauper* that fit or do not fit that definition. Pay particular attention to how coincidences and mistaken identities drive the action. Is it possible that the narrative could reach any resolution other than the one toward which all the action appears to point?

2. **Humor:** What role does humor play in the novel?

The Prince and the Pauper is obviously a very different kind of book than *The Adventures of Tom Sawyer* (1876), in which humor plays an important role in almost every scene. There is a great deal of humor in *The Prince and the Pauper,* but it appears to be of a different nature. For example, whereas Tom Sawyer looks for excuses to play jokes and undertake adventures that generate humorous situations, the central characters in *The Prince and the Pauper* seem to be driven by more serious concerns. How does this difference limit the role of humor in the novel?

James M. Cox argues that *The Prince and the Pauper* fails as a novel because it is, at heart, committed to humor but fails to be humorous, thanks to its excessive efforts to be serious. Is that a valid criticism of the book? What is there, if anything, about the novel to suggest that Mark Twain's intent was to write a humorous book? How might the book's serious themes have derailed that effort?

One of the first things to do before writing on this subject is to identify all the ways in which humor is used in *The Prince and the Pauper*. A good example with which to start is Tom Canty's first royal dinner (chapter 7), when his uncertainty about what to do about his itchy nose creates a humorous crisis. Perhaps more to the point, however, is the question of where humor is not used in the novel. How, for example, might Mark Twain have used mistaken-identity incidents to generate humor? Switched-identity stories are a staple of humorous fiction, and Mark Twain certainly got a lot of mileage from such stories. Could he have done anything differently to create more humorous situations in *The Prince and the Pauper*? Would mere humor necessarily be an improvement?

3. **Melodrama and the picaresque:** What role do melodramatic and picaresque elements play in the novel?

The essence of melodrama in literature is exaggerated and typically unrealistic dramatic moments and the use of physical action and plot devices, instead of character development, to advance stories. This definition clearly fits *The Prince and the Pauper*. The book is filled with melodramatic moments—such as Miles Hendon's flamboyant rescues of Edward, Edward's near-murder at the hands of a mad priest, and his last-minute interruption of the coronation ceremony—and it appears that plot is more important than character in the story.

A picaresque is a narrative about a character who goes through episodic adventures while moving from place to place and experiencing life at the lowest levels of society. Picaresque heroes are usually rascals, such as Henry Fielding's Tom Jones and Daniel Defoe's Moll Flanders, but the term seems to apply to the adventures Edward experiences in his travels. Edward is not the kind of rascal who is typically the protagonist of a picaresque story, but his companion, Miles Hendon, certainly is, and Hendon shares many of Edward's adventures.

If you write an essay on either or both of these subjects, you should begin by defining the terms you use to make it clear you understand the concepts of melodrama and picaresque. The essay should then adduce examples of those concepts from *The Prince and the Pauper* and show how they are used to advance the story. Perhaps the most important question to address is whether it is accurate to say that plot predominates over character in the novel.

Language, Symbols, and Imagery

The Prince and the Pauper is not a deeply nuanced work, so one would not expect to find multiple levels of meaning or subtle symbols and imagery. The most important symbol in the novel is probably the Great Seal of England, whose disappearance and eventual rediscovery provide crucial plot points. The fact that the seal represents the authority of the monarchy is so obvious, however, that it would be difficult to find much of interest to write about it. Differences in clothes among characters of different social classes represent a form of imagery, and that subject is discussed under the heading of Themes above. A richer subject for essay topics is the novel's language. Language is a central subject in most of Mark Twain's works and is of special interest here because of the unusual situation of his having to recreate 16th-century English.

Sample Topic:

1. **16th-century dialogue:** Does the dialogue in *The Prince and the Pauper* succeed in lending a feeling of authenticity to the novel?

The Prince and the Pauper was Mark Twain's first attempt to write a long fictional work set during a much earlier time period. In his efforts to write authentic 16th-century English dialogue, he read extensively in English history and toyed with experimental texts (including the ribald Elizabethan parody later published as *1601: Conversation as It Was by the Social Fireside in the Time of the Tudors*) to develop a feel for the sounds and rhythms of the language. The central question that an essay on this subject should address is not whether the novel's language is, in fact, an authentic reflection of 16th-century speech, but what Mark Twain's use of the language that he created contributes to the novel. Does it at least feel authentic? Is it rendered consistently? Does it assist or impede the flow of the narrative?

If you write on this subject, keep in mind the distinction between the language of the anonymous, third-person narrator and the language of the characters, as it is represented in dialogue. In fact, the language of the narration offers some points of interest itself. For example, several times in chapter 6, Mark Twain seems to forget himself by introducing nautical terminology that recalls his Mississippi River writings ("Snags and sandbars," "piloting a great ship through a dangerous channel").

Compare and Contrast Essays

While comparison subjects offer a wide scope for developing original ideas, they also make it easy to fall into the trap of doing the opposite. For example, you would probably prepare for a compare and contrast essay by compiling a list of similarities and differences between characters, between types of plots, between different points of view, or other aspects of *The Prince and the Pauper.* The danger in this approach is allowing yourself to be satisfied with the lists themselves, as if catalogs of comparisons reveal anything. It would not be enough simply to say that both Tom Sawyer and *The Prince and the Pauper*'s Tom Canty are adventurous boys with similar names and lively imaginations. You must also try to explain why these characters have these traits, how they affect each boy's behavior, and how they relate to other aspects of each boy's personality, and how these aspects of their personalities help to drive their stories' narratives.

A particularly attractive feature of compare and contrast essays is that they allow you to be creative on at least two levels: first, in finding aspects of one or more works to compare; second, in finding significant points to make about the similarities and differences you observe. True originality is often difficult to achieve, but one of your best chances of attaining it lies in innovative compare and contrast essays. Comparing Tom Sawyer and Tom Canty would give you a wide scope for an interesting essay, but the only chance for originality that subject would offer would be in the arguments you make, not in the basic question, which is so obvious that it is discussed in almost every analysis of *The Prince and the Pauper.* On the other hand, if you were to compare a less obvious combination of characters, such as Miles Hendon and *Huckleberry Finn*'s Jim (both of whom are traveling companions and father figures to boys), you would certainly be more likely to be on to something original.

Sample Topics:

1. **The prince v. the pauper:** In what ways are Tom Canty and Edward Tudor similar and different? How do these similarities and differences figure into the novel's plot?

   This subject may seem too obvious to leave anything original to be said, but with some effort and imagination, you might well come up with some fresh ideas. The two boys are superficially almost identical. They were born on the same day; they are physically indistinguishable; they apparently have similar mannerisms and patterns of speech; they come from structurally similar families (harsh, dictatorial fathers; older sisters); and they seem to have similar ideas about justice. Is this catalog essentially accurate and complete? If not, modify or add to it.

   What is important about the boys, however, is not so much what makes them similar, but what makes them different. One comes from a world of want and squalor, and the other comes from a world of almost unimaginable power, privilege, and wealth. One has had only the bare rudiments of an education and has been raised to expect nothing from life but knocks and disappointment. The other has been tutored by the finest minds in England and trained to assume the reins of the highest power in the land. Nevertheless, after they accidentally switch places and Tom Canty finds himself on the throne of England, he carries out the duties of the king as well as one might expect Edward to do. Does that seem possible? Does Tom have qualities that Edward may lack?

2. **The Prince and the Pauper v. Tom Sawyer and/or Huckleberry Finn:** What elements of Mark Twain's most famous Mississippi writings can be found in *The Prince and the Pauper*?

This is a rich subject on which to write an essay, but it requires familiarity with *The Prince and the Pauper* and *Tom Sawyer* or *Huckleberry Finn,* or both. This subject is particularly interesting because it will afford you the opportunity to place *The Prince and the Pauper* in the context of Mark Twain's two most famous Mississippi works—*Tom Sawyer,* which he published five years before *The Prince and the Pauper,* and *Huckleberry Finn,* which he published about four years later. Since *The Prince and the Pauper* falls almost midway between those two books, it would not be surprising to find connections between it and the other books.

You might start an essay on this subject by comparing settings in *The Prince and the Pauper* with those in the Mississippi books. Consider the similarities between Tom Canty's neighborhood of Offal Court, beside the River Thames, and Tom and Huck's village of St. Petersburg on the Mississippi. It seems fair to say there is nothing similar to Westminster Palace in *Tom Sawyer* or *Huckleberry Finn.* But can one argue that when Huck enters the Grangerford home in *Huckleberry Finn,* he experiences something like the transformation that the pauper Tom Canty goes through when he enjoys the "Limitless Plenty" of the royal palace?

The title characters in these three novels offer many points of comparison, but be careful not to be overly rigid in matching up pairs of characters. For example, the pauper Tom Canty seems a logical match for the indigent Huck Finn: Both boys are accustomed to living in desperate poverty; both have abusive fathers whom they wish to escape; and both are lifted into comfortable homes that they soon find to be wearisome prisons. At the same time, however, Tom Canty is a good match for Tom Sawyer, whose given name, approximate age, fascination with romantic literature, and lively imagination he shares. How do these two characters differ? To answer that question, you might consider how Tom Sawyer would fare, if he were accidentally placed on the throne of England. Leaving aside the fact that Tom Sawyer is a 19th-century American, is there anything about his makeup to suggest that he would do any better or worse as king than Tom Canty?

Prince Edward also offers important points of comparison with Huck Finn. Both boys become orphans early in their narratives (Huck does not know he is an orphan until the end, however) and go on long, picaresque journeys, during which they encounter human depravity and injustice in many different forms. Both travel with adult companions (Edward with Miles Hendon, Huck with Jim) who act as father figures. Much might be said about the similarities and differences in how Edward and Huck respond to their situations, based on their backgrounds and natures. Are there elements in Edward's story that might have influenced Mark Twain's writing of *Huckleberry Finn*?

Other points of comparison between *The Prince and the Pauper* and the Mississippi novels include structural similarities (such as Edward's and Huck's journeys) and similar incidents. For example, Edward's dramatic entrance at Tom's coronation in *The Prince and the Pauper* bears an unmistakable similarity to the sudden appearance of Tom and Huck and their friend Joe Harper at their own funeral in *Tom Sawyer*. The tests that Mrs. Canty applies to Edward, to determine if he really is her son are similar to the tests that Mrs. Loftus applies to Huck— disguised as a girl—to determine if he really is a girl. Are there other similar? Do they reveal anything about what Mark Twain was thinking when he was writing the books? The most obvious points of comparison among these books are the pairs of characters, settings, and incidents that are discussed above.

3. *The Prince and the Pauper* v. *Connecticut Yankee:* Do these two novels set in the English past reveal similar or different views about England, monarchy, and history?

In a sense, an essay on this subject would be something like the inverse of an essay comparing *The Prince and the Pauper* with *Tom Sawyer* or *Huckleberry Finn*. Whereas this essay would tend to focus on similarities between novels with radically different settings, an essay on *The Prince and the Pauper* and *Connecticut Yankee* would tend to focus on differences between novels with superficially similar settings in English history.

The Prince and the Pauper is set in the mid-16th century, while *Connecticut Yankee* is set in the early sixth century. That's a gap of more than 1,000 years, but Mark Twain was careless with his historical epochs, and the difference between the Englands of the two novels is not great. Indeed, if you compare the dialogue in the two books, you will find many similarities. What is important in the books, however, is not the window-dressing of speech and costumes but the depiction of institutions.

To write an essay on this subject, begin by outlining each book's views on the nature of monarchy, the injustice of inherited privilege, and the oppression of slaves and commoners. Is it fair to say that while *The Prince and the Pauper* offers criticisms of monarchical institutions, in the end it offers an optimistic view of monarchy by suggesting that King Edward will govern wisely? Do this book's views of England's institutions differ from those in *Connecticut Yankee,* or, does *The Prince and the Pauper* reveal some of the pessimism evident in the latter book?

Bibliography for *The Prince and the Pauper*

Bassett, John E. "The Prince, the Pauper, the Writers, and Mark Twain." *A Heart of Ideality in My Realism and Other Essays on Howells and Twain.* West Cornwall, CT: Locust Hill Press, 1991. 137–42.

Cox, James M. *Mark Twain: The Fate of Humor.* 2d ed. Columbia: U of Missouri P, 2002.

Emerson, Everett. Afterword. *The Prince and the Pauper.* By Mark Twain. New York: Oxford UP, 1996. 1–16 (Back matter has separate pagination.)

———. *Mark Twain: A Literary Life.* Philadelphia: U of Pennsylvania P, 2000.

Gerber, John C. *Mark Twain.* Boston: Twayne, 1988.

Lynn, Kenneth S. Afterword. *The Prince and the Pauper.* By Mark Twain. New York: Signet, 1964. 213–19.

Martin, Judith. Introduction. *The Prince and the Pauper.* By Mark Twain. New York: Oxford UP, 1996. xxxi–xli.

Morris, Linda A. "*The Adventures of Tom Sawyer* and *The Prince and the Pauper* as Juvenile Literature." *A Companion to Mark Twain.* Eds. Peter Messent and Louis J. Budd. Oxford, England: Blackwell, 2005. 371–86.

Paul, Kathleen. *The Prince and the Pauper.* Masterplots II: Juvenile and Young Adult Fiction Series. Ed. Frank N. Magill. Pasadena, CA: Salem Press, 1991. 3: 1,174–176.

Railton, Stephen. *Mark Twain in His Times.* etext.virginia.edu/railton/index2. html. (Includes full text of *The Prince and the Pauper* and numerous study aids.)

Rasmussen, R. Kent. "*The Prince and the Pauper.*" In *Critical Companion to Mark Twain.* New York: Facts On File, 2007. I: 365–389.

———. *The Prince and the Pauper. Cyclopedia of Literary Places.* Ed. R. Kent Rasmussen. Pasadena, CA: Salem Press, 2003. 3: 940–41.

Stone, Albert E., Jr. *The Innocent Eye: Childhood in Mark Twain's Imagination.* New Haven, CT: Yale UP, 1961.

Twain, Mark. *The Prince and the Pauper.* Eds. Victor Fischer and Lin Salamo. Berkeley: U of California P, 1979.

A CONNECTICUT YANKEE IN KING ARTHUR'S COURT

READING TO WRITE

I T IS nearly impossible to imagine Mark Twain writing a time-travel story sending a grown-up version of Tom Sawyer into the time of King Arthur that would not be a joy to read. *A Connecticut Yankee in King Arthur's Court* is just that and much more. An energetic, entertaining, and thought-provoking romp through early medieval England, the novel has delighted American readers since it was first published in 1889. It is so much fun, in fact, that it is sometimes seen as a children's book. The novel has also inspired numerous screen adaptations, most of which are comedies that play up the story's burlesque elements and comic contrasts between the distant past and the present. However, it should not be overlooked that the original novel contains disturbing elements of violence and cruelty that seem difficult to reconcile with the book's lighter moments. For example, in one scene, its hero—Hank Morgan—makes fun of an armor-clad knight wearing a ridiculous top hat; shortly afterward, Hank permits Queen Morgan Le Fay to hang every musician in her band simply because she does not like their music. Far more shocking is the immense contrast between Hank's playful humor in the early chapters and his callous slaughter of tens of thousands of English knights in the final chapters.

One of the first questions to ask of *Connecticut Yankee* is what the book is trying to do. Was Mark Twain's primary goal simply to get laughs?

Or did he write the book to condemn the cruelty, injustice, and primitive conditions of the medieval world so he could point up the superiority of modern America? Or might the book be trying to do something altogether different? After you find tentative answers to these first questions, you should ask whether the novel succeeds in achieving its purpose. This question might be more difficult than you suspect. For example, if you were to conclude that the book's primary purpose is to be humorous, you would have to reconcile that conclusion with the novel's cataclysmic ending, which has nothing funny about it.

To understand *Connecticut Yankee* properly, you should read it straight through before beginning to analyze it. If you have already read it, you would do well to read it again, all the while asking yourself whether it has a unifying message. The novel's complex and sprawling story can be divided into discrete and logical sections. If you were to study the book only one section at a time, you would almost certainly fail to grasp its overall unities. As much fun as the novel can be, it is not an easy book to understand on a first reading. It is, however, a book that can be more richly rewarding each time you read it.

A central challenge faced by first-time readers of *Connecticut Yankee* is making sense of the novel's apparently radical shifts in tone. Compare, for example, these two passages regarding Yankee Hank Morgan's conflicts with English knights. In the first passage, from chapter 9, Hank's comments about his impending duel with Sir Sagramor have a light, almost flippant, tone. His belittling remarks about knights ("the boys") make it hard to take his impending duel seriously.

> As soon as Sir Sagramor got well, he notified me that there was a little account to settle between us, and he named a day three or four years in the future . . . I said I would be ready when he got back. You see, he was going for the Holy Grail. The boys all took a flier at the Holy Grail now and then. It was a several years' cruise. They always put in the long absence snooping around, in the most conscientious way, though none of them had any idea where the Holy Grail really was . . .

Thirty chapters later, Hank finally confronts Sagramor in a tournament. After an amusing scene in which Hank uses a cowboy lasso to toy with Sagramor during their joust, the confrontation becomes deadly. Hank kills Sagramor with a revolver and then challenges *all* the knights to come at him at once. After he shoots nine more knights, the others break ranks and retreat. Hank then declares knight-errantry "a doomed institution" and says that the "march of civilization was begun." (Note, incidentally, how Hank's "civilization" springs from his use of a modern weapon to slaughter 10 people.) Later, Hank's march to civilization is blocked by the Roman Catholic Church, which turns "all England" against Hank. The novel reaches its climax when Hank, with his assistant Clarence and 52 boys, meet more than 25,000 knights in a final, cataclysmic battle. Using the weapons and technology of 19th-century "civilization," Hank and his followers massacre the knights. This extract from chapter 43 conveys the horrific nature of one phase of the slaughter:

> Land, what a sight! We were enclosed in three walls of dead men! All the other [electrified] fences were pretty nearly filled with the living, who were stealthily working their way forward through the wires. The sudden glare paralyzed this host, petrified them, you may say, with astonishment; there was just one instant for me to utilize their immobility in, and I didn't lose the chance. You see, in another instant they would have recovered their faculties, then they'd have burst into a cheer and made a rush, and my wires would have gone down before it; but that lost instant lost them their opportunity forever; while even that slight fragment of time was still unspent, I shot the current through all the fences and struck the whole host dead in their tracks! *There* was a groan you could *hear*! It voiced the death-pang of eleven thousand men.

When you read a scene such as that, you might well ask how a novel that starts out almost breezily can end in such an appalling nightmare. Does this apparently radical change reveal Mark Twain's carelessness or possibly a shift in his intentions? Or might there be an underlying structure that logically and consistently carries the story from beginning to end? A simple experiment will help you answer that question: As you read the novel, begin with the assumption that everything Mark Twain put into the book points toward the ending. In a sense, this approach will turn everything around. Instead of beginning with the assumption—which appears to be supported by the tone of the early chapters—that the novel is meant to be humorous, begin with the assumption that the book is supposed to be deadly serious. Thus, instead of needing to reconcile the extreme violence of the book's ending with the humor of the early chapters, you will need to reconcile the early humor with the later violence.

Pay particular attention throughout the novel to contrasts between what Hank says and what he actually does. In addition to the novel's many other qualities, it is full of irony. We have already seen Hank's connecting the "march of civilization" with deadly efficient modern weapons. Another example of irony is his excitement over introducing soap to England, while failing to notice that his polluting soap factory is actually making Camelot dirtier, instead of cleaner. The point to keep in mind as you read the novel is that *nothing* that its narrator says should be taken at face value. That is a sensible attitude to take toward everything Mark Twain wrote.

TOPICS AND STRATEGIES

A Connecticut Yankee in King Arthur's Court is Mark Twain's most complex novel and one of the richest in challenging ideas. There may well be no end to the number of essay topics the book can inspire. This section discusses both general and specific ideas for only a few possible topics, and you need not limit your essay choice to them. Whatever topic you select, keep in mind that the purpose of the discussions that follow is simply to help you develop your own ideas. Remember also that the broad categories under which possible topics are discussed are designed merely to help you find the subjects that interest you most; some topics might fit under other headings. It is the topics, not the categories, that matter.

Do not treat any of these suggestions as an outline of what you should write. In fact, you should even approach each suggestion skeptically by questioning whether the ideas it expresses are valid. Literature is never an exact science, especially when it comes to Mark Twain. Different authorities can, and usually do, disagree on issues, and *Connecticut Yankee* is an especially fertile field for disagreement.

Another thing to keep in mind is this: Although the discussions that follow raise many questions about *Connecticut Yankee,* these questions do not necessarily have right or wrong answers. Do not allow yourself to be stalled in fruitless attempts to prove a point. The strength of your essay will not come from the decisiveness of your conclusions, but from the power and clarity of your arguments. Whatever you choose to write about, use your imagination and try to consider all possible sides of every question.

A good way to stimulate your imagination is to outline evidence for arguments that take different sides on the same issues. For example, if you wish to argue that *Connecticut Yankee* is an attack on established religion, outline all the reasons you can find in the novel to argue the *opposite* point of view. The points you come up with may not alter your original conclusions, but some of them are likely to reveal weak spots in your preferred argument and thereby give you the opportunity to strengthen your case.

Themes

As Mark Twain's most didactic novel, *Connecticut Yankee* offers an abundance of strong opinions on a wide variety of themes, such as democracy versus monarchy, American versus British values, the proper place of religion, inherited titles and dignities, the importance of training, the benefits of modern technology, the power of custom, science versus magic and superstition, slavery, and the role of revolution in history. You should have no trouble finding a theme to write about.

Sample Topics:

1. **Science v. magic:** What does *Connecticut Yankee* say about the power of modern science over superstition and magic?

   On its surface, *Connecticut Yankee* appears to make a strong case for the superiority of late 19th-century science and technology over the superstition and magic of sixth-century England. At the beginning of the novel, Hank Morgan introduces himself as a practical, unsentimental Yankee with the knowledge and skills to manufacture virtually anything. After he establishes himself in the sixth century, he starts using those skills to lift England's commerce and technology up to the standards of his own time. All the while, he denigrates the people of the sixth century for their blind faith in superstition and magic and engages in what seems to be a personal vendetta against Merlin, the royal court magician and prophet. Hank's campaign raises several questions that would make good subjects for essays. For example, if he truly believes in the superior power of modern science, why does he publicly attribute his scientific and technological feats to magic and claim to be a better magician than Merlin? Why does he not explain the rational basis behind his feats, instead of fostering belief in magic? Is Hank really trying to promote modern science, or is he merely using science to establish himself as the most powerful magician in the land?

A second set of questions concerns the uses to which Hank applies his modern science. While he introduces electrical lighting, telegraphic and telephonic communications, steam power, printing, and other beneficial technologies, he also introduces modern weaponry: blasting powder, dynamite bombs and torpedoes, electrified fences, and machine guns (Gatling guns). What need has the sixth century for such weapons? The novel ends with Hank and his few remaining followers trapped in a cave, surrounded by the bodies of the tens of thousands of knights whom his modern science has slaughtered. Hank's weapons are all that remain of his modern science, and they end up benefitting no one. Finally, Merlin arrives and casts a spell that makes Hank sleep for 13 centuries. Which force triumphs in the end—science or magic? What point is Mark Twain trying to make?

2. **The English people:** How does Hank portray the people of sixth-century England? Does he sincerely regard them as worthy of the responsibilities they would have as citizens of the republic he promises to create?

Despite Hank's frequent protestations of his desire to abolish monarchy and inherited privilege in England and set up a republic that places all power in the hands of the people, the words he uses to describe sixth-century Britons frequently betray his contempt for them. Among the terms he uses are "more or less tame animals," "rabbits," "sheep," "worms," and "modified savages." He also frequently refers to English knights as "boys" and as "big children." Do his negative characterizations of the English people reflect his true feelings about them?

Within the context of the novel, are his remarks justified to any extent? Or is he merely demonstrating his arrogance as a 19th-century American, while failing to appreciate the true qualities of the people? Is his evident contempt limited to the people of the sixth century, or are there indications that he has a general contempt for humanity? If you write on this subject, try to read some of the scathing British reviews of the book, which you can find in Louis J. Budd's collection of contemporary reviews, the Norton Critical Edition of the novel edited by Allison R. Ensor, or in some other collections of essays and reviews.

Character

Hank Morgan, the "Yankee" of *Connecticut Yankee,* is one of Mark Twain's most complex and fully rounded fictional characters. He alone might provide grist for the mills of dozens of fascinating essays. Hank also makes a particularly rich essay subject because he essentially embodies the novel as a whole. However, if you choose to write about Hank, be careful not to identify him *too* closely with the novel. Remember that although he narrates the novel, Mark Twain is the novel's creator, and Mark Twain's and Hank's viewpoints are not necessarily the same. If Mark Twain is, in fact, using Hank to promote a hoax on his readers, we can be sure that he and Hank have vastly different views.

Beyond Hank, the novel is not a particularly fertile field for character studies, as few of its other characters are sufficiently developed to allow for meaningful analysis. For example, Hank's travel companion and eventual wife, Sandy, is little more than a cipher. Despite the frequency with which she appears, we never really learn enough about her to understand why Hank eventually becomes "her worshipper." Nevertheless, you might find a worthwhile essay topic in Sandy by looking at her in the context of the novel's general depictions of women. Or if you are interested in exploring Mark Twain's personal life, you might ask if Hank's sudden idealization of Sandy has something to do with Mark Twain's devotion to his own wife, Olivia Clemens.

Another character who offers some essay possibilities is King Arthur. You could, for example, compare his depiction in *Connecticut Yankee* with his depictions in other retellings of the Arthurian legends. Or if you prefer to stay within the confines of *Connecticut Yankee,* you could analyze Hank's descriptions of the king. Are the opinions that Hank expresses about Arthur consistent throughout the novel? If not, do Hank's changing views reflect changes in Hank himself or changes in the king?

Sample Topics:

1. **Hank Morgan's development as a character:** How much does Hank really change throughout the novel? Or is he essentially the same person at its conclusion that he is at its beginning?

Among Mark Twain's novels, no principal character, or protagonist, has greater control over his own destiny than *Connecticut Yankee*'s Hank Morgan, who makes himself the most powerful person in sixth-century England. He himself describes his power as "colossal" and tries to use that power to reshape England into the mold of 19th-century America. Through most of the novel, he appears to be succeeding, but eventually the church proves to be the greater power and forces Hank to admit he has failed. However, instead of acknowledging his defeat and quietly retiring to France, where he has left his wife and daughter, he retaliates against the church and its supporters by destroying all his modern factories and schools and using modern weapons and technology to kill more than 25,000 knights. By the end of the novel, Hank appears to have changed from an amiable and upbeat lover of freedom and democracy to a heartless tyrant bent on destroying every human being who does not subscribe to his beliefs—much as Adolf Hitler would later try to destroy Germany when he realized he was losing World War II.

The apparently radical shift in the novel's tone, from the early chapters to its cataclysmic ending, might suggest a parallel shift within Hank himself. Does he, however, really change? Or, is it possible that we, as readers, are simply failing to observe Hank's true nature from the beginning? In an essay on *Connecticut Yankee* written for *Making Mark Twain Work in the Classroom* (1999), Mark Twain scholar Lawrence I. Berkove argues that abundant evidence demonstrates that Hank's true nature "remains fixed through the novel." Is Berkove right? What kind of evidence supports or contradicts his contention? This subject is an especially important one, as it is central to the meaning of the novel as a whole.

2. **Hank as a performer:** What does the novel say about Hank's desire to show off, and what role does performance play in the novel?

Mark Twain is well known for liking to draw attention to himself by looking for opportunities to perform before audiences, both formal and casual. He gives the same traits to many of his characters, most notably Tom Sawyer and Hank Morgan. Tom loves being the center of attention; several dramatic moments in *The Adventures of Tom Sawyer* (1876) give him opportunities to show off before admiring audiences and afterward bask in glory. Hank Morgan has often been called a grown-up version of Tom Sawyer. Is that description accurate? To what extent does performance play a role in Hank's actions? What drives Hank more forcefully throughout the novel—his desire to reform sixth-century England or his need to win glory for himself? Are there moments when his impulse to show off gets in the way of his better judgment, causing him to create serious problems?

Before writing an essay on this subject, you should list the moments in the novel that demonstrate Hank's need to show off, beginning with his triumphant use of an eclipse to make people think he can blot out the sun. Pay particular attention to the language that Hank himself uses to describe how he "works" audiences, "gets up" his reputation, "shows off," and revels in glory.

If you prefer to build an essay around comparisons between Tom and Hank, you must read *Tom Sawyer*. You would do well also to read *Adventures of Huckleberry Finn* (1884), in which Huck frequently comments on Tom's showmanship and talent for "throwing in style" and "spreading himself." Indeed, the last 10 chapters of *Huckleberry Finn* revolve around Tom's efforts to complicate his and Huck's efforts to free the slave Jim with as much "style" as possible. Apart from Tom and Hank's shared impulse to show off, in what other ways are they similar or different?

3. **Merlin as a "humbug":** Is Merlin really the ineffectual magician and prophet that Hank claims he is?

After King Arthur, Merlin is probably the most famous figure in Arthurian legends. He is also one of the most enigmatic. In some traditions he is a great hero, in others a cunning villain. He is certainly a villain in Hank Morgan's estimation. Hank's narrative cites many instances of Merlin's ineptitude and repeatedly dismisses him as a "parlor-magic" artist, but is Hank always being honest? He reluctantly acknowledges that Merlin once prophesied that Arthur would become king of England and used enchantments to help him attain that office. Is it possible that Hank, in his hunger to raise his own stature at the court, is lying to himself about Merlin's true powers? After all, Merlin finally triumphs by casting a spell on Hank and correctly prophesying that Hank will sleep for 13 centuries. Throughout the novel, Hank complains repeatedly about having to prove his own powers. As you read *Connecticut Yankee*, look for evidence that Merlin may have greater powers than Hank admits—evidence that might reveal Hank as an unreliable narrator. Consider the possibility that Hank is jealous of Merlin's power, and that that is one of the reasons that he tries to make people think that he himself is a magician.

History and Context

Because it is set in sixth-century England, *Connecticut Yankee* is generally classified as a historical novel. However, the novel's setting is actually a time of legend, not one of recorded history, and little in its depiction of England conforms to what is known about the early Middle Ages. Most of the cultural, social, and political features that the novel describes come from much later time periods. Mark Twain admits as much in his preface to the novel. If you choose to write on a historical subject, you might consider the question of whether the novel's historical discrepancies matter. Do not, however, lose sight of your primary objective: to analyze *Connecticut Yankee* as literature, not as history. What matters most is not the authenticity of the novel's historical details but how the novel looks at history. In this regard, *Connecticut Yankee* is a very fertile subject for a history theme, as it constantly pits the past against the present and raises questions about the nature of change in history.

Sample Topics:

1. **Slavery:** *Connecticut Yankee* says a great number of harsh things about slavery in medieval England. Is it possible that the novel is also an indictment of slavery in 19th-century America?

Mark Twain wrote *Connecticut Yankee* less than a quarter century after slavery was abolished in the United States. He had grown up in Missouri, a slave state, and his own family had owned slaves when he was a boy. He was thus intimately familiar with the institution of slavery, but he eventually came to regard its existence as the worst mistake that the United States had ever made. Slavery had also existed in England in much earlier times, and it figures prominently in *Connecticut Yankee.* Hank even says that "most of King Arthur's British nation were slaves, pure and simple . . ." The novel's treatment of slavery offers a good subject for a variety of essay topics. For example, you might examine how Hank succeeds in getting King Arthur to abolish slavery. Or you could ask whether Hank, in declaring that slavery has been abolished, is possibly a victim of wishful thinking. What evidence does he provide to suggest that people who were formerly slaves are likely to experience any tangible improvements in their lives?

For a more challenging—and potentially more rewarding— essay subject, compare Hank's depictions of medieval English slavery with descriptions of slavery in the United States during Mark Twain's time. This topic will require your reading about slavery in a book such as Terrell Dempsey's *Searching for Jim: Slavery in Sam Clemens's World* (2003). You should also read what Mark Twain says about slavery in his autobiographical writings (which are published in many editions) and in some of his other fictional works, such as *Huckleberry Finn* and *Pudd'nhead Wilson* (1894).

2. **The immutability of history:** Does *Connecticut Yankee* attempt to say that history cannot be changed?

As Lawrence I. Berkove points out in a chapter of *Making Mark Twain Work in the Classroom,* an easily overlooked aspect of *Connecticut Yankee* is the fact that when the novel opens, everything that will happen in the story actually has *already* happened. The anonymous frame narrator meets Hank Morgan (whose name is not given until much later) during a tour of England's Warwick Castle, apparently in the year 1889. As Hank begins telling his story, the narrative shifts to a moment about 10 years earlier, when Hank was somehow transported from modern Connecticut to sixth-century England. Hank's narrative then continues in medieval England, where Merlin eventually casts a spell that causes Hank to sleep for 13 centuries. Hank evidently awakens shortly after we meet him in Warwick Castle. In a sense, his story goes full circle, starting and ending during the late 19th century.

The frame narrator's prelude to the novel ("A Word of Explanation") mentions an intriguing but apparently trivial fact: The sixth-century armor of Sir Sagramor le Desirous has an unexplained bullet hole in it. Hank immediately grabs the attention of both the frame narrator and the reader by saying that *he* made that hole himself. That is a nice hint of a dramatic moment to come in the novel, but what makes that bullet vastly more significant is the fact that is evidently the *only* tangible evidence that Hank Morgan was ever in the sixth century.

During the 10 or so years that Hank spends in medieval England, he builds modern factories, steam-powered trains and ships, and a host of other modern machines and devices. How is it possible that all those things have disappeared completely by the time he returns to his own era? Throughout his narrative, Hank often complains about the power of entrenched customs and institutions. Despite the huge technological revolution that Hank brings about in the sixth century, everything he changes reverts to its previous condition. Is the novel thereby saying that history cannot be changed? Is this the same thing as saying that everything is predestined? Might the novel also be saying that humankind has no hope for positive change and that it is an illusion to believe otherwise?

Philosophy and Ideas

If you were to close your eyes, open *Connecticut Yankee* to almost any page, and place your index finger there, you would probably find your finger touching a passage with an interesting philosophical observation. The novel literally teems with ideas. Its narrator, Hank Morgan, expresses strong opinions on almost every subject imaginable: the nature of free will, the power of customs and tradition, education and training, heredity versus environment, science versus superstition, religion, business and economics, politics and government, and the role of revolution in history. Every one of these subjects, and many others, would make excellent essay topics. The trick is not finding a topic but knowing what questions to ask about it. Whichever topic you select, you might start with a set of general questions, such as: What does Hank say on the subject? Are the views that he expresses on that subject consistent throughout his narrative? Do his opinions match the realities that he describes? Is he being honest with himself when he expresses his ideas?

Sample Topic:

1. **Human beings as "machines":** In what ways does *Connecticut Yankee* espouse a deterministic philosophy?

It is often observed that as Mark Twain grew older, he became more pessimistic and developed increasingly negative views of humankind. He channeled those views into a private, deterministic philosophy holding that human beings lack free will and are, in effect, machines controlled by outside forces. He would eventually outline his philosophy in a long, Socratic dialogue that he published anonymously as *What Is Man?*

(1906). Meanwhile, aspects of his deterministic philosophy can be found in many of his late writings, perhaps most notably in *Connecticut Yankee.*

An essay on this subject should open with a clear statement of what you mean by determinism, followed by examples of determinist viewpoints. You will find discussions of determinism in any good encyclopedia, and you would do well to read at least one of the two essays on the subject by Tom Quirk that are listed in the Bibliography below. As you become clear on what determinism is, look for examples in *Connecticut Yankee,* whose narrator, Hank Morgan, frequently expresses determinist views. A good example can be found in his remarks about Queen Morgan le Fay in chapter 18. (Note his use of the word "training"—a key word to watch for in the text):

> Training—training is everything; training is all there is *to* a person. We speak of nature; it is folly; there is no such thing as nature; what we call by that misleading name is merely heredity and training. We have no thoughts of our own, no opinions of our own; they are transmitted to us, trained into us.

Your essay naturally needs to go beyond a mere compilation of examples from the novel. Are there patterns to the manner and moments in which Hank expresses deterministic views? Does he express the same views on this subject consistently throughout the novel? Are his deterministic views consistent with other views he expresses, such as his wish to transform sixth-century England into a republic? As you read the novel, pay special attention to its use of "machine" terminology. Is it significant that Hank begins his story boasting of his responsibilities as superintendent of a giant factory and his ability to make virtually any kind of machinery? Also, what is Hank's "Man-Factory" all about? If he is sincere in his desire to "turn groping and grubbing automata into *men,*" why would he place them in a "factory"?

Form and Genre

Essays about the forms of works examine how the works are constructed, what literary techniques their authors use to create effects, and how and why the structures succeed or fail. The form of *Connecticut Yankee* is a first-person narrative set within a frame. The frame is the structure, or framework, that opens and ends the novel. *Connecticut Yankee*'s frame is set in what was the present time when Mark Twain wrote the novel and begins with the anonymous frame narrator (who might be Mark Twain himself) describing his meeting with a man—whom we later learn is Hank Morgan—who relates the novel's central story. After beginning his narrative orally, Hank gives the frame narrator a handwritten manuscript, which then forms the core of the novel. To appreciate the novel's structure, therefore, we need to keep in mind that it is supposed to be a handwritten record. A good question to ask of the novel's structure is how the story might differ if it were told in a different form, such as a third-person narrative similar to that of *The Prince and the Pauper.*

The term *genre* is used in a variety of ways but basically refers to the category into which a literary work fits. Any given work might belong to several different genres, and that is certainly true of *Connecticut Yankee,* which might be called a historical novel, a science-fiction novel, or a fantasy novel. The appropriateness of applying any of these terms to the novel would make a good subject for an essay, so long as the essay addresses the question of why the issue matters in the first place.

Sample Topics:

1. ***Connecticut Yankee* as a science-fiction story:** Should the novel be classified as a science-fiction story, a fantasy, or something else?

   Before jumping to conclusions on this question when you write an essay on this subject, you must define your terms carefully, and the definitions you use should be spelled out within your essay. The science-fiction and fantasy genres have much in common, so you will need to be clear on what it is that distinguishes them. In *Connecticut Yankee,* Hank Morgan goes from 19th-century America to sixth-century England and back, and for this reason the book has often been called the first time-travel novel. Time travel is generally regarded as a subgenre of science fiction, but does time travel actually occur in *Connecticut Yankee*? What usually sets science fiction apart from fantasy is the premise that things happen for rational reasons that can be explained in scientific terms, even if the science of the story is imaginary. You therefore might begin your essay by addressing the question of whether Hank's passage to the sixth century can be explained in science-fiction terms. If not, perhaps the novel is actually a fantasy. Is it possible that Hank dreams his entire story? To answer that question, you should examine the numerous dream symbols that permeate the novel. Indeed, the novel's dream motifs would make an excellent subject for an essay.

Keep in mind that although science fiction and fantasy may be distinct genres, they are not mutually exclusive. *Connecticut Yankee* might well have elements of both. Whatever conclusions you draw about the element of time travel, you should also consider other possible aspects of the novel that have science-fiction themes, such as Hank's efforts to make over sixth-century England on the model of 19th-century America.

2. ***Connecticut Yankee* as a frame story:** How might the novel differ if it had a different structure?

The introduction to this section discusses what makes *Connecticut Yankee* a frame story. The novel resembles *Huckleberry Finn* in having a first-person narrator, and the narratives of both novels are supposed to be books written by their narrators. However, *Connecticut Yankee* differs from *Huckleberry Finn* in being set in the form of a frame. Does its frame structure serve any purpose other than to provide an intriguing method of launching the novel's central narrative? Note that the two novels also differ in the way each establishes that its narrator has written his book. *Huckleberry Finn* makes so little of the fact that Huck's narrative comes from the book he has written that that particular aspect of the novel seems scarcely to matter. By contrast, the frame narrator of *Connecticut Yankee* not only sees Hank's book, he describes what it looks like and how he sits down and reads it. Do these details affect the nature of Hank's narrative itself or how we perceive his narrative as we read it?

To write an essay on this subject, try to imagine how the novel would read if it had a different structure—either an anonymous, third-person narrator, or the same first-person narrator but without a frame narrator or the pretense that the narrative comes from a book. How would such changes affect the ways we perceive Hank's story?

3. **Burlesque humor and satire:** What roles do burlesque humor and satire play in *Connecticut Yankee*?

As was pointed out at the beginning of this chapter, the comic elements in *Connecticut Yankee* are so unevenly distributed that the book as a whole appears to be badly unbalanced in tone. The early chapters are rich in burlesque humor, making fun of Hank's struggles adjusting to life in the sixth century and burlesquing medieval customs and beliefs. Much of the humor comes from contrasts between past and present, such as Hank's terrifying a band of tough knights by blowing tobacco smoke out of the helmet covering his entire head. With the exception of the long and hilarious description of armored knights playing baseball in chapter 40, most of the humor seems to be gone by the end of the book, when Hank's efforts to overthrow chivalric traditions and the power of the Roman Catholic Church become deadly serious. Is there a discernible reason for this dramatic shift in tone?

Burlesque humor and satire are closely related but are not the same thing, so the first thing an essay on this subject requires is a clear statement on how those terms are to be used in the essay. The essay should then cite representative examples of each type of humor in *Connecticut Yankee* and attempt to explain the purpose of each instance. For example, might the purpose of the burlesque baseball scenes be to make fun of the knights while pointing up their continued resistance to change, even after Hank has declared chivalry dead? A few chapters later, it becomes clear that chivalry is not dead, ludicrous though Hank has made it appear. If you write on this subject, look for patterns in Mark Twain's use of humor. Consider also the possibility that the book's humor is all part of a grand hoax, designed to draw in readers, misdirect them, and them shock them at the end.

4. ***Connecticut Yankee* as an illustrated novel:** How might illustrations in the book's first edition alter one's reading of the text?

During earlier eras, it was common for novels to contain illustrations. In some books the illustrations were like a fine condiment, lightly salted throughout the texts; in others, illustrations appeared on almost every other page. The first American editions of all Mark Twain's novels were profusely illustrated. With 220 exquisite line drawings by Dan Beard (1850–1941), the first American edition of *Connecticut Yankee* is one of Mark Twain's most beautifully illustrated books. However, the contributions of Beard's pictures go well beyond mere decoration. Many add original humor or provide graphic interpretations of ideas in the text, and some even add fresh ideas of their own. For example, the final illustration in the book shows Hank Morgan reunited with Sandy and their daughter, standing triumphantly over a prostrate Father Time. Beard also delighted in satirizing contemporary figures and used some of the most famous people of his time as models for the characters he drew. For example, the face of the "Slave Driver" on page 465 is unmistakably that of railroad tycoon Jay Gould (1836–92), a notorious robber baron whom Mark Twain regarded as a corruptor of American morals.

An essay on illustrations would be fun to write, but you would need to be careful to avoid falling into the trap of simply describing the pictures and adding admiring comments. Reading a heavily illustrated novel is very different from reading an unillustrated book. The most important question you should ask of the pictures in *Connecticut Yankee* is how they affect your reading of the novel. Do they tend to enhance your understanding of the text, or do they tend to be merely distracting?

Mark Twain himself greatly admired his novel's illustrations and called Beard "the only man who can correctly illustrate my writings, for he not only illustrates the text, but he also illustrates my thoughts." That quote would provide an excellent opening to an essay on *Connecticut Yankee*'s illustrations. Look for examples of pictures that support Mark Twain's remark, and also look for pictures that might contradict it. After you analyze examples of both, what can you say about the overall effect of the illustrations?

Despite the beauty of Beard's illustrations, most reprint editions of *Connecticut Yankee* have either used only a handful of Beard's pictures or have supplied entirely new illustrations. Happily, it should not be difficult to find all the pictures. The 1996 Oxford Mark Twain edition of *Connecticut Yankee* is a facsimile reprint with all Beard's illustrations exactly as they originally appeared. The 1979 University of California edition of the novel—which is available in paperback—also has all the original pictures. Finally, you can see many of the illustrations—along with comments by scholar Stephen Railton—on the *Mark Twain in His Times* Web site, at etext.virginia.edu/railton/index2.html. You may also find it useful to download some of the pictures to illustrate your essay.

Language, Symbols, and Imagery

An aspect of *Connecticut Yankee* that may not be immediately evident is the fact that the language spoken by most of its characters is not the same language that Hank Morgan records in his narrative. Modern English is largely a product of the Norman conquest of England in the 11th century; the language spoken in sixth-century England would have been more like German than what we now know as English. Hank acknowledges that fact in chapter 22, when he describes Sandy's speech patterns and adds, "It was borne in upon me that I was standing in the awful presence of the Mother of the German Language." Salted with words such as "seemeth," "prithee," "verily," and "forsooth," the flowery dialogue of *Connecticut Yankee*'s characters has no more to do with sixth-century England than it does with 19th-century America. Mark Twain borrowed much of it from Sir Thomas Malory's *Le Morte d'Arthur* (1485)—from which he quotes liberally in his novel's early chapters—and from other, later chroniclers of Arthurian England. To a large extent, that kind of language is mere decoration, and if you study it closely, you will find that it is very similar to the language spoken by Mark Twain's 16th-century characters in *The Prince and the Pauper*. Indeed, a comparison between the dialogue of the two novels could make a good subject for an essay. What makes *Connecticut Yankee* interesting is the rich imagery and figurative language that Hank introduces from 19th-century American English.

Sample Topics:

1. **The language of commerce:** What does Hank's commercial terminology and imagery contribute to the novel?

Of the various types of imagery that Hank uses in his modern language, perhaps the most evident is that of commerce. His narrative is full of words such as "business," "market," "shop," "stock," and "trade." This should not be surprising, as Hank promotes business schemes throughout the novel. Indeed, his position as King Arthur's chief minister rests on his promise to increase the revenue of the state. Almost every project he undertakes is designed to make a profit. However, although Hank often uses commercial terms in his discussions of actual commercial dealings, he also uses them frequently in other contexts. For example, after blowing up Merlin's tower, he says that "Merlin's stock was flat"—a metaphoric way of saying that Merlin's reputation as a magician was so badly damaged that if he were a commercial enterprise whose stock was being sold, no one would want to buy it. Similar images can be found throughout the novel. What purpose do they serve? And, what do they reveal about the values that Hank wishes to transplant from 19th-century America to sixth-century England?

If you write on this subject, you might start by inventorying Hank's uses of commercial terms, such as those mentioned above, while noting the contexts in which they appear. An efficient way to do this would be to download the electronic text of the novel from Project Gutenberg (www.gutenberg.org) and use a computer to search the text electronically. Look for patterns in the ways the terms are used, particularly in Hank's references to the status of his own reputation. Your discussion of the subject should take into account the actual commercial schemes that Hank develops.

2. **Dealing, taking tricks, bluffing, and decks of cards:** What use does the novel make of playing card imagery and symbolic numbers?

When Franklin D. Roosevelt became president of the United States in 1933, he called his government programs to relieve the hardships of the Great Depression the New Deal. He took the expression from *Connecticut Yankee*'s Hank Morgan, who denounces medieval England's unfair distribution of power and wealth and says that what the majority of people who do all the work and get none of the benefits need most is a "new deal." The word "deal," of course, comes from modern card games, such as poker; "new deal" is merely one of many allusions to card games throughout *Connecticut Yankee*. Other examples include terms such as "played his hand," "took every trick," and "bluff." Does such imagery suggest that Hank might regard his entire adventure as some kind of game?

Card game imagery is most evident in the novel's last chapters, in which Hank confronts the massed chivalry of England from a fortified cave. Note the apparent connections between numbers and playing cards. For example, Hank and his assistant, Clarence, are joined by exactly 52 boys (52 is the number of cards in a standard deck). Might Hank and Clarence be considered the deck's two jokers? Moreover, the boys fire 13 Gatling guns on the attacking knights; there are 13 cards in each suit in a deck. "Thirteen" is often considered a number with special powers, and Hank uses that number repeatedly throughout his narrative. An unspoken allusion to the same number can be found in Hank's references to the 12 electrified fences separating his supporters from their enemies. Counting from the inside circle to the knights outside the 12th fence, there are 13 divisions. Finally, when Merlin casts a spell on Hank, Hank sleeps for 13 centuries. Do all these numbers and allusions to card games mean anything?

Compare and Contrast Essays

Compare and contrast essays foster creativity on at least two levels: first, in finding aspects of one or more works to compare; then in finding significant points to make about the similarities and differences that are observed. One of your best chances of attaining true originality may lie in writing this type of essay—particularly on a subject that may not be obvious to others. A fairly obvious topic might be a comparison between *Connecticut Yankee* and *The Prince and the Pauper*—the two novels Mark Twain set in early England. That is a sufficiently broad subject to give you wide scope for an interesting essay, but your best chance for originality would be in the arguments you make, not in the basic question. A less obvious topic would be a comparison of the picaresque elements in *Connecticut Yankee* with those in *Huckleberry Finn.*

Compare and contrast topics offer wide scope for developing original ideas, but they also make it easy to fall into the trap of doing exactly the opposite. The danger lies in failing to develop your essay fully. You would likely begin your essay by compiling lists of similarities and differences between pairs of characters, types of plots, different points of view, or other aspects of *Connecticut Yankee.* That would be the logical place to start, but do not assume that catalogs of bare comparisons reveal anything. It would not be enough simply to say that both Hank Morgan and Tom Sawyer are adventurous characters with lively imaginations who love showing off and then catalog examples of their similarities. You would also need to explain why these characters have these traits, how the traits affect their actions, how they relate to other aspects of each character's personality, and how these aspects of their personalities help to drive their stories' narratives. The sample topics that follow represent only a fraction of possible compare and contrast topics.

Sample Topics:
1. **Hank Morgan v. Huck Finn:** How do they compare as reliable narrators of their own adventures?

Hank Morgan and Huckleberry Finn share the distinction of being Mark Twain's only fictional characters who narrate their own full-length stories. (*Personal Recollections of Joan of Arc* is narrated by Joan's friend, Sieur Louis de Conte, writing more than 60 years after the events he describes.) Hank and Huck obviously differ greatly in age, in education, in literacy, and in the duration and the nature of their experiences; however, they both write their narratives close to the time their adventures end and both are the central figures within their own stories. Many questions might be asked about how Hank and Huck compare as narrators, but the most interesting questions may be those concerning their reliability as narrators. Both seem always to tell the truth as they understand it, but is what they tell us always reliable? For example, Huck is too young and naive fully to understand everything going on around him and tends to underestimate the bad qualities of the adults he encounters. Hank, on the other hand, is older and much better educated and more experienced than Huck, but he is too much of a stranger in sixth-century England for us to trust his descriptions and judgments completely.

The question of whether any narrator is "reliable" can be a slippery one. Both Hank and Huck seem honest and forthright, but there are compelling reasons to distrust much of what they say. An essay on this subject needs to examine at least two dimensions of each character's narratives: who the characters are and what reasons we might have for distrusting their narratives, and the nature of what they are talking about at any given point in their narratives. Among the questions to consider are the possibility that either narrator is intentionally trying to deceive us, what reasons each of them may have for misunderstanding what he is observing, and what personal biases might be influencing what they say. If ever a fictional character were loaded with strong opinions and personal agendas, it is Hank Morgan.

2. ***Connecticut Yankee* v. *The Prince and the Pauper*:** Apart from being set in early England, what, if anything, do these two novels have in common?

Along with *Personal Recollections of Joan of Arc* (1896), the novels *Connecticut Yankee* and *The Prince and the Pauper* (1881) are generally classified as Mark Twain's historical novels (or historical romances). *Connecticut Yankee* is set in sixth-century England and *The Prince and the Pauper* in 16th-century England; however, more than the passage of time separates the two stories. *The Prince and the Pauper* is very much a true historical novel. It is based on an era of recorded history, it contains known historical figures, and it alludes to real historical events, such as the burning of Anne Askew and King Henry VIII's closing down of Roman Catholic monasteries. In contrast, while *Connecticut Yankee* is set in a definite time—the early sixth century—King Arthur and his court are figures of legend, not history. Evidence for their existence is so thin that they may as well be regarded as entirely fictional creations. Another fundamental difference between the two novels is their form. *Connecticut Yankee* is narrated by its title character, while *The Prince and the Pauper* has an anonymous third-person narrator. Differences such as these should be considered when comparisons of the two books are made.

An essay comparing these novels might explore a variety of questions. For example, how might differences between *The Prince and the Pauper*'s concrete historical setting and *Connecticut Yankee*'s setting in a time of legend have affected the way Mark Twain wrote the two stories? Did Arthurian England allow him to give his imagination more room to play than the confines of known history in the 16th century? Might it be argued that *Connecticut Yankee* should not even be regarded as a historical novel?

A subject that gets closer to the heart of both novels is the views that the books express about monarchies and inherited privilege, such as that enjoyed by members of the nobility. *Connecticut Yankee* consistently denounces systems of hereditary rule and privilege, but what does *The Prince and the Pauper* say on the same subject? Do the two books express similar or opposite views?

Bibliography for *Connecticut Yankee*

Baetzhold, Howard G. *"A Connecticut Yankee in King Arthur's Court." The Mark Twain Encyclopedia.* Ed. J. R. LeMaster and James D. Wilson. New York: Garland, 1993. 174–79. (The encyclopedia has separate entries on Hank Morgan, King Arthur, Sandy, and other related topics.)

———. *"A Connecticut Yankee:* Other British Literary Sources." *Mark Twain & John Bull: The British Connection.* Bloomington: U of Indiana P, 1970. 131–61.

———. "The Course of Composition of *A Connecticut Yankee:* A Reinterpretation." *American Literature* 33 (May 1961): 195–214.

Baldanza, Frank. "Historical Novels." *Mark Twain: An Introduction and Interpretation.* New York: Barnes & Noble, 1961. 68–85.

Bassett, John E. "The Troublesome Ending of *A Connecticut Yankee." A Heart of Ideality in My Realism and Other Essays on Howells and Twain.* West Cornwall, CT: Locust Hill Press, 1991. 151–58.

Berkove, Lawrence I. *"A Connecticut Yankee:* A Serious Hoax." *Essays in Arts and Sciences* 19 (May 1990): 28–44.

———. *"Connecticut Yankee:* Twain's Other Masterpiece." *Making Mark Twain Work in the Classroom.* Ed. James S. Leonard. Durham, NC: Duke UP, 1999. 88–109.

———. "The Gospel According to Hank Morgan's Newspaper." *Essays in Arts and Sciences* 20 (October 1991): 32–42.

———. "The Reality of the Dream: Structural and Thematic Unity in *A Connecticut Yankee in King Arthur's Court." Mark Twain Journal* 22, no. 1 (Spring 1984): 8–14.

Bochynski, Kevin. *"A Connecticut Yankee in King Arthur's Court." Masterplots II: Juvenile and Young-Adult Literature Series, Supplement.* Ed. Frank N. Magill. Pasadena, CA: Salem Press, 1997. 1: 255–58.

Budd, Louis J. Afterword. *A Connecticut Yankee in King Arthur's Court.* By Mark Twain. New York: Oxford UP, 1996. 1–16. (Back matter has separate pagination.)

———. *Mark Twain: Social Philosopher.* Bloomington: Indiana UP, 1962.

———, ed. *Mark Twain: The Contemporary Reviews.* New York: Cambridge UP, 1999.

Camfield, Gregg. *"A Connecticut Yankee in King Arthur's Court." The Oxford Companion to Mark Twain.* New York: Oxford UP, 2003. 130–36.

Carter, Everett. "The Meaning of *A Connecticut Yankee." American Literature* 50 (November 1978): 418–40.

Cox, James M. "Yankee Slang." *Mark Twain: The Fate of Humor.* 2d ed. Columbia: U of Missouri P, 2002. 198–221.

Cummings, Sherwood. *Mark Twain and Science: Adventures of a Mind.* Baton Rouge: Louisiana UP, 1988.

David, Beverly R., and Ray Sapirstein. "Illustrators and Illustrations in Mark Twain's First American Editions" and "Reading the Illustrations in *A Connecticut Yankee.*" *A Connecticut Yankee in King Arthur's Court.* By Mark Twain. New York: Oxford UP, 1996. 17–27. (Back matter has separate pagination.)

Dempsey, Terrell. *Searching for Jim: Slavery in Sam Clemens's World.* Columbia: U of Missouri P, 2003.

Driscoll, Kerry. "'Man Factories' and the 'White Indians' of Camelot: Re-reading the Native Subtext of *A Connecticut Yankee in King Arthur's Court.*" *Mark Twain Annual* 2 (2004): 7–24.

Emerson, Everett. *Mark Twain: A Literary Life.* Philadelphia: U of Pennsylvania P, 2000.

Ensor, Allison R., ed. *A Connecticut Yankee in King Arthur's Court.* New York: W. W. Norton, 1982.

Foote, Bud. *The "Connecticut Yankee" in the Twentieth Century: Travel to the Past in Science Fiction.* New York: Greenwood Press, 1991.

Foster, Edward F. "*A Connecticut Yankee* Anticipated: Max Adeler's *Fortunate Island.*" *Mark Twain's Humor: Critical Essays.* Ed. David E. E. Sloane. New York: Garland, 1993. 265–70.

Gerber, John C. "*A Connecticut Yankee in King Arthur's Court.*" *Mark Twain.* Boston: Twayne, 1988. 115–28.

Grant, William E. "*A Connecticut Yankee in King Arthur's Court.*" *Masterplots, Second Revised Edition.* Ed. Frank N. Magill. Pasadena, CA: Salem Press, 1996. 3:1,276–280.

Halliday, Sam. "History, 'Civilization,' and *A Connecticut Yankee in King Arthur's Court.*" *A Companion to Mark Twain.* Eds. Peter Messent and Louis J. Budd. Oxford, England: Blackwell, 2005. 416–30.

Harris, Susan K. *Mark Twain's Escape from Time: A Study of Patterns and Images.* Columbia: U of Missouri P, 1982.

Hoffman, Andrew Jay. "*A Connecticut Yankee in King Arthur's Court.*" *Twain's Heroes, Twain's Worlds.* Philadelphia: U of Pennsylvania P, 1988. 70–142.

Ketterer, David. "Epoch-Eclipse and Apocalypse: Special 'Effects' in *A Connecticut Yankee.*" *Publications of the Modern Language Association* 88 (October 1973): 1,104–114.

————, ed. *Mark Twain: Tales of Wonder.* Lincoln: U of Nebraska P, 2003 (first published in 1984 as *The Science Fiction of Mark Twain*).

Lacy, Norris J., et al., eds. *The New Arthurian Encyclopedia.* Chicago: St. James Press, 1991.

Leon, Philip. "'One of My Deepest Sorrows Was My West Point': West Point in *A Connecticut Yankee in King Arthur's Court.*" *Mark Twain & West Point.* Toronto: ECW Press, 1996. 80–99.

Leonard, James S. "*A Connecticut Yankee* in the Postmodern Classroom." *Making Mark Twain Work in the Classroom.* Ed. James S. Leonard. Durham, NC: Duke UP, 1999. 110–20.

Malory, Sir Thomas. *Le Morte d'Arthur.* New York: Modern Library, 1994.

Mandia, Patricia M. "Let There Be Darkness: *A Connecticut Yankee in King Arthur's Court.*" *Comedic Pathos: Black Humor in Twain's Fiction.* Jefferson, NC: McFarland, 1991. 84–101.

Melton, Quimby. "The British Reception of *A Connecticut Yankee:* Contemporary Reviews." *Mark Twain Journal* 39, no. 1 (Spring 2001): 2–24.

Messent, Peter. "Fantasy and *A Connecticut Yankee in King Arthur's Court.*" *Mark Twain.* New York: St. Martin's Press, 1997. 110–33.

Miller, Robert Keith. "Invincible Stupidity: *A Connecticut Yankee in King Arthur's Court.*" *Mark Twain.* New York: Frederick Ungar, 1983. 113–35.

Quirk, Tom. "Determinism." *The Mark Twain Encyclopedia.* Eds. J. R. LeMaster and James D. Wilson. New York: Garland, 1993. 216–17.

————. "Mark Twain and Human Nature." *A Companion to Mark Twain.* Eds. Peter Messent and Louis J. Budd. Oxford, England: Blackwell, 2005. 21–37.

Railton, Stephen. *The Life & Work of Mark Twain.* Chantilly, VA: Teaching Company, 2002 (includes three lectures on *A Connecticut Yankee*; available in audio and video formats).

————. "Lost in Time: *A Connecticut Yankee in King Arthur's Court.*" *Mark Twain: A Short Introduction.* Malden, MA: Blackwell, 2004. 75–95.

————, *Mark Twain in His Times.* etext.virginia.edu/railton/index2.html (Includes full text of *A Connecticut Yankee* and numerous study aids).

Rasmussen, R. Kent. "*A Connecticut Yankee in King Arthur's Court.*" *Magill's Guide to Science Fiction and Fantasy Literature.* Ed. T. A. Shippey. Pasadena, CA: Salem Press, 1996. 1: 171–73.

————. "*A Connecticut Yankee in King Arthur's Court.*" *Cyclopedia of Literary Places.* Pasadena, CA: Salem Press, 2003. 1:233–34.

————. "*A Connecticut Yankee in King Arthur's Court.*" In *Critical Companion to Mark Twain.* New York: Facts On File, 2007. I: 59–96.

Robinson, Douglas. "Revising the American Dream: *A Connecticut Yankee.*" *Mark Twain.* Ed. Harold Bloom. New York: Chelsea House, 1986. 183–206.

Salomon, Roger B. *Twain and the Image of History.* New Haven, CT: Yale UP, 1961.

Sloane, David E. E. *Student Companion to Mark Twain.* Westport, CT: Greenwood Press, 2001.

Smith, Henry Nash. *Mark Twain's Fable of Progress: Political and Economic Ideas in "A Connecticut Yankee."* New Brunswick, NJ: Rutgers UP, 1964.

————. "An Object Lesson in Democracy." *Mark Twain: The Development of a Writer.* Cambridge, MA: Belknap Press, 1962. 138–70.

Twain, Mark. *A Connecticut Yankee in King Arthur's Court.* Ed. Bernard L. Stein. Introduction by Henry Nash Smith. Berkeley: U of California P, 1979.

————. *A Connecticut Yankee in King Arthur's Court.* Ed. Shelley Fisher Fishkin. New York: Oxford UP, 1996.

————. *Mark Twain's Own Autobiography.* Ed. Michael J. Kiskis. Madison: U Wisconsin P, 1990.

————. *What Is Man?* 1906. Reprint, New York: Oxford UP, 1996.

Vonnegut, Kurt, Jr. "Introduction: Some Comments on Mark Twain's *A Connecticut Yankee in King Arthur's Court* by Kurt Vonnegut at the Age of Seventy-two." *A Connecticut Yankee in King Arthur's Court.* New York: Oxford UP, 1996. xxxi–xxxiii.

Welland, Dennis. "*A Connecticut Yankee* in England." *Mark Twain in England.* London: Chatto & Windus, 1978. 127–44.

Wilson, James D. "The Use of History in Mark Twain's *A Connecticut Yankee.*" *Publications of the Modern Language Association* 80 (March 1965): 102–10.

PUDD'NHEAD WILSON

READING TO WRITE

*P*UDD'NHEAD *WILSON* (1894) holds a special place in Mark Twain's fiction, as many critics regard it as his last major novel. Moreover, although the book is not directly tied to any of his other fiction, it is often seen as the final part of what has been called his Mississippi River trilogy. This informal trilogy begins with *Tom Sawyer* (1876), which offers a somewhat nostalgic depiction of life in an early 19th-century riverfront town modeled on Mark Twain's boyhood home of Hannibal, Missouri. With its more serious themes and strong attack on slavery, the second part of the trilogy, *Huckleberry Finn* (1884), offers a darker view of the same fictional town of St. Petersburg. *Pudd'nhead Wilson* takes that dark view several steps further by bringing closer to the surface the evils of slavery and racism in another riverfront town, Dawson's Landing. That town is also modeled on Hannibal, but unlike the St. Petersburg of the other two novels, it is *south* of St. Louis. As you read the novel, pay attention to that geographical shift; it is significant because it reflects the novel's emphasis on the idea that the evils of slavery intensify farther "down the river."

Of the five novels discussed in the present volume, *Pudd'nhead Wilson* is much the shortest. Despite its brevity, it may be the most challenging one to write about. Thanks to its complex web of ironies, you will find that little of what you read can be taken at face value. The novel deals with serious issues, but it is not clear what messages, if any, it tries to convey. For example, does it offer powerful condemnations of slavery and racism? Or does its resolution of the conflicts created by those evils sanction the values of white slaveholding culture? A first question to ask while reading *Pudd'nhead Wilson*, therefore, is whether it presents a mixed message about race and slavery. If you conclude it does, is that mixing intentional or merely the result of careless writing? Or might the novel's irony run so deep that readers have trouble deciphering its messages? *Pudd'nhead Wilson* is a very different kind of book than *Huckleberry Finn,* but it shares the latter's power by using irony to condemn slavery and contemporary ideas about what constitutes race. The novel deals with other important issues, of course, but slavery and race are at its center and tie into almost every theme.

As you read the novel, be careful not to draw quick conclusions. *Pudd'nhead Wilson* presents readers with difficult challenges, but those very challenges are what make it exciting to read and write about. Scholars and critics are still grappling with the novel's layers of meaning and have reached little consensus. The field is wide open for fresh interpretations.

Before beginning any essay on *Pudd'nhead Wilson,* make sure you understand what is meant by irony. That word is used in more than one way, and each of its uses can be slippery to grasp. In its narrowest sense, irony is the use of words to express ideas that mean something other than what the words themselves appear to mean. The true meaning of the words may even be the exact opposite of their literal meaning. David Wilson, the title character of *Pudd'nhead Wilson,* is a master of irony. In fact, his use of irony permanently marks him. When he first arrives in Dawson's Landing in 1830, he makes an ironic remark that the villagers cannot understand. Distracted by the annoying yelping of an unseen dog, he says, "I wished I owned half of that dog." When asked why, he replies, "Because I would kill my half." He does not really want to own half the dog, and he probably does not really want to kill it; he merely wants to silence it and knows killing half the dog would kill the whole animal and achieve the desired effect. His remark is a simple example of irony, and the failure of the villagers to understand it causes them immediately to brand Wilson a fool and nickname him "pudd'nhead." The very title of the novel is, therefore, based on irony, and that irony is compounded by the fact that Wilson is anything but a fool.

Wilson's remark about the dog sets him permanently apart from the other villagers. It also lays the groundwork for the complex layers of irony permeating the book. Wilson's personal partiality for irony runs throughout the novel, every chapter of which opens with one or two aphorisms from "Pudd'nhead Wilson's Calendar," a sort of whimsical almanac that Wilson maintains for his own amusement and that of the Free-thinkers' Society, of which he and Judge Driscoll are the only members. Indeed, the fact that the "society" has only two members is itself a subtle form of irony, as one would expect any organization with so grand a name to have many members.

A second and broader meaning of irony applies to situations in which a series of events leads to results that differ greatly from—and may even be the opposite of—what one expects. The central story line of *Pudd'nhead Wilson* is a perfect example of this kind of irony. In chapter 3, the slave woman Roxy becomes so afraid her infant son, Chambers, might one day be sold down the river that she switches him with her master's baby so he will grow up a free man and never face that peril. However, Roxy's switching of the babies sets in motion events that eventually lead to her son's being sold down the river—the exact opposite of what she intends. That is powerful stuff. Scholar John Gerber likens Roxy's story to a Greek tragedy, in which everything leads to the very thing the tragic heroine most wants to avoid.

One might suppose that no outcome of Roxy's switching of the babies could be more strongly ironic than her son's ultimately being sold down the river. However, something else that happens as a result of her action might be just that. In chapter 16, her adult son—known to the world as Tom Driscoll—sells Roxy herself down the river. That is something that he could never do if Roxy had not made it possible for him to grow up as a free man. This happens because Roxy allows Tom to sell her back into slavery temporarily to raise money to pay his gambling debts. Tom betrays her by selling her *down* the river. His betrayal is doubly ironic because his mother—unlike he—is legally free at the moment he sells her. The situation thus has a slave pretending to be a free man selling a free woman who is pretending to be a slave.

These incidents are strong examples of irony, but the novel contains many more, some of which are so subtle that they will go unnoticed with a casual reading. A particularly subtle example occurs in chapter 5's description of Tom's return from an eastern university when he is a young man:

> Tom's Eastern polish was not popular among the young people. They could have endured it, perhaps, if Tom had stopped there; but he wore gloves, and that they couldn't stand, and wouldn't; so he was mainly without society. He brought home with him a suit of clothes of such exquisite style and cut and fashion,—Eastern fashion, city fashion,—that it filled everybody with anguish and was regarded as a peculiarly wanton affront. He enjoyed the feeling which he was exciting, and paraded the town serene and happy all day; but the young fellows set a tailor to work that night, and when Tom started out on his parade next morning he found the old deformed negro bell-ringer straddling along in his wake tricked out in a flamboyant curtain-calico exaggeration of his finery, and imitating his fancy Eastern graces as well as he could.
>
> Tom surrendered, and after that clothed himself in the local fashion.

Tom abandons his newly acquired eastern clothes because he finds it intolerable to be mocked by a black man pretending to be a white man. Tom's embarrassment is understandable, but the situation is ironic because Tom himself is—by the conventions of slave society—a black man imitating a white man. Thus, the old negro bell-ringer is a black man imitating another black man imitating a white man. The novel is full of similar ironies, all of which serve to point up the absurdities of racial classifications.

In addition to being an attack on slavery and racism, *Pudd'nhead Wilson* can also be read as an indictment of southern culture generally. Scholar John Gerber sees the book as depicting that culture as "the ultimate absurdity of human existence" and calls it a "sermon on the hopelessness of a society that accepts slavery."

An example of that absurdity is the novel's depiction of southern attitudes toward honor. The most distinguished resident of Dawson's Landing is Judge Leicester Driscoll, the uncle of Tom Driscoll—whom he never learns is actually the slavewoman Roxy's son. In chapter 13, he is appalled to learn that Tom has settled a dispute with the Italian Luigi Capello by taking him to court on assault charges, instead of challenging him to a duel. To salvage the family honor, the judge challenges Luigi to a duel himself and is thrilled by the Italian's quick acceptance: "'He's a darling! Why, it's an honor as well as a pleasure to stand up before such a man.'" Although the duel is fought with no one being hurt but the spectators, the villagers of Dawson's Landing regard it as a glorious event.

Afterward, Tom Driscoll tries to mask his cowardice by telling his uncle that he did not challenge Luigi to a duel because the man is a "confessed assassin." It is a blatant lie, but the judge swallows it whole and then feels shame for having fought a duel against such a person:

> The old man sat a while plunged in thought; then he looked up with a satisfied light in his eye, and said: "That this assassin should have put the affront upon me of letting me meet him on the field of honor as if he were a gentleman is a matter which I will presently settle—but not now. I will not shoot him until after election. I see a way to ruin them both [Luigi and his brother, Angelo] before; I will attend to that first.

The multiple absurdities in this episode should be obvious. When the judge still regards Luigi Capello as a splendid fellow, he thinks it an honor to have the privilege to try to kill him in a duel. However, when he thinks that Luigi is an assassin, he is ashamed to have met him on the "field of honor." Moreover, he plans to exact a revenge against Luigi for bringing this shame upon him. The form of his intended revenge? Assassination. If the full absurdity of all this is not enough, the judge bases his views on the unsubstantiated claims of his cowardly nephew, Tom, whom he should have good reason to doubt. However, in his eyes, Tom is a southern gentleman, and that is enough to make what he says trustworthy.

The absurdity of southern notions of honor and pride in racial heritage extends even into the slave quarter. Roxy, Tom's true mother, regards herself and her son as niggers. Nevertheless, she takes an inordinate pride in their white aristocratic ancestry and particularly in the fact that Tom's father was Colonel Cecil Burleigh Essex, who "'wuz de highest quality in dis whole town—ole Virginny stock.'" Roxy, like the judge, is appalled by Tom's failure to challenge Luigi to a duel. In her eyes, however, Tom's failing is due to the minute amount of African blood in his ancestry:

> "Whatever has come o' yo' Essex blood? Dat's what I can't understand. En it ain't on'y jist Essex blood dat's in you, not by a long sight—'deed

it ain't. My great-great-great-gran'father en yo' great-great-great-great-gran'father was ole Cap'n John Smith, de highest blood dat Ole Virginny ever turned out, en *his* great-great-gran'mother or somers along back dah, was Pocahontas de Injun queen, en her husbun' was a nigger king outen Africa—en yit here you is, a slinkin' outen a duel en disgracin' our whole line like a ornery low-down hound! Yes, it's de nigger in you!" (chapter 14)

In considering issues such as slavery, race, and southern honor, a general question to keep in mind as you choose an essay topic is whether the views expressed in *Pudd'nhead Wilson* reflect Mark Twain's own thinking or if they are expressed to present ironic statements on the subjects. As we have noted, there is no consensus on Mark Twain's intent in this novel, so there are no set answers to many of the questions that the novel raises.

TOPICS AND STRATEGIES

The general and specific ideas for possible essay topics on *Pudd'nhead Wilson* that are discussed below are intended merely to suggest approaches that will help you develop your own ideas, not to outline what you should write. As always, the keys to successful essay writing are originality of thought and clearness and force of argument. Many of the questions suggested below may have no right or wrong answers. The strength of your essay will come not merely from the conclusions you reach, but from the power and clarity of the arguments you advance to reach those conclusions. *Pudd'nhead Wilson* is a wonderfully complex novel to write about and one that offers you a wide scope to find your own approach.

Themes

Race and slavery are clearly the two most central issues in *Pudd'nhead Wilson*. These subjects are closely related and tie into issues about personal identity, such as what it means to be white or black, free or slave. In the antebellum American South, distinctions between slaves and free persons were clear. However, the relationship between slavery and African ancestry was not always equally clear. Newborn children inherited their legal status from their mothers. Children of slave women were legally slaves, regardless of the status of their fathers. Likewise, the children of free women were free, even if their fathers were slaves. This is why Roxy is considered a negro slave, even though she is described as being only one-sixteenth black. She is the descendant of four generations of white fathers and slave mothers, just as her son, Chambers (the false Tom Driscoll), is the son of a slave mother and a white father, Colonel Essex.

Sample Topics:

1. **Twins and changelings:** How does the switching of the babies Chambers and Tom Driscoll in chapter 3 drive the plot?

A strong current running through Mark Twain's writings is his obsession with twins, changelings, and switched identities. *The Prince and the Pauper* (1881), for example, is about a young heir to the English throne and a lowly commoner who look so much alike that after they swap clothes for fun, no one believes that they have changed places. *Pudd'nhead Wilson* is built around a similar theme. After Roxy switches the clothes of her baby son, Chambers, and the master's son, Tom Driscoll, no one detects the switch until the end of the novel, more than 20 years later. A crucial difference between the two novels, however, is the fact that the boys in *The Prince and the Pauper* are fully aware of their switch, and each struggles to be restored to his previous condition, while the boys in *Pudd'nhead Wilson* are unaware they have been switched until they are adults, and then each, for quite different reasons, is reluctant to reverse his condition. Another important difference is that while each of the boys in *The Prince and the Pauper* is improved by his changeling experience, the lives of both the boys in *Pudd'nhead Wilson* are ruined. Many interesting essays could be written on what Mark Twain may have been trying to say in his changeling stories.

Pudd'nhead Wilson actually has two pairs of "twins," if we allow that Chambers and Tom are, in a sense, twins. Angelo and Luigi Capello, the Italians who settle in Dawson's Landing, make up the second pair of twins. What makes the two pairs of twins especially interesting is the fact that when Mark Twain began writing his book, the Capellos were his central characters. However, the brothers were not quite the same kind of twins who appear in *Pudd'nhead Wilson.* In Mark Twain's original manuscript, the Capellos are conjoined, or "Siamese," twins, and Mark Twain's original intent was to write a farce exploiting all the comic possibilities of two men with diametrically opposed personalities who are literally forced to stick together. By Mark Twain's own account, he abandoned that story line as other characters began taking over, and *Pudd'nhead Wilson* turned out to be a very different kind of book.

The theme of twins and changelings suggests a number of intriguing essay topics that could examine comparisons of the theme in *Pudd'nhead Wilson* with Mark Twain's treatment of the same theme in his other works. However, it is not necessary to go beyond *Pudd'nhead Wilson* to find interesting essays topics on the subject. Perhaps the most obvious would be an essay exploring how Mark Twain's shift from a farce about conjoined twins to a more serious work on slavery and race influenced the way *Pudd'nhead Wilson* treats Chambers and Tom as changelings. Does it make sense to see them as twins? Are there parallels within the novel between them and the Capello brothers? To handle this subject adequately, you should read an edition of *Pudd'nhead Wilson* that contains the remnants of Mark Twain's original story, which was published at the same time as "Those Extraordinary Twins."

2. **Heredity v. environment:** Does the novel make a case for either heredity or environment being more important in the ways individuals grow up?

Pudd'nhead Wilson provides a kind of laboratory case study in which to consider this question. The central case is, of course, the false Tom Driscoll, who grows up to be a cowardly, lazy, gambling, thieving, and lying wastrel and even a murderer. What makes him grow up that way? Is the novel saying that it is the conditioning he receives as a pampered and petted child to whom no one can say no and whose excesses no one tries to curb until it is too late? Or does the novel suggest that something in his inborn nature makes him bad? And, if the latter is the case, is the novel saying that his flaws are due to his African ancestry? If Chambers and Tom were not switched as babies, is there any reason to believe that the true Tom would develop as the false Tom does?

These are tricky questions to answer, as the novel seems to present contradictory points of view. For example, when Roxy berates her son for his cowardice in avoiding a duel with Luigi Capello in chapter 14, she says, "It's de nigger in you, dat's what it is. Thirty-one parts o' you is white, en on'y one part nigger, en dat po' little one part is yo' *soul*. Tain't wuth savin' . . ." Does that view reflect Mark Twain's own thoughts on the subject, or is he merely putting into her mouth a racist view that he wishes to condemn. To begin to answer that question, consider the views on the importance of training that the novel expresses elsewhere. For example, in this Pudd'nhead Wilson maxim: "Training is everything. The peach was once a bitter almond; cauliflower is nothing but cabbage with a college education." As that maxim opens chapter 5, which describes Tom's brief stint at Yale University, we might infer that the false Tom is the "cabbage with a college education." In fact, the chapter explicitly states that Tom acquires some of his worst habits during his time at Yale.

An essay on the subject of heredity versus environment should also look beyond the case of the false Tom Driscoll. Virtually all the characters in the novel are driven, to some extent, by their training. Roxy, though physically virtually a white person, has been conditioned to think of herself as a slave. The true Tom Driscoll is wholly white by ancestry, but is hopelessly adapted to a black slave mentality. Judge Driscoll is conditioned by his Virginia heritage and the southern code of honor and other villagers are also conditioned by their training.

3. **Parenting instincts:** What does the novel say about the need of men and women to have children? Is there such a thing as a parenting instinct?

Another curious aspect of Mark Twain's fiction is the scarcity of healthy nuclear families. Tom Sawyer is an orphan, Huck Finn becomes an orphan after his abusive father dies, and the prince of *The Prince and the Pauper* quickly becomes an orphan. In *Pudd'nhead Wilson,* the mother of the true Tom Driscoll dies shortly after Tom is born, and Tom's father, Percy Driscoll, pays so little attention to him that he fails to notice when Roxy switches Tom with her own son, Chambers. After Percy dies, his childless brother, Judge Driscoll, adopts Tom. With the help of his widowed and equally childless sister, Mrs. Rachel Pratt, the judge unintentionally contributes to Tom's development as a wastrel by foolishly indulging him. In chapter 19, David Wilson explains the judge's blindness to Tom's obvious faults as the product of "'a parental instinct that has been starving'" for so long that it "'will be entirely satisfied with anything that comes handy; its taste is atrophied, it can't tell mud-cat from shad.'" Roxy also contributes to Tom's development during the years that she spends raising him. Despite "her splendid common sense and practical everyday ability, Roxy was a doting fool of a mother." An essay on this subject might ask whether there is any truth in Wilson's assertion that childless adults can become so desperate to have children that they are inclined to overlook their adopted children's faults and thereby bring them up badly.

4. **Motherly love:** What does the novel say about the power of a mother's love?

Although broken and dysfunctional families seem to be the norm in Mark Twain's fiction, his writings also generally depict mother figures as strong characters willing to make great sacrifices out of love for their children. In *Tom Sawyer,* for example, Tom's devoted surrogate mother, Aunt Polly, bears a strong resemblance to Mark Twain's own mother, Jane Lampton Clemens, who was a strong figure in Mark Twain's life. Motherly love is, in fact, one of the strongest themes in *Pudd'nhead Wilson.* Roxy repeatedly makes sacrifices and is willing to abase herself out of her devotion to her son. How realistic is her behavior? To what extent does the theme of motherly love drive the novel's plot?

Aside from undertaking a careful reading of the novel, you might prepare for an essay on this subject by reading about Mark Twain's relationship with his mother. Any major biography of Mark Twain would be a good starting point, but Mark Twain's own tribute to his mother, "Jane Lampton Clemens" (see Bibliography below) would be ideal. Comparisons with Mark Twain's depictions of mothers in other writings would be illuminating too. Of particular interest are the mothers whom Prince (later King) Edward encounters during his travels in *The Prince and the Pauper.*

5. **Clothes:** What does the novel say about the importance of clothes to a person's identity?

Another of Mark Twain's favorite themes is the notion that an individual's identity is determined by the clothes that he or she wears. That theme is central to *The Prince and the Pauper,* and it plays important roles in *Huckleberry Finn* and *Connecticut Yankee,* in both of which characters repeatedly change their identities along with their clothes. In *Pudd'nhead Wilson,* Roxy gets the idea of switching her infant son with that of her master only after she switches their clothes. The point that most people can distinguish the two babies only by their clothes is made repeatedly. The novel also has other instances of clothes changes, most of which involve changed identities. For example, the false Tom Driscoll wears women's clothing when he goes on his burglary raids, and Roxy wears a man's outfit when she confronts Tom after escaping from her Arkansas master.

To write an essay on this subject, you might begin by cataloging every instance in the novel that describes a character's dress. Then, analyze the passages in which the descriptions occur to determine whether the novel is making a point about the significance of the clothes themselves.

6. **Unredeemable scoundrels:** Tom Driscoll constantly vows to reform but instead goes from one dastardly act to another, steadily elevating the magnitude of his crimes until he commits murder. Is the novel saying that criminals are beyond redemption? Does Tom's criminal nature symbolize the hopelessness of a slave society?

Mark Twain had a lot of fun with scoundrels—or rapscallions as he often called them—in his fiction, most notably, perhaps, in *Huckleberry Finn*. He particularly enjoyed playing with the idea that members of respectable society are ever ready to coddle and try to reform miscreants and social outcasts, such as Pap Finn in *Huckleberry Finn* and Injun Joe in *Tom Sawyer*. *Pudd'nhead Wilson*'s Tom Driscoll fits into the mold of a scoundrel who appears to be beyond redemption, despite his repeated vows to reform.

To develop this subject, examine all the instances in which Tom promises to reform and determine whether there are patterns in the relationships between his words and his deeds. Look, also, for other examples of efforts at reform in the novel, such as the effect on Roxy of attending a Methodist revival in chapter 2. Comparisons between *Pudd'nhead Wilson* and other Mark Twain works would suggest additional ideas.

Character

As we have seen, a central concern of *Pudd'nhead Wilson* is the question of the identities of its diverse characters. Racial identity is obviously important in the novel; however, it is not the only identity issue. John C. Gerber argues that "There is no major character in *Pudd'nhead Wilson* without a problem of identity." Consider, for example, the title character, David Wilson: Who is he, really? As an upstate New Yorker who studied law at an eastern school, he is an outsider in his adopted southern town of Dawson's Landing. However, he appears eventually to accept the values of that slaveholding town and even seems to subscribe to the southern code of honor, although it clashes with his legal training and his northern upbringing. Is he, by temperament, a northerner or a southerner? A progressive thinker or a conservative? Does he have any interest in social reform? Or, he is concerned only with self-aggrandizement?

A question that one should always consider when reading any novel is the extent to which its characters are, in fact, *characters,* and not merely one- or two-dimensional figures inserted as props to move the story along. True characters are complex and more three-dimensional (or fully rounded) people, figures about whom readers learn enough not to expect always to behave predictably. The distinction between round and flat characters is particularly important in analyses of *Pudd'nhead Wilson,* as most of its characters are comparatively flat. In fact, Mark Twain himself said of his book's title character, "I have never thought of Pudd'nhead as a *character,* but only as a piece of machinery—a button or a crank or a lever, with a useful function to perform in a machine, but with no dignity about that." Is that a fair analysis of Wilson, or was Mark Twain being too harsh on him?

Sample Topics:

1. **David Wilson:** How fully developed a character is he and what is his role in the novel?

The introduction to this section raises several troublesome questions about Wilson as a character, and each of these questions suggests a variety of good essay subjects. For example, from Wilson's first appearance in the novel, it is clear that he is intelligent, perceptive, and imaginative. Why would a person with his talents and background settle in a backwater village like Dawson's Landing? And why would he stay there after realizing that the simple-minded villagers are unlikely ever to give him a chance to practice law? After he finally does get a chance to demonstrate his skills and his brilliance, he scores a sensational success but afterward seems satisfied merely to be accepted and shows no interest in bettering the town by challenging its values. Was Mark Twain correct in describing Wilson as merely a piece of machinery who exists only to move the plot along? Without necessarily investigating the history of how Mark Twain wrote this novel, try to answer why he used Wilson's name for its title.

Another approach to writing about Wilson would be to consider whether he is, in some sense, an alter ego of Mark Twain himself. Wilson occasionally steps into the center of action but is usually at the fringes of the narrative, reacting to the unfolding events much as the novel's anonymous narrator, who is, in fact, Mark Twain. In his afterword to the Oxford edition of *Pudd'nhead Wilson,* David Lionel Smith calls Mark Twain "the quintessential ironic observer" and points out the close ties between the sentiments Wilson expresses in his calendar aphorisms and the views of Mark Twain himself. An essay linking Wilson to Mark Twain would benefit from a reading of some of the biographical works on Mark Twain's later years.

2. **Roxy:** Is she the only fully developed character in the novel? Is she consistently portrayed?

Often described as the strongest female character Mark Twain ever created, Roxy clearly dominates *Pudd'nhead Wilson*'s action. Indeed, David Lionel Smith calls her the novel's "catalytic figure" because she establishes the terms on which its plot is resolved. It can also be argued that Roxy is the only character in the novel who directly challenges the social order of Dawson's Landing. As you read the novel, play close attention to the role that Roxy plays and ask yourself how much of what happens derives from things that Roxy consciously does. Also, ask yourself whether she is portrayed as a fully rounded character. How would you describe her? What are her strengths and weaknesses? Are her thoughts and behavior consistent? If not, are the inconsistencies and contradictions in her behavior realistic? For example, why might a person of her strength of personality be so foolish as to trust her duplicitous son? Why would she misread signs of his selfishness as signs of his caring for her? Is there more to these inconsistencies than strong motherly love? Are there any other characters in the novel who approach Roxy's complexity?

An essay on Roxy should also examine all the ironies bound up in her complex character. John Gerber calls her "irony personified": She looks white but talks and acts black; she shares white prejudices about African Americans but accepts the role of a black slave. All her best intentions are also filled with irony. For example, she switches her own baby with the master's in order to ensure that her son can never be sold down the river, but her very action eventually results in the exact thing that she wants to avoid. Aside from that act, Roxy appears to be honest through the first part of the book. After she is freed from slavery, she works hard and saves her earnings in a bank, only to see it go "smash," leaving her with nothing.

3. **Tom Driscoll (the true Chambers):** What kind of character is he? Is he entirely one-dimensional?

Roxy's natural son is arguably the second-most important character in *Pudd'nhead Wilson.* He appears in virtually every chapter and his criminal acts drive much of the plot. Selfish, vain, and lazy, he drinks heavily, gambles foolishly, steals to pay his gambling debts, betrays those who try to love him, and ends up murdering his principal benefactor. A man with no apparent redeeming qualities, he is an evil character, much like Injun Joe in *Tom Sawyer.* Is he, however, truly one-dimensional? Despite the centrality of slavery in the novel, Tom is the only character in the book who even reflects on the injustice of slavery. Shortly after he learns the truth about his parentage in chapter 10, he asks himself,

> "Why were niggers *and* whites made? What crime did the uncreated first nigger commit that the curse of birth was decreed for him? And why is this awful difference made between white and black? ... How hard the nigger's fate seems, this morning!—yet until last night such a thought never entered my head."

This passage raises a number of questions that might be addressed in an essay. For example, is the sensitivity that Tom demonstrates in the passage simply an aberration in his naturally selfish behavior? Or, are there other reasons to believe that he has some good qualities? Is Mark Twain possibly trying to say that Tom's privileged upbringing in a slaveholding society is what has corrupted him? Why might Mark Twain have put those thoughts only in Tom's head and not in the minds of another character, such as Roxy or Wilson?

4. **The Capello twins:** What does the novel really tell us about them, and what is their role in the novel?

To understand the Capellos' role in *Pudd'nhead Wilson* fully, you must read the novel's companion story, "Those Extraordinary Twins," which is published alongside *Pudd'nhead Wilson* in some editions. The published version of that story is the remnant of the novel that Mark Twain originally intended to write. When he started that book, the Italian twins were to be its central characters; however, they were not exactly the same twins who appear in *Pudd'nhead Wilson.* Instead, they were conjoined, or Siamese, twins. Moreover, they were highly unusual conjoined twins: Each had a head and two arms, but they shared the same torso and the same set of legs. Together, the Capellos looked like a two-headed, four-armed man—extraordinary twins indeed. Always interested in twins, Mark Twain was particularly taken by the comic possibilities of conjoined twins. Except for their extra pair of arms, his original Capello brothers resembled real conjoined twins whom he saw in Italy in 1891. His original novel was to be a farce built around the comic antagonisms arising from the twins' sharply contrary personalities and habits.

By his own account—which appears in his preface to "Those Extraordinary Twins," Mark Twain eventually abandoned his unfinished farce and recast his novel as a tragedy built around other characters. He physically separated the conjoined twins but left them in the novel; however, a careful reading of *Pudd'nhead Wilson* will reveal traces of the twins' original conjoined condition. The first question you might address is why Mark Twain left the twins in his final novel. What purpose do they serve? Is there anything about their being twins, their being Italian, their purportedly being noblemen, or anything else about them that serves the needs of the novel? As twins, do the Capellos serve as some kind of symbolic reflection of the novel's other pair of "twins," Tom and Chambers? Would the novel lose anything of value if the Capellos were removed altogether and their functions assumed by other characters, perhaps local villagers? Do their given names, Angelo (as in angelic?) and Luigi (read "Lucifer"?), have any significant meaning?

5. **Chambers (the true Tom Driscoll):** What does this almost forgotten character reveal about the nature of racial differences?

A neglected central character of the novel is the true Tom Driscoll, the rightful heir to the Driscoll fortune who is brought up as the slave Chambers. Unlike the false Tom, he has no idea of his true identity until the novel reaches its dramatic climax in the murder trial. Although his plight would make him a perfect character in a Charles Dickens novel about lost birthright, *Pudd'nhead Wilson* gives him little to do. Apart from being an object of readers' pity, Chambers seems merely to serve as a symbol of the role of environment and training on human development. Although he is physically and genetically 100 percent white, he is mentally entirely a black slave, with all the stereotyped limitations and disabilities associated with slaves. The full pathos of his degraded condition does not emerge until after he is restored to this rightful place in white society and it becomes evident that he faces a dismal future.

The novel's last remark about Chambers is suggestive: "But we cannot follow his curious fate further—that would be a long story." What is likely to become of Chambers as a free man might provide the basis of an interesting essay in speculation; however, a more fruitful essay subject would be an analysis of what his degradation reveals about the nature of slavery and its relationship to race.

History and Context

To appreciate the historical context of *Pudd'nhead Wilson,* you should familiarize yourself with the antebellum South in which the novel is set and the late 19th century when Mark Twain wrote the book. It would be nearly impossible to discuss the issue of slavery in the novel without first understanding the general nature of slavery in the South. It is also necessary to understand something about changing American attitudes toward race relations during the post-Civil War era. As the 19th century approached its end, white attitudes toward African Americans, in both the North and the South, hardened. In 1896, only two years after *Pudd'nhead Wilson* was published, the U.S. Supreme Court approved the legal segregation of the races in its notorious *Plessy v. Ferguson* ruling. Over the next half century, racial segregation was the law of the land.

Sample Topics:

1. **Slavery:** *Pudd'nhead Wilson*'s plot turns on the idea that what Missouri slaves most feared was being "sold down the river." That notion rests on the premise that the conditions of slavery worsened as one moved ever deeper into the South. How is that idea expressed throughout the novel and how does it help to drive the plot?

   This subject can be approached through several perspectives. First, one should read *Pudd'nhead Wilson* carefully and note all its allusions to the fear of being sold down the river, beginning in chapter 2, which equates selling slaves down the river to "condemning them to hell! No Missouri negro doubted this." Does the novel express this idea as a fact or as a reflection of what its characters believe?

   A second perspective is historical and might begin with asking whether there was any truth to the idea that the conditions for slaves were harsher down the river than in Missouri. Mark Twain—whose parents owned slaves—evidently believed that to be true. His autobiographical writings describe the slavery of his part of Missouri as being of the "mild domestic" variety, "not the brutal plantation article. Cruelties were very rare, and exceedingly and wholesomely unpopular." That view, however, seems to have been colored by Mark Twain's nostalgia for the past. Slavery in and around Hannibal may actually have been every bit as brutal as that farther south. To research this subject, you can do no better than start with Terrell Dempsey's *Searching for Jim: Slavery in Sam Clemens's World* (2003), an entirely unsentimental investigation into the realities of Missouri slavery that pays special attention to Mark Twain's experience with slavery.

2. **"One-drop" theory of race:** *Pudd'nhead Wilson* has been criticized for propagating the "one-drop" theory of race, that is, the idea that any person with a trace of African ancestry is a negro. Is this criticism valid? What does the novel say on this subject?

One of the ambiguities of *Pudd'nhead Wilson* is what it may be trying to say about the nature of racial differences. Roxy is only one-sixteenth African and her son is only one-thirty-second, yet both are legally regarded as negro slaves. When the novel says that Chambers is "by a fiction of law and custom a negro" (chapter 2), it appears to be attacking social conventions about race and caste. At the same time, however, the novel appears to support the one-drop theory by attributing the shortcomings of the false Tom Driscoll to his African ancestry. When Roxy confronts her son about his cowardice for refusing to defend his honor in a duel, she accuses him of disgracing his birth, and by that, she means his white ancestry. Her implication seems to be that all virtuous traits are inherited from one's white ancestors and what one inherits from one's African ancestors is essentially negative. In her son's case, those things are negative indeed, as he has no redeeming qualities. Is *Pudd'nhead Wilson* suggesting that Tom Driscoll's faults are due to his racial makeup? Keep in mind that Roxy has twice as much African blood as Tom, but she is a stronger and, arguably, morally superior character.

The treatment of race in *Pudd'nhead Wilson* is a rich subject for an essay. What is needed is a particularly close reading of the text to dig out what messages, if any, the novel intends. What views does it express on the nature of race and the proper relationships between white and black people. Do views on the subject such as those expressed by Roxy reflect Mark Twain's own views? Or is his book an attempt to depict the views on race held by either pre–Civil War southern whites, post–Civil War white Americans generally, or both? To get at answers to such questions, you will need to read about Mark Twain's attitudes toward race. A good place to start is with the books by Shelley Fisher Fishkin, particularly *Was Huck Black?*

3. **North v. South:** Although *Pudd'nhead Wilson* presents a harsh view of southern slaveholding culture, it does not exempt northerners from criticism. Is the novel an attack mainly on southern society or is it a broader attack on American society—or perhaps the human race generally—for condoning slavery?

After Roxy escapes from the Arkansas plantation to which her son has sold her, she says that her Arkansas master is a kindly man who was disposed to treat her gently, but that his wife is a northerner (a "Yank"), who insisted that she work in the fields and got the overseer to treat her harshly. Moreover, the overseer himself was also a northerner, who "knows how to work a nigger to death, en dey knows how to whale 'em, too—whale 'em till dey backs is welted like a washboard."

Do passages such as this indicate that Mark Twain was trying to say that it was not just white southerners who were responsible for the evils of slavery? In addressing that question, you should also do a little research on the historical role of northerners in the antebellum South. Does Roxy's comment about the terrible reputation of northerner overseers among slaves have any historical validity?

If you choose to write on this subject, keep in mind that David Wilson, the novel's title character, is himself a northerner. Is there anything about his northern roots that sets him apart from the southerners among whom he is living? Why might Mark Twain have made him a northerner? Would he serve any different purpose in the novel if he were instead a southerner?

4. **Fingerprinting:** *Pudd'nhead Wilson* was the first major fictional work to make a significant use of fingerprints in its plot. What do fingerprints contribute to the novel? Does their anachronistic use in any way spoil the novel? Does the novel contain other examples of anachronisms?

Mark Twain was always fascinated by new technologies. Fingerprint identification was a brand new forensic tool at the time *Pudd'nhead Wilson* appeared. Francis Galton had put it on a scientific basis only two years earlier, with his publication of *Finger Prints* (1892). The fictional Wilson's collecting of fingerprints during the early 19th century is thus an example of an anachronism—the placing of something outside its proper historical time. An essay on this subject might look at *Pudd'nhead Wilson* in the context of the development of forensic science and the growing fascination with detective fiction. Among the questions that this subject raises is whether the mystery elements in the novel were an attempt to capitalize on the popularity of Sherlock Holmes stories, which Arthur Conan Doyle had started publishing in 1887.

5. **The not-so-gay Nineties:** The decade of the 1890s is popularly perceived as a relatively prosperous and carefree time in American history. However, the decade was actually an economically troubled and stressful period, and some of that stress found its way into *Pudd'nhead Wilson*.

Mark Twain published *Pudd'nhead Wilson* at a bad time in American economic history. After the boom years of the so-called Gilded Age (an era that he helped to name), the United States was headed for a crash in what became known as the Panic of 1893. Mark Twain himself owned a publishing firm that went into bankruptcy the following year—the same year in which he published *Pudd'nhead Wilson.* In fact, because of the failure of his firm, *Pudd'nhead Wilson* was the first book he published with someone else's firm since he had started his own company a decade earlier. It is probably not a coincidence that he gave many of the characters in his new novel serious financial problems. Percy Driscoll's land speculations fail before he dies; Roxy loses her life savings when her New Orleans bank fails; Tom Driscoll is in perpetual financial trouble; the Capello brothers have a history of struggling to make ends meet; and David Wilson abandons his efforts to build a law practice and turns to other work to get by. David Lionel Smith describes the setting of the novel as "a world terrorized by the depredations of laissez-faire capitalism run amok." Mark Twain projects the culture of the 1890s into the antebellum period, but Smith finds the linkage apt.

An essay on this subject requires three lines of research. The first, of course, is a careful reading of what the novel says about money matters. The second is some investigation into Mark Twain's personal history, which was characterized by a constant struggle to get rich and repeated investment failures. Indeed, the specter of bankruptcy loomed over him throughout his life, and his own father—like Percy Driscoll—died after failing in a major land investment. Charles H. Gold's *"Hatching Ruin," Or, Mark Twain's Road to Bankruptcy* (2003) is the fullest study of Mark Twain's business dealings yet published, but almost any biography of Mark Twain would be useful. The third line of research is to look into the historical forces leading to the Panic of 1893.

Philosophy and Ideas

Another way to look at *Pudd'nhead Wilson* is to explore the philosophical ideas that are expressed within it. This approach is related to the study of themes described above, but it operates at a more general level.

Sample Topics:

1. **Hypocrisy:** What does *Pudd'nhead Wilson* say about the human tendency toward hypocrisy and moral relativism?

Because hypocrisy is generally understood to mean pretending to be something that one is not or believing something that one does not believe, it can be closely associated with irony. For example, a man who claims to be a teetotaller who is actually a secret drinker is a hypocrite. Moreover, because he is the opposite of what he pretends to be, there is an ironic aspect to his behavior. Since, as we have already seen, *Pudd'nhead Wilson* is filled with irony, we should not be surprised to find many instances of hypocrisy in the novel.

A prime example of hypocrisy in Dawson's Landing is the existence of a organization called the Sons of Liberty in the midst of a slaveholding town. The townspeople pride themselves on their democratic ideals, but those ideals do not extend to their chattels. Hypocrisy is also often allied with moral relativism, the personal belief that the moral and ethical standards of others do not necessarily apply to oneself. For example, Percy Driscoll's slaves do not regard stealing from him as sinful because he daily robs them of their liberty. Driscoll naturally sees the matter differently; he cannot abide theft, but it does not occur to him that he, as a slaveowner, might be the greater thief. In fact, he regards himself as noble and magnanimous for selling his thieving slaves locally, instead of down the river. The town's leading citizens—particularly those of Virginian ancestry—pride themselves on their adherence to the southern code of honor, while seeming oblivious to the fact that their society is built on slavery and their code rests on violence.

Because hypocrisy and moral relativism are open-ended concepts, they lend themselves to a wide variety of approaches in an essay. If you decide to write on this subject, you might begin by looking for examples of hypocritical behavior and moral relativism throughout the novel to show how Mark Twain uses them to develop irony.

2. **Unrecognized genius:** What does Mark Twain mean by unrecognized genius and how does he use it as a theme in his writings?

Mark Twain had a particular fascination with the idea of exceptionally talented people going unrecognized by the communities in which they live. In *Life on the Mississippi* (1883), for example, he wrote about a boy from his hometown of Hannibal whom everyone thought was a "perfect chucklehead" until he astonished everyone by going off to St. Louis and becoming the "first lawyer in the State of Missouri." One of his favorite historical figures was Joan of Arc, the 15th-century savior of France, about whom he wrote a novel after finishing *Pudd'nhead Wilson.* In that novel, Joan's fellow Domremy villagers are too dense to recognize her greatness. The last book Mark Twain published during his lifetime, *Captain Stormfield's Visit to Heaven* (1909), tells about a Tennessee tailor whom heaven honors as the greatest poet the world has ever produced, although he was regarded as a fool during his time on Earth. David Wilson fits very much into this category. Indeed, Mark Twain may have modeled him on that unnamed "chucklehead" lawyer—probably Samuel Taylor Glover (1813–1884)—of *Life on the Mississippi.*

To build an essay on this subject, begin by looking closely at *Pudd'nhead Wilson*'s depiction of David Wilson. What is the basis for the villagers' dismissal of him as a fool? What happens through the course of the novel to confirm or contradict the villagers' low regard for his intelligence? Is it significant that Roxy and Judge Driscoll are the only villagers who do not share that opinion?

This subject would also lend itself well to a comparative approach by looking at Mark Twain's treatment of the unrecognized-genius theme in some of his other works. For example, does Tom Sawyer fit the same mold? Another character who almost certainly does is Tom Canty, the beggar boy in *The Prince and the Pauper* who accidentally becomes king of England. With a little research into the life of Mark Twain, you might also see if you can find reasons for his fascination with this subject. Is it possible that he regarded himself as an example of unrecognized genius?

Language, Symbols, and Imagery

This category encompasses the choices of words, symbols, and images that writers use to enhance their texts. In contrast to literal language, which uses words to mean exactly what they are assumed to mean, figurative language uses words to mean things other than their literal meanings. *Pudd'nhead Wilson* does not use a great deal of this type of figurative language; however, it does employ symbols to convey ideas. A more subtle form of figurative language, symbols employ the names of familiar objects, ideas, and even characters to create moods or enhance atmosphere.

Sample Topics:

1. **Symbols of social order:** *Pudd'nhead Wilson* opens with an almost idyllic portrait of Dawson's Landing. As the narrative unfolds, however, it is clear that the town is anything but idyllic. What symbols and images does Mark Twain use to portray the town and southern society generally, and how do they change as the novel progresses?

   The second paragraph of the novel offers an almost rapturous picture of Dawson's Landing as a "snug little collection of modest one- and two-story frame dwellings whose whitewashed exteriors were almost concealed from sight by climbing tangles of rose vines, honeysuckles and morning-glories. . . ." The symbolism in the full paragraph is so powerful that the passage itself even uses the word *symbol* in reference to contented house cats. That paragraph would make a strong starting point for an essay, which should begin by identifying what its symbols—and others that follow in the chapter—signify about the people and institutions of Dawson's Landing. John Gerber regards the curled-up cat as a symbol of the town's "mindless contentment." Is that view valid? Look for other examples of symbols and images throughout the novel and try to determine whether there is a pattern to their relationship with the changing narrative.

2. **Animal symbols:** What symbolic uses of animals does the novel make?

The curled-up cat image of the novel's second paragraph is one of many significant allusions to animals in the novel. More than half the chapters contain references to dogs, and some of these references clearly have symbolic meanings. A striking example is the "Pudd'nhead Wilson's Calendar" maxim that opens chapter 16: "If you pick up a starving dog and make him prosperous, he will not bite you. This is the principal difference between a dog and a man." The relevance of that maxim to the chapter that follows seems clear: In it, Roxy makes an extraordinary sacrifice to save her son from financial disaster, only to have him betray her.

An obvious first step in writing on this subject would be to list every reference to animals in the novel, along with comments about the possible symbolic meanings of the passages in which they appear. Chapter 1's cat passage is a good starting point, and it is followed by the passage in which Wilson arrives in Dawson's Landing and makes his ironic remark about wanting to own half a barking dog so that he could kill his half. That passage is so full of symbolism that an entire paper could be written on it alone. The concept of killing half a dog relates closely to the theme of twins and dualism that pervades the novel. Consider also whether there may there be a connection between that passage and the Old Testament story of Solomon's proposal to split an infant child in half. That biblical story has a remarkable parallel to the central story line in *Pudd'nhead Wilson*. In the first book of Kings (3:16–28), two women appear before King Solomon, each claiming to be the mother of the same child. One claims that after the other woman's own child died, that woman swapped babies, keeping the live child for herself. Solomon proposes to settle the dispute by cutting the baby in two and giving half to each woman. The woman in possession of the baby accepts the proposal, but the other opts to relinquish her claim in order to spare the baby. Is it possible that Mark Twain had this biblical story in mind when he wrote the dog passage? He was certainly familiar with the story, as he has Huck and Jim discuss it in *Huckleberry Finn*, whose chapter 14 you should read.

3. **The haunted house:** When Roxy confronts her son, the false Tom, with the truth about his parentage, she does it in the town's haunted house. What special symbolism does that house convey?

In his excellent recorded lecture course on Mark Twain, Stephen Railton argues that Dawson's Landing's haunted house is a dark place that symbolizes what goes on behind the scenes in a slave society and makes possible miscegenation. Since both Roxy and Tom are products of racial mixing, the haunted house provides a natural meeting place for them to share their secrets. Stating that much may be obvious—an essay on this subject needs to go further. Consider the ways in which all the homes in Dawson's Landing are described. What other symbols do their descriptions contain? Look at the locations of the homes as well. Is it significant that the house nearest to the haunted house is Wilson's home?

Form and Genre

We have already commented on the novel's unusual history. By his own account, Mark Twain started the book as a farce about grotesque conjoined twins, only to see several minor characters take over and transform his story into a tragedy. He then dropped the farcical elements and rebuilt his story around different characters. There are reasons to doubt the honesty of Mark Twain's account of his book's genesis, but if we leave that matter aside, other questions about the book's construction remain.

Sample Topics:

1. **Tragedy, farce, or something else?:** Although *Pudd'nhead Wilson* is now accepted as an important classic, it is generally regarded as a poorly constructed novel. Is it? Are its problems related to Mark Twain's shift from farce to tragedy? In what way is the novel a tragedy?

So many elements go into a novel, that there are many ways in which its construction can go wrong. Among the flaws that

David Lionel Smith observes in *Pudd'nhead Wilson* are its insufficiently related narrative threads, many self-indulgent digressions, and lack of structural symmetry. Are such criticisms valid? To address this question, you will need to outline the novel's main narrative threads, identify the links among them, and determine what is meant by a lack of structural symmetry and self-indulgent digressions. Do not try to account for every problem in the novel's structure. Instead, focus your essay on what you believe to be the main problems. Among the elements to examine are narrative continuity, consistency of tone, and the ways in which characters fit into the plot.

2. **"Pudd'nhead Wilson's Calendar":** What is the function of the maxims that open chapters?

An unusual feature of the novel is Mark Twain's use of witty and ironic maxims to open each chapter. For example, chapter 4 opens with "Adam and Eve had many advantages, but the principal one was, that they escaped teething." That allusion to the biblical story of Adam and Eve's coming into the world as fully formed adults is witty, but does it or other Pudd'nhead Wilson maxims have a useful function in the structure of the novel? If the maxims have no larger purpose, might they be examples of what David Lionel Smith calls "self-indulgent digressions"?

The best approach to writing an essay on this subject is evident: After you read each chapter, reread the maxims and ask yourself how they relate to the main content of the chapter. For example, the first maxim for chapter 5 states: "Training is everything. The peach was once a bitter almond; cauliflower is nothing but cabbage with a college education." The chapter goes on to discuss Tom Driscoll's two years at Yale University, so the possible relevance of the maxim should be clear. The relevance of many other maxims is less obvious, but if you use your imagination, you may be surprised by what you find. After you have compiled a list of relevant and apparently irrelevant maxims, study it carefully and ask whether there are any coherent patterns in how the maxims are used or the types of maxims that are most relevant. Keep an open mind in looking for relevance, which might be very subtle. Your goal should be to assess the contributions that the maxims make to the book. Would the novel be weaker or stronger without them? Why?

Compare and Contrast Essays

Compare and contrast essays offer a wide scope for developing original ideas but can also make it easy to fall into the trap of doing the opposite. Preparation for such essays usually begins with compiling lists of similarities and differences—between characters, plots, points of view, and so on. The danger in this approach is concluding that the lists themselves reveal anything. For example, simply observing that *Pudd'nhead Wilson*'s title character shares Tom Sawyer's flair for showmanship in public forums says little. You should also explain what you mean by that statement, give examples of each character's public performances, say something about how their predilections relate to their overall personalities, and perhaps also show how their performances help to drive the plots of their stories.

One of the most attractive aspects of compare and contrast essays is that they permit you to be creative on two levels: first, in finding aspects of one or more works to compare; second, in finding significant points to make about the similarities and differences you observe. True originality can be difficult to achieve, but one of your best chances of attaining it lies in finding an innovative compare and contrast topic.

Sample Topics:

1. **Dawson's Landing v. St. Petersburg:** In what ways does *Pudd'nhead Wilson*'s town resemble, or differ from, the town in *Tom Sawyer*?

Like the fictional hometown of Tom Sawyer and Huck Finn, Dawson's Landing is modeled on Mark Twain's boyhood home of Hannibal, Missouri. Both are Missouri towns on the Mississippi River and appear to be about the same size and to have similar commercial enterprises. However, they also have some striking differences. For example, Dawson's Landing is much farther south than St. Petersburg. Why should that difference matter in a novel revolving around slavery? Another, perhaps more subtle, difference is that in *Tom Sawyer*, St. Petersburg is seen through the eyes of boys, while *Pudd'nhead Wilson* views Dawson's Landing from an adult perspective. How do these different perspectives color the ways that the towns are depicted?

To write on this topic, you will need to read *Tom Sawyer*, as well as *Pudd'nhead Wilson*. As you take notes on the most important characteristics of each town, try to look beyond tangible facts by assessing the emotional feeling, or mood, that each town projects. Pay special attention to the ways in which people relate to one another.

St. Petersburg is also the setting of the early chapters of *Huckleberry Finn*, but that book says much less about the town than *Tom Sawyer* does. Mark Twain modeled other fictional towns on Hannibal. If you wish to broaden your essay's scope or shift its focus, you might read his short story "The Man That Corrupted Hadleyburg" (1898), which is discussed in another chapter in this book. You will find that Hadleyburg bears interesting points of comparison to Dawson's Landing. Stephen Railton points out that each time Mark Twain created a new version of his boyhood hometown, his depiction of it became less attractive.

2. **Roxy v. her son:** In what ways are Roxy and her son, the false Tom, similar or different? What accounts for their similarities and differences?

Roxy and Tom offer an intriguing pair of characters to compare. Although they are considered "negroes" only by "fiction of law and custom," according to *Pudd'nhead Wilson*'s anonymous narrator, they represent the novel's only important African American characters. For this reason, most of what the novel says about African Americans and slaves revolves around them. As mother and son, Roxy and Tom are biologically related but apparently quite different characters. For example, while Tom is weak and cowardly, Roxy is strong and courageous. What makes them so different in this regard? What aspects of their makeups make them similar or different? Might the novel be implying that their different personalities are shaped by the fact that Roxy has twice as much African blood in her veins as Tom? Could it be saying that Roxy's life as a slave has made her stronger? Or is there no discernible explanation for their differences? To find answers to questions such as these, read the book closely, as the evidence you need is likely to be found in nuances, particularly in what the characters say. Keep in mind that in the matter of racial stereotypes, you are looking for explanations within the context of the novel.

Bibliography for *Pudd'nhead Wilson*

Berger, Sidney E., ed. *Pudd'nhead Wilson and Those Extraordinary Twins.* By Samuel Langhorne Clemens. New York: W. W. Norton, 1980. (Norton Critical edition, with revised texts, supporting editorial notes, and reprints of critical articles.)

Brewton, Vince. "'An Honour as Well as a Pleasure': Dueling, Violence, and Race in *Pudd'nhead Wilson*." *Southern Quarterly* 38, no. 4 (Summer 2000): 101–18.

Chadwick, Jocelyn. "Forbidden Thoughts: New Challenges of Teaching Twain's *The Tragedy of Pudd'nhead Wilson*." *Mark Twain Annual* 1 (2003): 85–96.

Dempsey, Terrell. *Searching for Jim: Slavery in Sam Clemens's World.* Columbia: U Missouri P, 2003.

Fishkin, Shelley Fisher. *Lighting Out for the Territory: Reflections on Mark Twain and American Culture.* New York: Oxford UP, 1997.

———. "Mark Twain and Race." *A Historical Guide to Mark Twain.* New York: Oxford UP, 2002. 127–62.

———. *Was Huck Black? Mark Twain and African-American Voices.* New York: Oxford UP, 1993.

Gerber, John C. "*The Tragedy of Pudd'nhead Wilson* and *The Comedy of Those Extraordinary Twins*." *Mark Twain.* Boston: Twayne, 1988. 129–38.

Gillman, Susan, and Forrest G. Robinson, eds. *Mark Twain's "Pudd'nhead Wilson": Race, Conflict and Culture.* Durham, NC: Duke UP, 1990.

Gold, Charles H. *"Hatching Ruin," Or, Mark Twain's Road to Bankruptcy.* Columbia: U of Missouri P, 2003.

Harrington, Paula. "Dawson's Landing: On the Disappearance of Domesticity in a Slaveholding Town." *Mark Twain Annual* 3 (2005): 91–97.

Hoffman, Andrew Jay. *Twain's Heroes, Twain's Worlds.* Philadelphia: U of Pennsylvania P, 1988.

Hughes, Langston. Introduction. *Pudd'nhead Wilson.* By Mark Twain. New York: Bantam Books, 1959.

Mandia, Patricia M. "Children of Fate and Irony in *Pudd'nhead Wilson.*" *Comedic Pathos: Black Humor in Twain's Fiction.* Jefferson, NC: McFarland, 1991. 51–67.

Messent, Peter. "Severed Connections: *Pudd'nhead Wilson and Those Extraordinary Twins.*" *Mark Twain.* New York: St. Martin's Press, 1997. 134–56.

Morris, Linda A. *Gender Play in Mark Twain: Cross-Dressing and Transgression.* Columbia: U of Missouri P, 2007.

Pinckney, Darryl. Introduction, Notes. *Pudd'nhead Wilson and Those Extraordinary Twins.* By Mark Twain. New York: Barnes & Noble Classics, 2005. xv–xl.

Railton, Stephen. *The Life & Work of Mark Twain.* Chantilly, VA: Teaching Company, 2002. (Includes a lecture on *Pudd'nhead Wilson*; in both audio and video formats.)

———. "Looking for Refuge: *Pudd'nhead Wilson* and 'Hadleyburg.'" *Mark Twain: A Short Introduction.* Malden, MA: Blackwell, 2004. 96–115.

———. *Mark Twain in His Times.* etext.virginia.edu/railton/index2.html (Includes full text of *Pudd'nhead Wilson* and numerous study aids).

———. "The Tragedy of Mark Twain, by Pudd'nhead Wilson." *Nineteenth-Century Literature* 56, no. 4 (March 2002): 519–44.

Rasmussen, R. Kent. "*Pudd'nhead Wilson, The Tragedy of.*" In *Critical Companion to Mark Twain.* New York: Facts On File, 2007. I: 392–419.

———. "The Tragedy of Pudd'nhead Wilson." *Masterplots II: Juvenile and Young Adult Literature Series, Supplement.* Ed. Frank N. Magill. Pasadena, CA: Salem Press, 1997. 3:1,253–256.

Sloane, David E. E. *Student Companion to Mark Twain.* Westport, CT: Greenwood Press, 2001.

Smith, David L. Afterword, For Further Reading. *The Tragedy of Pudd'nhead Wilson and the Comedy Those Extraordinary Twins.* By Mark Twain. New York: Oxford UP, 1996. 1–19. (Back matter has separate pagination.)

———. "Humor Sentimentality, and Mark Twain's Black Characters." *Constructing Mark Twain: New Directions in Scholarship.* Eds. Laura E. Skandera Trombley and Michael J. Kiskis. Columbia: U of Missouri P, 2001. 151–68.

Twain, Mark. "Jane Lampton Clemens." *Huck Finn and Tom Sawyer Among the Indians and Other Unfinished Stories.* Berkeley: U of California P, 1989. 82–92.

———. *The Tragedy of Pudd'nhead Wilson and the Comedy Those Extraordinary Twins.* New York: Oxford UP, 1996. Facsimile reprint of the first American edition of *Pudd'nhead Wilson.*

Williams, Sherley Anne. Introduction. *The Tragedy of Pudd'nhead Wilson and the Comedy Those Extraordinary Twins.* By Mark Twain. New York: Oxford UP, 1996. xxxi–xliii.

Wonham, Henry B. "The Minstrel and the Detective: The Functions of Ethnic Caricature in Mark Twain's Writings of the 1890s." *Constructing Mark Twain: New Directions in Scholarship.* Eds. Laura E. Skandera Trombley and Michael J. Kiskis. Columbia: U of Missouri P, 2001. 122–38.

THE JUMPING
FROG STORY

READING TO WRITE

T HE JUMPING frog story may well be Mark Twain's most famous short work. That is fitting, because it helped make him famous and advanced his writing career. He wrote the story while living in California in 1865, in response to humorist Artemus Ward's request for a contribution to a book of humorous stories he was editing. Mark Twain had actually started writing his story before he received Ward's invitation but delivered his manuscript too late for inclusion in Ward's book. Ironically, that mishap proved to be a lucky break, as Ward passed the story along to the editor of the weekly magazine *The Saturday Press,* in whose November 1865 issue it appeared. Magazines were a major form of entertainment in those days, and the story attracted so much attention that it was reprinted in magazines and newspapers all over the United States, thereby making the name Mark Twain nationally known for the first time. If the story had arrived in time to appear in Ward's book, it would probably have disappeared into obscurity, and Mark Twain's subsequent writing career might have been very different.

Before you consider the jumping frog story itself, you should understand that Mark Twain revised it more than once, and it was published under several different titles. It is probably best known as "The Celebrated Jumping Frog of Calaveras County," although it was first published as "Jim Smiley and His Jumping Frog." It has also been published as "The Notorious Jumping Frog of Calaveras County." To avoid confusion, it may be best simply to call it the jumping frog story (without quotation marks), regardless of which version you read. If you need to look up information on it, keep in mind that you may have to search under more than one title.

The jumping frog story was widely reprinted during the 1860s because readers of that era found it exceptionally funny. Modern readers might get a chuckle or two out of it, but few are likely to find it as hilarious as 19th-century readers did. As you read the story, you should ask yourself why that is. Tastes in humor naturally change over time, but do changing tastes alone account for the different reactions of past and present readers? Another reason for different reactions to the story to consider is what role changing conventions in fiction and story structures play in how we react to humor.

The jumping frog story is a classic example of a type of tall tale that characterized Southwest American humor during the early to mid-19th century. Its structure, like that of many other tall tales of its era, is a frame within which a genteel—presumably eastern—narrator relates his encounter with a vernacular western character, who in turn narrates the central story. In the story's original version, Mark Twain himself is the frame narrator and tells his story in the form of a signed letter addressed to "Mr. A. Ward." Later versions drop the letter format and names, leaving the frame narrator anonymous. Later versions also altered a few other details, but the core part of the story is essentially the same. The question of whether Mark Twain's dropping of his own and Ward's names is significant might itself provide the basis of an essay topic; that possibility is discussed in the section on Character below.

The jumping frog story has been retold in so many forms that it has taken on a life of its own. Indeed, it has become so closely associated with Northern California's Calaveras County that an annual frog-jumping contest is held in the county's town of Angels Camp, whose local high school's teams are nicknamed the Jumping Frogs.

The core of the story is simple: Jim Smiley, a resident of Angel's Camp ("Boomerang" in the original version), claims that his pet frog, Dan'l Webster, "can outjump any frog in Calaveras county." A stranger in the camp expresses his willingness to bet against Dan'l Webster, so Smiley hunts up a frog for the stranger to wager on. While Smiley looks for a frog in a swamp, the stranger fills Dan'l Webster with "quail shot" (lead pellets used in shotgun shells). After Smiley returns, the stranger's frog easily wins the jumping contest; the stranger then pockets Smiley's money and disappears.

An interesting aspect of the frog story is that it appears to have been based on an incident that really occurred in a California mining camp during the mid-19th century. Mark Twain heard the story from a bartender in the dilapidated tavern of a mining camp, where he and a friend spent a week in early 1865. Moreover, at least one version of the story had been published before Mark Twain wrote his own version. Do these facts make Mark Twain's version any less original? Perhaps. However, as you read the story, notice how much of it has nothing to do with the frog. Everything leading up to the frog incident is Mark Twain's invention. Most of the first 60 percent or so of the story concerns the frame narrator, Simon Wheeler, and Jim Smiley. Would the passages about the frog read differently without the preliminary buildup?

The content of the story is obviously important to its humorous effect. However, the *manner* in which it is told may be even more important. This is an aspect of storytelling that was of great interest to Mark Twain throughout his writing and lecturing career. He makes that clear in the story's first paragraph, in which the frame narrator expresses his suspicion that he is the victim of a hoax—that he has been sent to look for a man, "Leonidas W. Smiley," who does not really exist merely to get Simon Wheeler to tell him about "Jim Smiley," "and he would go to work and bore me to death with some exasperating reminiscence of him as long and as tedious as it should be useless to me. If that was the design, it succeeded." That passage tells us immediately that the frame narrator has no sense of humor and warns us that we are in for a boring story.

The frame narrator's description of Simon Wheeler as a storyteller reinforces our expectation that the story will be boring:

> Simon Wheeler . . . reeled off the monotonous narrative which follows this paragraph. He never smiled, he never frowned, he never changed his voice from the gentle-flowing key to which he tuned his initial sentence, he never betrayed the slightest suspicion of enthusiasm; but all through the interminable narrative there ran a vein of impressive earnestness and sincerity, which showed me plainly that, so far from his imagining that there was anything ridiculous or funny about his story, he regarded it as

a really important matter, and admired its two heroes as men of transcendent genius in finesse. I let him go on in his own way, and never interrupted him once.

That paragraph may be the key to the power of the story's humor. The story is inherently funny, but the contrast between its humor and Wheeler's deadpan earnestness in reciting it makes it funnier still. In "How to Tell a Story," an essay that he wrote 30 years after the jumping frog story, Mark Twain said, "The humorous story is told gravely; the teller does his best to conceal the fact that he even dimly suspects that there is anything funny about it; . . ." He used the same technique himself when he worked the lecture circuit. He would tell humorous or even ludicrous stories in a deadpan manner. When audiences erupted in laughter, he would act surprised and confused, as if he had no idea he may have said anything funny; that reaction never failed to make his audiences laugh even louder.

TOPICS AND STRATEGIES

The pages that follow offer both general and specific ideas for essay topics about the jumping frog story. You need not limit your choices to topics discussed here, but if you do select one of them, treat its discussion merely as a starting point for your own essay. Do not hesitate to challenge points made here and never adopt anyone else's views unless you are satisfied you understand them and can advance arguments of your own to support them.

As you develop your essay, you may find you are raising questions for which no definite answers seem possible. That is not necessarily a bad thing, as difficult questions often have no right or wrong answers. Be careful not to fall into the trap of becoming mired in fruitless quests to prove points that may not be provable. The strength of your essay will come not merely from the decisiveness of its conclusions, but from the power and clarity of the arguments that it advances to reach those conclusions. Whatever topics on which you choose to write, use your imagination and try to consider all possible sides of every question. The keys to successful essay writing are originality of thought and clearness and force of argument.

A technique for coming up with new ideas that almost always works is outlining evidence supporting contrary points of view on the same issues. For example, assume you wish to make a case for regarding Jim Smiley as a con man. You would naturally begin by outlining every detail in the jumping frog story that lends support to that view (be sure to keep track of page references). What you should do next is outline all the evidence you can find that supports the *opposite* point of view. Whatever contrary evidence you collect may not alter your original conclusion, but some of it may reveal weaknesses in your argument and thereby give you the opportunity to strengthen your essay. In any case, your goal should not be merely to win an argument, but to get at the truth, and doing that always requires looking at all sides of issues.

Themes

As discussed in the section on Form and Genre below, the jumping frog story is more a sketch than a true short story. As such, it is not rich in themes. Gambling and con men are obvious themes, but additional themes may be hard to find. This limitation may appear to be a drawback to your essay writing; however, it also presents a stimulating challenge. The jumping frog story is short enough to be read multiple times in a brief period; each time you read it, you are likely to find points you have not noticed before. With a little persistence, you may well find an interesting theme that no one else has noticed. For example, you might make a case that the story is, in part, a subtle protest against animal abuse (the frog is not the only animal in the story that suffers). That argument would require some major stretching, but it would gain strength if you were to compare the story to *A Dog's Tale* (1903) and *A Horse's Tale* (1906)—emotionally powerful animal rights stories that Mark Twain wrote many years later.

Sample Topics:

1. **Gambling:** Is Jim Smiley addicted to gambling?

It might be difficult to argue that Mark Twain wrote the jumping frog story as a critique of the lax morals of men living on the frontier or to lament the moral degradation of men addicted to gambling, but it is clear that the story revolves around Jim

Smiley's compulsive gambling habits. Is Smiley what today is called a gambling addict? Or is his gambling habit merely his way of coping with the boredom of living in an isolated mining community? If you write on this subject, study the story carefully for indications of what motivates Smiley to gamble and what rewards he may derive from it. Keep in mind that gambling is a social behavior, as it takes at least two people to make wagers, and consider the question of whether the story is, in fact, commenting on mining camp morals.

2. **Frontier con men:** Which, if any, of the characters in the jumping frog story should be regarded as confidence men, or tricksters?

One of the stock characters of Southwest humor and tall tales is the trickster—a person who takes advantage of the credulity or ignorance of others. We call such people "con men," short for "confidence men," because they take people into their confidence and cheat them. Two of the most famous con men in literature are the Duke and King of *Huckleberry Finn,* who have a dazzling variety of schemes for cheating people. Is the jumping frog story's Jim Smiley another example of a con man? It is clear that he wants constantly to make bets, but does the story indicate anything about how honestly he treats the people with whom he wagers? When he goes off into a swamp to find a frog to jump against his own frog, do we have any reason to believe that he will not take advantage of the stranger by selecting an inferior frog? Is the stranger himself a con man? We know that he cheats Smiley by filling his frog with quail shot, but what motivates him to do that? Could it be that he assumes that Smiley intends to cheat him?

Character

Aside from names that it mentions in passing, the jumping frog story has only four human figures who can properly be considered characters: the frame narrator ("Mark Twain" in the original version of the story; anonymous in later versions), Simon Wheeler, Jim Smiley, and the unnamed stranger who wagers against Smiley's frog. More a sketch than a true short story, the narrative appears not to reveal much about any of these characters. However, a careful reading may reveal more about them than you expect.

Sample Topics:

1. **Simon Wheeler:** What does Wheeler's narrative reveal about Wheeler himself?

   In his brief opening remarks, the frame narrator describes Simon Wheeler as "good-natured," "garrulous," "old," "fat," and "bald" and adds that he found Wheeler "dozing comfortably" in a dilapidated old tavern in a mining camp. Those comments allow us to form a mental picture of Wheeler, but to assess his character, we must rely on Wheeler's own remarks. Fortunately, those are extensive, as he narrates every word in the story except the frame narrator's opening and closing remarks. To write on this subject, read Wheeler's narrative closely and look for comments that reveal aspects of his personality and values. The frame narrator says that Wheeler regarded his story as "a really important matter, and admired its two heroes as men of transcendent genius in finesse." What, if anything, does Wheeler say to merit that description? If that description is accurate, what does it reveal about Wheeler as a person? Another thing to look for in Wheeler's narrative is patterns in his selection of facts to relate. For example, does he differentiate between trivial and important details or treat them all the same? Like the frame narrator, Wheeler himself appears to be humorless, as he seems to find nothing funny about his story. Is there anything in the profile of Wheeler you are building to account for his evident lack of humor and his deadpan delivery of his narrative? (For more on this subject, see the Compare and Contrast section below.)

2. **"Men of transcendent genius":** According to the frame narrator, Simon Wheeler regards the "two heroes" of his narrative "as

men of transcendent genius in finesse." What basis is there for that generous assessment?

The two central characters of Simon Wheeler's narrative are Jim Smiley and the stranger who bests him in the frog-jumping contest. We learn little from Wheeler's narrative about the stranger beyond the fact that he is clever enough to outsmart Smiley. On the other hand, Wheeler tells us a great deal about Smiley. What does Wheeler say about him to support the conclusion that he regards Smiley as a genius? To address that question, you will need to study the story carefully for evidence of Smiley's traits, such as his persistence in making and following through with wagers and his patience in training animals. You should also do some extra reading about the nature of Southwest humor to get a broader sense of what characteristics might have been considered admirable in a Western mining camp. Among the works in the Bibliography below that you will find most helpful are the articles by W. Craig Turner and books by Walter Blair, Tom Quirk, Kenneth S. Lynn, and James M. Cox.

History and Context

Thanks in large part to the jumping frog story, Mark Twain's name is often associated with the California gold rush. The story is set in a California gold-mining camp, but it has only a peripheral relevance to the state's gold rush days. Before coming to California, Mark Twain had lived for several years in the epicenter of Nevada's silver-mining region during its boom years. By contrast, he spent only a few months in California's gold region. Moreover, by the time he arrived there, the gold rush was already largely over. He is thus relating his own view when he has the jumping frog story's frame narrator describe Angel's Camp as a "decayed mining camp" when he meets Simon Wheeler. Wheeler's own narrative pushes the timetable back further. In fact, Wheeler puts dates on his story: "the winter of '49—or . . . the spring of '50"—years that place the time of Jim Smiley's story near the beginning of the California gold rush, which began in 1849.

Sample Topic:

1. **Frontier mining camps:** What does the jumping frog story reveal about mid-19th-century life on the Western frontier?

You might regard an essay on this subject as something akin to gold mining: Dig through the story as thoroughly as you can and sluice out every fact and nuance that reveals something about life on the frontier in general or about life in mining camps in particular. Some details are explicit, such as Simon Wheeler's allusion to the unfinished "big flume" in Angel's Camp at the beginning of the gold rush. Other details are more subtle, such as the activities that kept residents of mining camps entertained. Pay special attention to the frame narrator's observations and try to say something about the deterioration of the mining camp between Jim Smiley's time and that of the narrator's meeting with Simon Wheeler.

Form and Genre

Mark Twain was no respecter of literary genres. Consequently, much of what he wrote is difficult to classify. He himself called most of his early writings *sketches,* but used the word to mean something slightly different than what the term is generally understood to mean now. In the modern sense, a *sketch* is a brief fictional work that is distinguished from a true short story in being built around a single incident with little attempt at complex narrative structure or developed characters. Mark Twain's jumping frog story fits this definition, as it focuses on one event: the confrontation between Jim Smiley and the stranger. Everything else in the story is essentially background information that does not appear to be integral to the story.

Sample Topic:

1. **The sketch form:** If the background material of the jumping frog story were missing, what would remain?

Mark Twain did not invent the core of the jumping frog story, as it was based on an incident that may have really happened in a California mining camp. He did, however, make at least one major contribution to the story: He gave its protagonist, Jim Smiley, a background that establishes him as a compulsive gambler. Apart from amusing anecdotes about Smiley's colorful gambling history, what does this background material add to the sketch?

To write on this subject, begin by considering the frog anecdote as a self-contained sketch. If you are reading the story for the first time, start with the paragraph that begins, "Well, thish-yer Smiley had rat-tarriers, and chicken cocks . . ." and stop after the paragraph in which the stranger gets away. If you have already read the story, read the frog section again and try to forget everything else in the story. Does the frog sketch work by itself? Or does some essential element seem to be missing? After you have considered those questions, go back and read the entire story from its beginning. How do the other parts of the story change your reading of the frog sketch? Does their additional information make the sketch any funnier or make Jim Smiley any more or less sympathetic? What does the overlay of the frame narration contribute to the story's humor?

Compare and Contrast Essays

Compare and contrast essays offer opportunities to express creativity on at least two levels: first, in finding aspects of one or more works to compare; then in finding significant points to make about whatever similarities and differences are noted. If you wish to strive for true originality, look for subjects that may not be obvious to others. A fairly obvious pair of characters to compare within the jumping frog story are Jim Smiley and the stranger who bets against his frog. An essay comparing the two of them would probably look for evidence that either or both of them is a trickster. They might make a good topic for a compare and contrast essay, but the topic itself would not be very original.

An example of a far more original topic would be a comparison of Jim Smiley's bull-pup, Andrew Jackson, and Emmeline Grangerford, the young obituary poet of *Huckleberry Finn*. That subject might sound unpromising, but consider these points: Both Andrew Jackson and Emmeline possess genius in their specialized fields, and both die of apparent heartbreak after failing at what they do best. The dog loses a fight because its opponent has no hind legs to grab hold of; Emmeline leaves a poem unfinished because she cannot find a rhyme for *Whistler*. The challenge in writing on such a subject would be finding deeper levels of meaning.

Sample Topic:

1. **Simon Wheeler and Huck Finn as deadpan narrators:** What do Simon Wheeler and Huck's inclinations to be humorless contribute to the humor of their stories? In what ways are they similar as narrators?

   As discussed above, much of the humor in the jumping frog story derives from the failure of both the frame narrator and Simon Wheeler to see anything funny in the frog story. In this respect, they both resemble Huck Finn, who narrates his own story in *Adventures of Huckleberry Finn* (1884). Much of *Huckleberry Finn*'s power derives from having its story told by an ignorant and naive, but good-hearted, boy who is oblivious to the large moral issues surrounding him. Indeed, he is so naive that he often thinks that he is doing the wrong thing when he is actually doing the right thing. Huck's naïveté also extends to his general obliviousness to humorous situations. For example, in chapter 22 of *Huckleberry Finn,* he sees a circus stunt-riding act that he completely misunderstands. An apparently drunk member of the audience who insists on displaying his riding skill on a spirited horse eventually reveals himself to be one of the circus's professional riders. Everyone in the audience is thrilled by his performance except Huck, who never understands that the man's ruse is a planned act and instead worries that the man may fall off the horse because he is drunk. Other examples of Huck's humorlessness can be found throughout the novel.

   A comparison of Huck Finn and Simon Wheeler should cite examples of several passages that each narrates without expressing any recognition of the humor or irony that they contain. Explain how you can tell that neither narrator sees humor in what he describes. What does their deadpan manner of narrating contribute to their stories? What would the effect on their stories be if they made it clear that they thought their stories were funny?

Bibliography for The Jumping Frog Story

Blair, Walter. *Native American Humor, 1800–1900.* Boston: American Book Co., 1937.

Blount, Roy, Jr. Introduction. *The Celebrated Jumping Frog of Calaveras County, and Other Sketches.* By Mark Twain. New York: Oxford UP, 1996. xxxi–xliv.

Branch, Edgar M. *The Literary Apprenticeship of Mark Twain.* Urbana: U of Illinois P, 1950.

———. "'My Voice Is Still for Setchell' A Background Study of 'Jim Smiley and His Jumping Frog.'" *Mark Twain's Humor Critical Essays.* Ed. David E. E. Sloane. New York: Garland, 1993. 3–29.

Bucci, Richard. Afterword, For Further Reading. *The Celebrated Jumping Frog of Calaveras County, and Other Sketches.* By Mark Twain. New York: Oxford UP, 1996. 1–20. (Back matter has separate pagination.)

Cox, James M. "Discovery." *Mark Twain The Fate of Humor.* 2d ed. Columbia: U of Missouri P, 2002. 3–33.

Emerson, Everett. *Mark Twain A Literary Life.* Philadelphia: U of Pennsylvania P, 2000.

Florence, Don. *Persona and Humor in Mark Twain's Early Writings.* Columbia: U of Missouri P, 1995.

Lynn, Kenneth S. *Mark Twain and Southwestern Humor.* 1959. Reprint, Westport, CT: Greenwood Press, 1972.

Messent, Peter. *The Short Works of Mark Twain A Critical Study.* Philadelphia: U of Pennsylvania P, 2001.

Miller, Robert Keith. "The Growth of a Misanthrope Representative Short Fiction." *Mark Twain.* New York: Frederick Ungar, 1983. 161–95.

Quirk, Tom. *Mark Twain A Study of the Short Fiction.* New York: Twayne Publishers, 1997.

Rasmussen, R. Kent. "Jumping frog story." In *Critical Companion to Mark Twain.* New York: Facts On File, 2007. I: 286–289.

Smith, Henry Nash. *Mark Twain The Development of a Writer.* Cambridge, MA: Belknap Press, 1962.

Smith, Lawrence R. "Mark Twain's 'Jumping Frog' Toward an American Heroic Ideal." *Mark Twain Journal* 20, no. 1 (1979): 15–18.

Turner, W. Craig. "The Celebrating Jumping Frog of Calaveras County." *The Mark Twain Encyclopedia*. Eds. J. R. LeMaster and James D. Wilson. New York: Garland, 1993. 133–135.

———. "Southwestern Humor." *The Mark Twain Encyclopedia*. Eds. J. R. LeMaster and James D. Wilson. New York: Garland, 1993. 705–07.

Twain, Mark. "The Celebrated Jumping Frog of Calaveras County." *The Celebrated Jumping Frog of Calaveras County, and Other Sketches*. New York: Oxford UP, 1996. 7–19.

———. *Early Tales and Sketches. 1851–1864*. Vol. 1. Eds. Edgar Marquess Branch and Robert H. Hirst. Berkeley: U of California P, 1979.

———. *Early Tales and Sketches. 1864–1865*. Vol. 2. Eds. Edgar Marquess Branch and Robert H. Hirst. Berkeley: U of California P, 1981.

———. "How to Tell a Story: The Humorous Story an American Development; Its Difference from Comic and Witty Stories." *Collected Tales, Sketches, Speeches, & Essays, 1891–1910*. Ed. Louis J. Budd. New York: Library of America, 1992. 201–06.

———. "Jim Smiley and His Jumping Frog." *Collected Tales, Sketches, Speeches, & Essays, 1852–1890*. Ed. Louis J. Budd. New York: Library of America, 1992. 171–07. (Original version of Mark Twain's story.)

Williams, George J., III. *Mark Twain and the Jumping Frog of Calaveras County How Mark Twain's Humorous Frog Story Launched His Legendary Writing Career*. Carson City, NV: Tree by the River Publishing, 2000.

Wilson, James D. "'Jim Smiley and His Jumping Frog.'" *A Reader's Guide to the Short Stories of Mark Twain*. Boston: G. K. Hall, 1987. 163–76.

Wonham, Henry B. *Mark Twain and the Art of the Tall Tale*. New York: Oxford UP, 1993.

Zaid, Rhona E. "The Celebrated Jumping Frog of Calaveras County." *Masterplots II: Short Story Series, Revised Edition*. Ed. Charles May. Pasadena, CA: Salem Press, 2004. 1: 563–65.

"THE MAN THAT CORRUPTED HADLEYBURG"

READING TO WRITE

O N ITS surface, "The Man That Corrupted Hadleyburg" (1898) is about revenge: the brilliantly successful scheme of an outsider to humiliate an entire town for having done him some unspecified wrong. The story's very title sums up what the stranger appears to do to the town: He corrupts it. He does that by using the bait of a rich reward to tempt the town's leading citizens to abandon their principles by lying to claim a fortune they know they do not deserve. The story's tight, symmetrical structure neatly gathers all Hadleyburg's citizens in a public forum, where the liars are exposed and their reputations ruined. Because Hadleyburg itself has long had the reputation of being the most honest and upright town in the region, its treasured reputation for incorruptibility is destroyed, and the stranger's revenge is complete.

If revenge were all that the story were about, it might be difficult to find an interesting subject on which to write an essay. However, the story is more complex than may at first appear, so it requires an especially thoughtful reading. A first question to ask is what it means to say that Hadleyburg is "corrupted." As that word is generally understood, to corrupt people is to cause them to change their moral or ethical behavior from honorable to dishonorable. Is that what actually happens in "The Man That Corrupted Hadleyburg"? If the people

241

of Hadleyburg are truly upright and honest, then the answer would appear to be yes: The leading townspeople do abandon their moral standards and are corrupted. However, aside from frequently quoted platitudes about Hadleyburg's sterling reputation, what does the story really say about Hadleyburg's citizens? What has the town done to deserve its reputation for incorruptibility? In fact, has any of its citizens ever done anything praiseworthy? Is it possible that the stranger's scheme merely exposes corruption that exists before his arrival in Hadleyburg?

A decidedly negative view of the town is expressed by one of the story's main characters, Mrs. Richards, the wife of Edward Richards, the bank cashier to whom the stranger's original letter is addressed. Shortly after the Richardses receive the stranger's sack of coins, Mr. Richards gives the letter to a newspaper editor to publish. He relishes the thought of how the letter will enhance his community's reputation:

> "Think what a noise it will make! And it will make all the other towns jealous; for no stranger would trust such a thing to any town but Hadleyburg, and they know it. It's a great card for us. I must get to the printing-office now, or I shall be too late."

At the same moment that Richards expresses pride in his town, he also conveys a mean thought in his wish to make other towns jealous. This should give us reason to suspect that Hadleyburg's pride in its incorruptibility may be tied to arrogance and a lack of charity. As we read on, that suspicion is confirmed. After Richards delivers the stranger's message about the sack of gold to a newspaperman, the story is relayed to other towns. Almost immediately afterward, Richards and his wife regret their rashness in jumping to spread the news. They both agree that the only person in the town who might have done the good deed to which the stranger's letter alludes—giving a stranger 20 dollars—is Barclay Goodson. Since Goodson is dead, the Richardses could easily keep the money for themselves. Mrs. Richards scolds her husband for rushing off to publicize the letter, then realizes that what she is suggesting is dishonest. In a moment of clarity, she sums up Hadleyburg's true nature:

"God knows I never had shade nor shadow of a doubt of my petrified and indestructible honesty until now—and now, under the very first big and real temptation, I—Edward, it is my belief that this town's honesty is as rotten as mine is; as rotten as yours is. It is a mean town, a hard, stingy town, and hasn't a virtue in the world but this honesty it is so celebrated for and so conceited about; and so help me, I do believe that if ever the day comes that its honesty falls under great temptation, its grand reputation will go to ruin like a house of cards. There, now, I've made confession, and I feel better; I am a humbug, and I've been one all my life, without knowing it. Let no man call me honest again—I will not have it."

Yes, there appears to be something rotten in Hadleyburg, and Mrs. Richards's words may prove to be prophetic. As you examine the story more closely, you should find other reasons to suspect that the town's sterling reputation is a sham. If Hadleyburg proves to have been corrupt before the stranger perpetrates his hoax, then what transformation is really taking place? What message is the story trying to convey?

TOPICS AND STRATEGIES

This section offers both general and specific ideas for possible essay topics and provides suggestions about how to approach them. As a central goal of any essay assignment is to encourage writers to express their own ideas, it is up to you to develop whatever topic you choose. Regard these suggestions merely as starting points and look for ways to introduce your own ideas. Also do not assume that every point made here is necessarily valid. Never use anyone else's ideas until you have reasons of your own to regard them as sound.

Themes

As is true of most short stories, "The Man That Corrupted Hadleyburg" deals with a limited number of themes. The opening section of this chapter alludes to several: revenge, greed, honesty, integrity, incorruptibility, pride, and arrogance. Several of these themes are so closely interrelated that they might best be considered together.

Sample Topics:

1. **Revenge:** Is "The Man That Corrupted Hadleyburg" primarily a story about vengeance? The driving impulse behind the stranger's plan to corrupt Hadleyburg is revenge for what he calls "a deep offense which I had not earned."

   According to the story, the stranger is a "bitter man and revengeful" who spent a year developing a sweeping plan to ruin Hadleyburg. An intriguing aspect of the story is that the deep offense that he once suffered is never specified; would the story be any stronger if it were explained? Or is it possible to guess what that offense might have been? To develop an essay on this topic, extract from the story every detail revealing something about both the mentality of the stranger and the meaner aspects of Hadleyburg's citizens. Note that while the story emphasizes the stranger's bitterness toward the town, it also reveals a softer side of his nature. For example, might the fact that he is willing to spare the Richardses from his revenge reveal anything about the offense that angered him and the kind of person he really is?

2. **Greed and illusory wealth:** After all Hadleyburg's leading citizens—the "Nineteeners"—receive identical letters from "Howard L. Stephenson," each of them believes that he holds the key to claiming the $40,000 prize in the stranger's sack. These men and their wives begin spending this money in their imaginations and some actually start spending for real and go into debt. What does the story say about the human proclivity for greed and the foolhardiness of relying on illusory riches?

   Searching for illusory wealth is a theme to which Mark Twain frequently returned in his writings and is, in fact, the central theme of his first novel, *The Gilded Age* (1874), which he cowrote with Charles Dudley Warner. Partly autobiographical, *The Gilded Age* explores the damage done to a poor family by unfulfilled expectations of easy riches. Mark Twain's formal autobiographical writings tell how his own family expected eventually to become rich from his father's investment in a huge tract of land. That expectation, he wrote,

> kept us hoping and hoping during forty years, and forsook us at last. It put our energies to sleep and made visionaries of us—dreamers and indolent. We were always going to be rich next year—no occasion to work. It is good to begin life poor; it is good to begin life rich—these are wholesome; but to begin it poor and prospectively rich! The man who has not experienced it cannot imagine the curse of it.

The events in "The Man That Corrupted Hadleyburg" unfold within a period of only a few weeks, but that appears to be long enough for the prospect of sudden riches to begin doing similar damage to the members of the Nineteeners' families. Greed is the motive force behind the lies that Hadleyburg's citizens tell so they can claim the treasure sack. Is the story suggesting that these people are any greedier than others? Or, is it, perhaps, a commentary on human nature generally? Do any important Hadleyburg citizens not share in that greed?

An essay on this subject might take a wide variety of approaches. Perhaps the simplest would be to address the topic solely from within the context of the "The Man That Corrupted Hadleyburg." Carefully examine every allusion to greed within the story and try to determine whether the story exempts anyone. Another approach would be to look at the subject within the broader context of Mark Twain's other writings. *The Gilded Age* would be a good book to read, but it is an exceptionally long and sprawling book that wanders off in other directions. More to the point are two other short stories by Mark Twain that focus on the theme of illusory wealth: "The £1,000,000 Bank-Note" (1893) and "The $30,000 Bequest" (1904). Both these stories should provide insights into the theme of illusory wealth in "The Man That Corrupted Hadleyburg."

3. **Hypocrisy:** Are the citizens of Hadleyburg hypocrites or is their greed consistent with their pride in their town's reputation?

As hypocrisy is generally understood to be the pretense of having a virtue or belief that one does not really have, the people of Hadleyburg would appear to be hypocrites. Is that a fair assessment? Or might it be argued that the town deserved its reputation for incorruptibility until it undergoes a transformation when its previously virtuous citizens succumb to unprecedented temptation?

To write on this subject, begin by reviewing everything the story says, or hints at, about the town's past. For example, is the fact that Richards regards himself as "another man's slave" in Pinkerton's bank compatible with the town's reputation for incorruptibility? Look also for examples of characters' rationalizations of their dishonest attempts to claim the money sack.

Character

"The Man That Corrupted Hadleyburg" is very much a story about character, but we cannot expect a short story to develop its characters as fully as a novel. Nevertheless, to appreciate what this story is about, we need to learn as much as we can about its main characters—the Richardses and other "Nineteeners," Burgess, Halliday, and the stranger himself. To do that, look for every hint about these characters that the story provides.

Sample Topics:

1. **The Richardses:** Are they as innocent as they appear?

   Edward Richards and his wife are the central characters in the story, which opens with the stranger leaving his sack at their house and ends with their deaths. Like the town's other "Nineteeners," the Richardses succumb to temptation by knowingly lying to claim the treasure sack. However, they appear to be less venal than the others. Their conversations reveal them to be remorseful for their actions, and, if their words are to be believed, neither of them has ever before done anything of which they are ashamed. Moreover, because they are elderly, poor, and without family to contribute to their support, we may be inclined to make allowances for their solitary lapse in this story. However, we should ask if the Richardses are really any more deserving of sympathy than their fellow Nineteeners. And, if we conclude that they are equally corrupt, what does that say about human nature?

Susan K. Harris has argued that the Richardses are not only representative of their town but are actually the town's "most corrupt characters." She argues that whenever the Richardses are forced to choose between right and wrong, they consistently choose wrong. Is that observation valid? If it is, what moral points about human nature is "The Man That Corrupted Hadleyburg" trying to make?

2. **The Reverend Burgess:** Why does the stranger select Burgess to preside over the town meeting? What unnamed offense might Burgess be suspected of having committed? Does it matter to the story what that offense was?

Burgess occupies a curiously anomalous position within the story. Richards describes him as the "best-hated man" in Hadleyburg, as Burgess is reviled for an unspecified past offense that nearly got him run out of town. Nevertheless, the stranger instructs that Burgess be the person to preside over the town meeting at which the money sack is to be awarded, and Burgess's authority to conduct the meeting is not challenged.

A number of questions can be asked about Burgess. What offense may he have committed? Why has he stayed in Hadleyburg, even though he "will never get another congregation here"? Since it appears his innocence in the unnamed offense has never been established, why does the town now tolerate his presence and even meekly acquiesce to his authority in the town meeting? Is this behavior inconsistent? Or is it possible that the citizens of Hadleyburg feel some shame about their past treatment of Burgess? Is Burgess being sincere when he extols the virtues of Hadleyburg at that town meeting?

3. **The mysterious stranger:** Is the stranger a true character or merely a catalyst in the story?

Although the stranger's actions drive the story's plot, the story reveals little about him. What can be said about him? How might the story differ if more were known about him? To write on this subject, sift the entire story for every clue that reveals something about the kind of person the stranger is. Does all this information add up to anything resembling a character sketch? Try assuming that the story says much more about him and consider how that additional information might affect the story's plot. Does the element of mystery surrounding the stranger (who is sometimes called one of Mark Twain's "mysterious stranger" figures) strengthen or weaken the story, and, if so, how?

Philosophy and Ideas

"The Man That Corrupted Hadleyburg" treats a number of broad philosophical ideas, such as pride, greed, and personal ethics. Any of these would provide the basis for a good essay topic. This approach is related to the study of themes discussed above, but it operates at a more general level.

Sample Topic:

1. **Professional ethics:** Among the minor characters who figure most prominently in this story are Pinkerton the banker and Wilson the lawyer. Mark Twain depicts both disapprovingly, drawing on negative stereotypes of their professions. Is he offering a general condemnation of the ethics of the banking and legal professions?

Pinkerton is depicted as a mean, money-grubbing banker who has made life miserable for Richards, one of his cashiers. Wilson is a glib lawyer gifted "in the tricks and delusions of oratory." Both men are obviously greedy and unprincipled, as are all Hadleyburg's Nineteeners, but in contrast to the others, these men appear to serve as representatives of their professions.

In view of Mark Twain's known disillusionment with what he regarded as the excesses of the Gilded Age, it is fair to ask if he wanted to single out banking and law as particularly reprehensible professions.

This might be a fun subject on which to write an essay, as it would require you to dig up all the dirt on Pinkerton and Wilson you can find. Does the story treat these men any more harshly than representatives of any other professions? Some investigation into Mark Twain's attitude toward lawyers and bankers would help, but you should be able to craft an essay on this subject with what you find in the story.

Form and Genre

"The Man That Corrupted Hadleyburg" adheres to certain conventions of the short story form and might be regarded as a representative example of the short fiction Mark Twain wrote during his later years. As is typical of short fictional works, the story revolves around a narrow range of themes, provides limited background to its events, and does not attempt to develop its characters fully. In the end, it seems to leave unanswered more questions than it answers. If you wish to write an essay focusing on the short story form, you might do well to read this story along with Mark Twain's "The $30,000 Bequest" and "The £1,000,000 Bank-note" and look for common themes and structural devices in all three stories. James D. Wilson's *A Reader's Guide to the Short Stories of Mark Twain* would be a useful guide.

Sample Topic:

1. **Unresolved mysteries:** The story raises several questions that are never answered. What role do they play in the story's structure?

The most obvious unresolved question is the identity of the stranger. He appears at the beginning and end of the story and uses the name "Howard L. Stephenson," but who he really is and where he is from is never made certain. Moreover, the story never reveals the offense the town committed against him that moved him to undertake its corruption. Another and curiously parallel mystery is what great offense the townspeople believe the Reverend Burgess once committed. If, as Richards confesses to his wife, Burgess was truly innocent, why should Richards have feared that standing up for Burgess would turn the town against him? What kind of people would turn on a respected neighbor merely for proving an accused person innocent?

Compare and Contrast Essays

Compare and contrast subjects offer a wide scope for developing original essay ideas. However, if they are not approached properly, the results can be anything but original. The first step in preparing a compare and contrast essay is usually the compilation of lists of similarities and differences—between characters, between plots, between points of view, and so on. What makes this approach dangerous is the trap of allowing oneself to be satisfied with the lists themselves, as if these points mean anything alone. You must try to explain what makes the similarities and differences significant.

What makes compare and contrast essays especially attractive is that they allow you to be creative on two levels: first, in finding aspects of one or more works to compare; second, in finding significant points to make about the similarities and differences you observe. True originality is often difficult to achieve, but one of your best chances of attaining it lies in finding meaningful points of comparison.

Sample Topics:

1. **Hadleyburg v. other towns:** Does Hadleyburg resemble other towns in Mark Twain's fiction?

   The St. Petersburg of *Tom Sawyer* is often viewed as a wonderful model of an American town, with the best traits of small-town life. Indeed, Hannibal, Missouri, upon which St. Petersburg is modeled, now calls itself "America's Hometown." With all its evident faults, Hadleyburg seems not to fit the same model. Or is it possible that elements of the vanity, hypocrisy, greed, and small-mindedness that characterize Hadleyburg are also present in St. Petersburg and others of Mark Twain's important fictional towns?

One way to approach this subject is by cataloging the virtues and faults of Hadleyburg to construct the most balanced portrait of the town possible. Then, choose another Mark Twain work, such as *Tom Sawyer* or *Pudd'nhead Wilson,* and give its town a similar analysis. Dawson's Landing in *Pudd'nhead Wilson* would probably provide the easier comparison with Hadleyburg. However, St. Petersburg in *Tom Sawyer* would offer a more challenging comparison and be the better choice for a provocative essay. A side issue to consider is how analyzing a town in one story might help to illuminate the town in another story. Are there common elements in Hadleyburg, Dawson's Landing, and St. Petersburg that suggest that Mark Twain may have been thinking of the same place when he wrote about all three?

2. **The Richardses v. other Nineteeners:** What characteristics set the Richardses apart from Hadleyburg's other leading citizens?

As an alternative to the essay focusing solely on the Richardses suggested above, an essay comparing the Richardses to the town's other leading families would require a little more digging. You might begin by listing all the characters mentioned by name and noting every important fact about each of them. Make another list of the story's general observations about the town's Nineteeners—the 19 leading citizens who include the Richardses. What traits do they have in common? What, if anything, sets the Richardses apart from the others? Is there anything special about the Richardses that makes them better fitted to play a leading role in the story?

3. **Other Mark Twain stories:** How does "The Man That Corrupted Hadleyburg" compare to Mark Twain's other stories about illusory wealth?

As we observed in the discussion of greed and illusory wealth, Mark Twain frequently returned to the subject of seeking easy riches in his writings. Another of his stories that bears a particularly close resemblance to "The Man That Corrupted Hadleyburg" is "The $30,000 Bequest," which he published in 1904. Like "Hadleyburg," that story concerns a hoax involving a letter holding out the promise of great wealth. A young married couple, Saladin and Electra Foster, receive the letter from a distant relative, who tells them they will inherit $30,000 when he dies. Until then, however, they must tell no one and must not even inquire into his health. The Fosters are happy and well off at the time they receive the letter, but the expectation of immense wealth so disorders their values and alters their behavior that it gradually ruins their lives. Eventually, they learn that their relative's letter was merely a cruel joke. Afterward, they—like the Richardses of "Hadleyburg"—die from the shock.

Before writing on this subject, outline the main points of both stories, paying particular attention to important similarities and differences. Among the questions to ask are what the central theme of each story is and what each story says about human nature. Are the stories attempting to make the same points? If not, how do they differ?

If you would like to range further, look also at "The £1,000,000 Bank-note." This story, which Mark Twain wrote about six years earlier than "The Man That Corrupted Hadleyburg," is about a penniless American in London who is the guileless subject of a wager between two rich brothers, who give him custody of a banknote so large that he cannot possibly spend it. One brother bets that the man will starve within 30 days, the other that he will survive that period without being arrested. As in the other two stories, the man is given a letter of instructions.

Bibliography for "The Man That Corrupted Hadleyburg"

Briden, Earl F. "'The Man That Corrupted Hadleyburg.'" *The Mark Twain Encyclopedia*. Eds. J. R. LeMaster and James D. Wilson. New York: Garland, 1993. 484–86.

———. "Twainian Pedagogy and the No-Account Lessons of 'Hadleyburg.'" *Studies in Short Fiction* 28 (Spring 1991): 125–234.

Cope, Janice B. "The Man That Corrupted Hadleyburg." *Masterplots II: Short Story Series, Revised Edition.* Ed. Charles May. Pasadena, CA: Salem Press, 2004. 6: 2,523–525.

Emerson, Everett. *Mark Twain: A Literary Life.* Philadelphia: U of Pennsylvania P, 2000.

Harris, Susan K. "'Hadleyburg': Mark Twain's Dual Attack on Banal Theology and Banal Literature." *American Literary Realism, 1870–1910* 16, no. 2 (Autumn 1983): 240–52. Reprinted in *Mark Twain's Humor: Critical Essays.* Ed. David E. E. Sloane. New York: Garland, 1993.

Macnaughton, William R. *Mark Twain's Last Years as a Writer.* Columbia: U of Missouri P, 1979.

Mandia, Patricia M. "Greed Machines in 'The Man That Corrupted Hadleyburg' and 'The $30,000 Bequest.'" *Comedic Pathos: Black Humor in Twain's Fiction.* Jefferson, NC: McFarland, 1991. 68–83.

The Man That Corrupted Hadleyburg. PBS television dramatization (1981).

Messent, Peter. *Mark Twain.* New York: St. Martin's Press, 1997.

——. *The Short Works of Mark Twain: A Critical Study.* Philadelphia: U of Pennsylvania P, 2001.

Ozick, Cynthia. Introduction. *The Man That Corrupted Hadleyburg and Other Stories and Essays.* By Mark Twain. New York: Oxford UP, 1996. xxxi–xlix.

Quirk, Tom. *Mark Twain: A Study of the Short Fiction.* New York: Twayne Publishers, 1997.

Railton, Stephen. "Looking for Refuge: *Pudd'nhead Wilson* and 'Hadleyburg.'" *Mark Twain: A Short Introduction.* Malden, MA: Blackwell, 2004. 96–115.

——. "Mark Twain Tries to Get the Last Laugh: Hadleyburg and Other Performances." *Mark Twain Annual* 3 (2005): 23–36.

Rasmussen, R. Kent. *"The Man That Corrupted Hadleyburg."* In *Critical Companion to Mark Twain.* New York: Facts On File, 2007. I: 320–28

Rubin-Dorsky, Jeffrey. Afterword, For Further Reading. *The Man That Corrupted Hadleyburg and Other Stories and Essays.* By Mark Twain. New York: Oxford UP, 1996. 1–20. (Back matter has separate pagination.)

Rucker, Mary E. "Moralism and Determinism in 'The Man That Corrupted Hadleyburg.'" *Studies in Short Fiction* 14 (Winter 1977): 49–54.

Rule, Henry B. "The Role of Satan in 'The Man That Corrupted Hadleyburg.'" *Studies in Short Fiction* 6 (Fall 1977): 619–29.

Scharnhorst, Gary. "Paradise Revisited: Twain's 'The Man That Corrupted Hadleyburg.'" *Studies in Short Fiction* 18 (Winter 1981): 59–64.

Smith, Henry Nash. *Mark Twain: The Development of a Writer.* Cambridge, MA: Harvard UP, 1962.

Twain, Mark. "The Man That Corrupted Hadleyburg." *Collected Tales, Sketches, Speeches, & Essays, 1891–1910.* Ed. Louis J. Budd. New York: Library of America. 390–438.

———. *Mark Twain's Autobiography.* Ed. Albert Bigelow Paine. 2 vols. New York: Harper & Brothers, 1924.

Wilson, James D. "'The Man That Corrupted Hadleyburg.'" *A Reader's Guide to the Short Stories of Mark Twain.* Boston: G. K. Hall, 1987. 199–215.

"THE WAR PRAYER"

READING TO WRITE

"THE WAR Prayer" is nearly as simple as a story can be and still be regarded a story. After a Christian pastor delivers an impassioned prayer for the military success of men about to go off to war to his rabidly patriotic congregation, a stranger enters his church. This man stuns the congregation with an expanded version of the pastor's prayer that calls graphic attention to the horrific realities of war. Nothing else happens in the story.

This powerful antiwar statement occupies a curious place among Mark Twain's published works. After he wrote it in 1905, his daughter Jean and several friends warned him not to publish it because its message was "sacrilegious." He was satisfied to leave it unpublished during his lifetime. According to Albert Bigelow Paine, his biographer and personal confidant, Mark Twain feared that publication of the story might brand him a lunatic in the public eye. "I have told the whole truth in that," he reportedly said, "and only dead men can tell the truth in this world. It can be published after I am dead." Paine was also Mark Twain's literary executor; he published part of "The War Prayer" in his massive 1912 biography of Mark Twain, and he later published the full story, for the first time, in a collection titled *Europe & Elsewhere* (1923). The story has been reprinted many times since then, and since 1968, it has been continuously in print as a self-contained and illustrated book.

"The War Prayer" presents special challenges to essay writing. Its short length may be an attractive feature to a would-be essay writer, but that same brevity also limits the range of topics on which you can write. To find an interesting and worthwhile topic, you will have to be receptive to subtle points as you read the story. You may discover that only a few words will suggest a topic you can develop into something meaningful. Note the richness of language and imagery in the story's first two sentences alone:

> It was a time of great and exalting excitement. The country was up in arms, the war was on, in every breast burned the holy fire of patriotism; the drums were beating, the bands playing, the toy pistols popping, the bunched firecrackers hissing and spluttering; on every hand and far down the receding and fading spread of roofs and balconies a fluttering wilderness of flags flashed in the sun; daily the young volunteers marched down the wide avenue gay and fine in their new uniforms, the proud fathers and mothers and sisters and sweethearts cheering them with voices choked with happy emotion as they swung by; nightly the packed mass-meetings listened, panting, to patriot oratory which stirred the deepest deeps of their hearts . . .

A great deal is going on in that passage. Words such as "bands," "beating drums," "toy pistols," "firecrackers," and "flags" evoke vivid images, but if you read the passage more carefully, you will sense that other things are going on beneath the surface. For example, the word "proud," which also appears elsewhere in the story, describes the feelings of the relatives and friends of the soldiers going off to war. The story seems to be saying that pride is the driving force behind wartime patriotism and that soldiers volunteer to fight and risk their lives primarily to make their "dear ones" proud. Pride might make a good essay topic. To write about that, study the story carefully for other evidence that pride is behind wartime fever. At the same time, avoid jumping to overly narrow conclusions. Even if pride is a driving force behind patriotic behavior, it is not necessarily the only one that is important.

Though brief, the stranger's oration is another rich source of ideas for essays. Consider this passage that he utters before beginning his formal prayer:

> "God's servant and yours has prayed his prayer. Has he paused, and taken thought? Is it one prayer? No, it is two—one uttered, the other not. Both

have reached the ear of Him who heareth all supplications, the spoken and the unspoken. Ponder this—keep it in mind. If you would beseech a blessing upon yourself, beware! lest without intent you invoke a curse upon your neighbor at the same time. If you pray for the blessing of rain upon your crop which needs it, by that act you are possibly praying for a curse upon some neighbor's crop which may not need rain and can be injured by it."

This passage can be read as an attack on the selfishness and narrow-mindedness of people who are concerned with only their own interests. It might also be read as an attack on Christians for having the conceit to believe that God looks after their interests alone. It might further be read as an attack on members of the clergy, who presumably should know better.

As you study the story, you will find many nuanced passages that are similarly suggestive. If you have trouble settling on a topic, try picking one at random. Ideas generally generate more ideas, so if you start to write about an idea, there is a good chance that the mere act of writing will begin to stimulate new ideas.

TOPICS AND STRATEGIES

This section offers both general and specific ideas for possible essay topics, but you certainly need not limit your choice to those discussed here. If you do select one of these topics, you should not regard this discussion as an outline of what you should write. The purpose of these discussions is simply to help you develop your own ideas. Moreover, the broad categories here are only to help you find subjects that interest you most; some topics could be discussed under other headings. It is the topics, not the categories, that matter.

The discussions that follow raise many questions about "The War Prayer," but few of these questions—or those that you raise yourself—have right or wrong answers. Try to avoid the trap of getting bogged down in fruitless attempts to prove a point. The strength of your essay will come not merely from the decisiveness of the conclusions it reaches, but from the power and clarity of the arguments that it advances. Whatever topics you choose to write about, use your imagination and try to consider all possible sides of every question. The keys to successful essay writing are originality of thought and clearness and force of argument.

A good way to stimulate your imagination is to outline arguments that take different sides on the same issues. For example, if you were to take the position that "The War Prayer" is, at least in part, an attack on Christian arrogance and complacent belief in the notion that "God is on our side," you would doubtless begin by outlining all the points in the story that support that position. You should also outline all the points you can find to argue the *opposite* point of view. Whatever points you find may not alter your original opinion, but some of them may reveal weaknesses in your chosen argument and thereby give you the opportunity to strengthen your case.

Themes

Despite the brevity of "The War Prayer," it touches several themes that could make compelling essay topics. What makes these themes especially compelling is their timelessness. The central message of Mark Twain's story is as relevant today as it was during his time. Whenever any nation goes to war, it is natural for its citizens to hope for victory and to see the soldiers fighting for their country as heroes. If the description of the patriotic fervor swelling up within the unnamed country of "The War Prayer" strikes you as exaggerated, compare it to what has happened during military conflicts in which the United States has been engaged during your own lifetime. For example, at the start of both the Gulf War and the Iraq War, patriotism rose to a fever pitch in the United States. American flags popped up everywhere, millions of yellow ribbons wrapped around trees mysteriously appeared, billboards and bumper stickers bearing patriotic slogans proliferated, and Americans were constantly exhorted to pray for victory. Smartly uniformed soldiers may not have marched down city streets accompanied by exhilarating martial music as in times past, but the soldiers going off to the Middle East were constantly celebrated on television broadcasts.

As you read Mark Twain's story, think about recent events and ask yourself if there is any fundamental difference between modern attitudes toward war and patriotism and those of Mark Twain's time. The focus of whatever essay you write should be on "The War Prayer" itself. However, you will find the story more meaningful if you think about its relevance to events such as the Gulf War of 1991 and the Iraq War of 2003. (For personal opinions of how the story is relevant to current events, read some of the customer reviews of the book edition of "The War Prayer" on Amazon.com on the Web.)

Sample Topics:

1. **War:** Is what the stranger says about the overlooked consequences of victory in war relevant to real-life conflicts?

"The War Prayer" is very much a read-between-the-lines kind of story. It is brief and its few words deal mostly in generalities and symbols. However, its short form works well for its central message, which appears to be this: In our passionate desire to see our own side victorious in war, we should not overlook the dreadful suffering that our victory will bring to the innocent. Is that an accurate description of the stranger's message? What does that message imply in a conflict such as the modern Iraq War?

   To write on this subject, read up on a modern conflict, such as the U.S. invasion of Iraq in 2003, and analyze it within the context of "The War Prayer." Did the citizens of at least one nation in the conflict go into the war with a patriotic fervor similar to that described in the story? Did they seem to have their attitude that God was on their side and that prayer would aid their cause? Were the consequences of their quest for victory as devastating to the innocent and weak as those described by the story's strange orator?

2. **Religious faith:** What does "The War Prayer" say about religious beliefs, faith in prayer, and the notion that "God is on our side"?

"The War Prayer" says nothing explicit about the denomination of the unnamed church in which the story is set. The fact that the story takes place within a "church" with a "pastor" almost certainly makes the people in the story Christians, and they are very likely Protestants. Does that matter? Would their spiritual leader's prayer be different if the congregationalists were Roman Catholics, Jews, Muslims, Buddhists, or something else? As with other aspects of this story, Mark Twain seems to be trying to make universal points about religion and about faith in the power of prayer. What points does the story make?

If you write on this subject, you should consider it from at least three perspectives. The first is what the pastor's prayer implies about his followers' beliefs. Next is the stranger's rejoinder to that prayer. And, finally, what does the congregation's dismissal of the stranger as a "lunatic" imply about its members' religious beliefs? Is the story suggesting that when nations go to war, their citizens tend to believe that God is on their side and their side alone? As you read the story, look for every hint, every nuance, that suggests something about the religious beliefs of the people in the unnamed country.

For additional ideas on Mark Twain's attitude toward religion, read some of his other writings on the subject. Of particular value are his posthumously published *Letters from the Earth* (1962) and Howard Baetzhold and Joseph B. McCullough's collection, *The Bible According to Mark Twain* (1995).

Character

The only figure approximating anything that can be called a character in "The War Prayer" is the stranger who appears in the church and stuns the congregation with his oration. It would be difficult, but not impossible, to squeeze a substantial essay out of the few details about him that the story provides. However, the very difficulty of that challenge could make for an exceptionally original essay.

Mark Twain is believed to have modeled the story's stranger on Henry Clay Dean (1822–87), an eccentric, self-educated man he met while living in Iowa during the mid-1850s. When the Civil War was stirring up patriotic fervor in Iowa in early 1861, a lecture agent hastily grabbed a scruffy and tattered Dean off a Keokuk street to fill in for a lecturer who missed his speaking engagement. According to Mark Twain's second-hand account of the incident, the audience initially thought that Dean was an "escaped lunatic." However, his powerful oratory eventually won over his listeners, who concluded that he was an "escaped archangel."

This background information may or may not color your ideas about the stranger in "The War Prayer."

Sample Topic:

1. **The aged stranger:** What can be said about the orator in "The War Prayer"? Does it matter who he really is?

"The War Prayer" is such a short work that you should read it several times to ferret out every detail and nuance regarding the stranger. A first question to consider is whether the stranger is supposed to be a real human being, some kind of a heavenly angel, or a figment of the congregation's imagination. Does the fact that Mark Twain apparently modeled the stranger's oratorical performance on Henry Clay Dean's Keokuk speech have any bearing on this question? If you conclude that the story's stranger is supposed to be a real human being, could the congregation's surmise that he is a "lunatic" be correct? And, if that is correct, does that fact have any bearing on the validity of the message that the stranger delivers? Does the congregation regard him as a lunatic solely because of the content of his message? Or might they be influenced by his personal appearance and the manner in which he seized control of the meeting?

What clues does the story provide to suggest that the stranger is either an angel or an imaginary figure? The brief physical description provided gives him somewhat ethereal qualities, but could a lunatic fit the same description?

History and Context

Mark Twain wrote this story in 1905, after he had become disenchanted with the growing U.S. drift toward becoming an imperial power around the turn of the 20th century. He opposed imperialism in all parts of the world and strongly believed that America, above all other nations, had no business trying to be an imperial power. During the Spanish-American War of 1898, he had welcomed the U.S. role in ending Spanish rule over Cuba and the Philippines and hoped to see both those countries attain self-rule. However, he was quickly disillusioned by the ugly turn that the Philippine independence struggle took when it became clear that the United States had no intention of giving up its power in the Philippines after driving the Spanish out. He responded by beginning to publish angry articles condemning American imperialism. "The War Prayer" can be read within the context of those anti-imperialist writings, which Jim Zwick collected in *Mark Twain's Weapons of Satire* (1992).

Although Mark Twain most likely had the U.S. conflict in the Philippines in mind when he wrote "The War Prayer," a notable aspect of its construction is the absence of any clear references to time or place. Apart from the story's allusions to ostensibly Christian "churches" and "pastors" and its hints about modern firearms, the story could be set in virtually any country during virtually any time period. In fact, during the 1960s, interest in the story in the United States grew along with opposition to the Vietnam War. American military incursions into the Middle East during the 1990s and early 21st century renewed interest in "The War Prayer."

Sample Topic:

1. **A universal antiwar story?:** Should "The War Prayer" be regarded as a universal story? To what extent is it tied to the period in which Mark Twain wrote it?

A truly universal story is one that could be set in virtually any time or place. As was pointed out earlier, "The War Prayer" has the clear markings of a universal story. Or, more accurately, it lacks markings that typically tie stories to specific times and places. It does not reveal where it takes place, it gives no hint what war is being fought, and it provides only loose hints that its setting may be a modern Christian country. Aside from those clues, is there anything in the story that limits its universality? Perhaps more to the point—is there anything in the story to suggest that Mark Twain wrote it during the early 20th century to condemn American interference in the Philippines?

To lend substance to an essay on this subject, you should familiarize yourself with descriptions of the patriotic manifestations with which the United States and other countries have gone into wars. Select at least three different conflicts and focus on at least two different nations involved in those conflicts. At least one of the conflicts you examine should come from a war fought *after* Mark Twain died in 1910. Gather enough information to sketch portraits of how citizens responded to their countries' entries into the wars, then compare your sketches with the descriptions of patriotic fervor in "The War Prayer." Is the story an accurate model of how patriots have responded to war in different times and places?

Interesting data could come from both the Union and the Confederate sides of the U.S. Civil War, the American side of the Spanish-American War, the German and French sides of World War I, and the American side of both the 1991 Gulf War and the 2003 Iraq War. You need not, however, limit yourself to these choices. You should be able to find sufficient information in any good general history of each conflict.

Philosophy and Ideas

Because the line between themes and philosophical ideas in "The War Prayer" is a thin one, you will find topics on war and religion in the Themes section above that might equally belong in this section. The most prominent idea in the story concerns the consequences of excessive, blind patriotism, a subject of great interest to Mark Twain, especially during the last years of his life when he fumed over American interventions in other nations. His anti-imperialist writings contain many scathing remarks about unthinking patriotism. He loved to distill his thoughts into brief maxims, in one of which he defines a patriot as "the person who can holler the loudest without knowing what he is hollering about." Does that observation apply to the churchgoers in "The War Prayer"?

Mark Twain saw blind patriotism as one of the forces behind the greed for land and the imperialist impulses of national governments, including that of the United States. In an 1896 journal entry, he wrote that patriotism is

a word which always commemorates a robbery. There isn't a foot of land in the world which doesn't represent the ousting & re-ousting of a long line of successive "owners" who each in turn, as "patriots," with proud &

swelling hearts defended it against the next gang of "robbers" who came to steal it & *did*—& became swelling-hearted patriots in *their* turn.

Note the similarity of that passage's imagery to the language used in "The War Prayer." Other observations on unthinking patriotism can be found in Jim Zwick's collection of Mark Twain's anti-imperialist writings, *Mark Twain's Weapons of Satire* (1992), and in several of Mark Twain's posthumously published stories in *Letters from the Earth* (1962).

Sample Topic:

1. **The holy fire of patriotism:** How does "The War Prayer" make a case against excessive patriotism?

As the prefatory remarks in this section point out, the dangers of excessive and unthinking patriotism constitute the central idea in "The War Prayer." The story opens with vivid descriptions of joyous demonstrations of patriotic fervor throughout some unnamed country about to go to war. The next paragraph shifts the focus to a single church, whose pastor pours his congregation's patriotic feelings into an impassioned prayer asking God for victory. The mood then suddenly shifts, when a newly arrived stranger elaborates on the pastor's prayer, articulating the unspoken and horrific implications of a patriotic victory in a prayer of his own.

The story as a whole seems to condemn the concept of patriotism, yet it is difficult to find any passages that explicitly criticize or denounce patriotism. Is the story, then, truly an attack on unthinking patriotism? If so, how does it deliver that message? Can a different interpretation be read into the story?

Form and Genre

An important aspect of the construction of "The War Prayer" is the virtual absence of dialogue. The story divides almost exactly in half: The first half is a description of the setting related by an anonymous third-person narrator; almost all the second half is the stranger's monologue, most of which is taken up by his prayer. The story is so brief and so narrowly focused on a single incident that it might be more accurate to classify it as a sketch. The distinctions between sketches and short stories might serve as the basis for an essay on "The War Prayer," but debating the work's proper classification would be a sterile exercise, unless some greater significance can be attached. You would have to demonstrate why it matters which classification applies. On the other hand, questions about classifying the story might take on new and more interesting dimensions if you were to read it in its illustrated book edition.

Sample Topic:

1. **"The War Prayer" as a prose poem:** Does the story's publication in the form of an illustrated book alter its message or power?

As American involvement in the Vietnam War escalated during the late 1960s, a powerful antiwar movement arose. In response to this movement, Harper & Row—Mark Twain's official publisher since the late 1890s—issued "The War Prayer" in a small volume. Containing about 80 unnumbered pages (many of which are blank), the book was profusely illustrated by John Groth (1902–88), an artist and combat veteran of World War II. The book appears to have remained in print continuously since 1968. Groth's vigorous line drawings add starkly graphic interpretations to Mark Twain's text. Perhaps more impressive, however, is the effect achieved by spreading the text out over a large number of pages. Each page at the beginning of the story contains 19 brief lines that have the appearance of a poem, with each page facing one of Groth's drawings. The amount of text on pages containing the stranger's prayer ranges from a single word to several lines. This format seems to have the effect of giving each line, sometimes even individual words, greater power. The format may not be what Mark Twain had in mind when he wrote the story, but if it strengthens his message without altering his words, is it reasonable to think that he might have approved of the book?

If you write on this subject, you must read "The War Prayer" in both its standard prose form and in its illustrated book form. There are doubtless many equally valid ways to approach this subject, but you cannot go far wrong if you start by studying the story in its standard textual form in any of the many books in which it has been published. After you form some conclusions about the nature of the story's message and the effectiveness of its prose, read the story in its illustrated edition to judge how the radically different format alters the story's message. Does the story work effectively as a prose poem? Are there elements in Mark Twain's original language that are naturally suited for poetry? Did the book's editors make wise choices by dividing sentences into separate lines and breaking text between pages? Your essay should give examples of where such editorial decisions strengthen the text and where better decisions might have been made. You might also examine the contributions of Groth's illustrations to the text.

Language, Symbols, and Imagery

It has been pointed out elsewhere in this chapter that "The War Prayer" is rich in symbols and imagery. Three types of imagery predominate: patriotic, religious, and military. The most obvious images are the many patriotic symbols mentioned at the beginning of the story. The first paragraph alone mentions "drums," "bands," "toy pistols," "firecrackers," "flags," "uniforms," "mass-meetings," and "oratory." A close reading of the story will find other types of imagery. If you choose to write on this subject, you will need to identify the imagery that is used and explain what it contributes to the story.

Sample Topic:

1. **Symbolism:** How does "The War Prayer" use symbols to obtain effects?

   In a brief story that revolves around a single incident and lacks both characters and dialogue, symbolic language takes on greater meaning. An essay on this subject should examine the story's language carefully and identify the symbols and imagery that it uses. The patriotic symbols lacing the story's opening paragraphs are so powerful you should be careful not to overlook others that appear in the story. Can the story's symbols be classified in a meaningful way? Does any one set of symbols seem more effective than any other?

Compare and Contrast Essays

Because of its brevity, "The War Prayer" provides a limited range of subjects for meaty essay topics. To find more fruitful subject matter, you may need to go outside the story and find other Mark Twain writings to compare it with. The most obvious subjects to build compare and contrast essays on are war, religion, and patriotism. Mark Twain wrote comparatively little about war, but a Civil War story he wrote in 1885—20 years before "The War Prayer"—would make an ideal counterpoint for a comparative essay.

Mark Twain did write a great deal on religion, so religious themes can be found in many of his other works. To find ideas, browse through a book such as *Letters from the Earth* (1962) or *The Bible According to Mark Twain* (1995). If you are up for a particularly ambitious challenge, read Mark Twain's *Personal Recollections of Joan of Arc* (1896), a novel about the early 15th-century French maiden who claimed she was directed by God to command French armies against English invaders. An essay examining the relevance of "The War Prayer" to Mark Twain's admiring portrait of Joan of Arc could be fascinating, but writing it would be a major challenge.

Sample Topics:

1. **A Civil War story:** How does Mark Twain's "The Private History of a Campaign That Failed" foreshadow the themes of "The War Prayer"?

   Written for a magazine series of true-life memoirs of men who fought in the Civil War, Mark Twain's "The Private History of a Campaign That Failed" appears to be a genuine account of his brief experience as a soldier in an irregular Confederate unit in Missouri at the start of the war. The story chronicles the confusion, disorder, and monotony of untrained soldiers continually retreating from an unseen enemy until they ambush a stranger on a horse, and the narrator decides that he is not cut out for war. The fact that the story's narrator is anonymous is significant—Mark Twain was never in the Confederate army. Moreover, Missouri was never part of the Confederacy. Mark Twain had a brief experience in a state militia unit, but he simply invented most of his story. However, what matters here is not the facts of his story, but its theme—namely, that war is an ugly business and that killing strangers is a terrible thing. Comparisons between this story and "The War Prayer" should provide the basis for an interesting essay. If you choose to write on this subject, a central question to ask is whether the core ideas of "The War Prayer" are to be found in the 1885 story. Conversely, does the earlier story contain any ideas that contradict themes in "The War Prayer"? If you wish to broaden the scope of your essay, read "A Curious Experience," a wholly fictional story set in the Civil War that Mark Twain wrote in 1881; you can find it in many collections of Mark Twain's stories. For more of Mark Twain's observations about the Civil War, see the later chapters (especially chapter 35) of *Life on the Mississippi* (1883).

2. **"Mysterious strangers"**: Does the stranger in "The War Prayer" resemble "mysterious stranger" figures in other Mark Twain writings?

A recurrent motif in Mark Twain's later writings is the appearance of strangers who enter what are typically small or closed communities, upset the existing social orders, and then disappear. Mark Twain wrote a series of interrelated and mostly unfinished manuscripts that have come to be known as the "Mysterious Stranger" stories. In each of these stories—which include *No. 44, the Mysterious Stranger* (1982)—the stranger figure is an angel with miraculous powers who poses as a human boy. Another story with a stranger who lacks such powers but who nevertheless upsets the social order in a town is "The Man That Corrupted Hadleyburg" (1899)—the subject of another chapter in this book. Some critics have even classified the novel *A Connecticut Yankee in King Arthur's Court* (1889) as a mysterious stranger story because its late 19th-century protagonist is, in effect, a mysterious stranger whose miraculous powers upset the existing order in sixth-century England.

If you write on this subject, you should read at least two other Mark Twain stories with important stranger figures. (Do *not*, however, include the frequently reprinted novel *The Mysterious Stranger* that was first published under Mark Twain's name in 1916, as it is not a completely authentic Mark Twain work.) Your goal should be to examine affinities between the stranger of "The War Prayer" and other strangers in Mark Twain writings. You should also look beyond the strangers to find similar patterns in other elements of the stories. For example, the members of the congregation in "The War Prayer" appear to be complacent and smugly confident of their own virtues and rightness. Can the same be said for members of the communities that Mark Twain's other strangers enter? Do any of those other stories share the same sense of purpose that "The War Prayer" has? Use your imagination to find other parallels among the stories. Does Mark Twain's frequent use of this motif say anything about his views on how changes are effected in communities?

Bibliography for "The War Prayer"

Amazon.com (www.amazon.com) (Commercial Web site on which many reviews of "The War Prayer" are posted.)

Baetzhold, Howard G., and Joseph B. McCullough, eds. *The Bible According to Mark Twain: Irreverent Writings on Eden, Heaven, and the Flood by America's Master Satirist.* Athens: U of Georgia P, 1995.

Britton, Wesley. "Tom Paine and Mark Twain: 'Common Sense' as a Source for 'The War Prayer.'" *Conference of College Teachers of English Studies* 54 (1989): 13–19.

Fisher Fishkin, Shelley, and Tatsumi Takayumi, eds. "New Perspectives on 'The War-Prayer': An International Forum." *Mark Twain Studies* (Japan) 2 (October 2006): 7–118 (Includes corrected text of "The War Prayer," a facsimile of Mark Twain's original manuscript, and 25 essays).

Garrett, Greg. "'The War Prayer.'" *The Mark Twain Encyclopedia.* Eds. J. R. LeMaster and James D. Wilson. New York: Garland, 1993. 769–70.

Gibson, William M., ed. *Mark Twain's Mysterious Stranger Manuscripts.* Berkeley: U of California P, 1969.

Paine, Albert Bigelow. *Mark Twain, A Biography: The Personal and Literary Life of Samuel Langhorne Clemens.* 3 vols. New York: Harper & Bros., 1912.

Rasmussen, R. Kent. *"The War Prayer."* In *Critical Companion to Mark Twain.* New York: Facts On File, 2007. I: 551–53

Smith, Janet, ed. *Mark Twain on the Damned Human Race.* New York: Hill & Wang, 1962.

Twain, Mark. *Letters from the Earth.* Ed. Bernard DeVoto. New York: Harper & Row, 1962.

———. *No. 44, The Mysterious Stranger.* Berkeley: U of California P, 1982.

———. *The War Prayer.* Illustrated by John Groth. New York: Perennial Library, 1971.

———. *"The War Prayer." Collected Tales, Sketches, Speeches, & Essays, 1891–1910.* Ed. Louis J. Budd. New York: Library of America, 1992. 652–55.

Tuckey, John S., ed. *Mark Twain's "The Mysterious Stranger" and the Critics.* Belmont, CA: Wadsworth Publishing, 1968.

Zwick, Jim, ed. *Mark Twain's Weapons of Satire: Anti-imperialist Writings on the Philippine-American War.* Syracuse, NY: Syracuse UP, 1992.

ROUGHING IT

READING TO WRITE

A LIVELY AND often riotous account of Mark Twain's real experiences in Nevada, California, and Hawaii during the early 1860s, Roughing It is one of Mark Twain's most enduring books. There are many reasons why people still read it more than 135 years after its first publication. It is packed with amusing tall tales, memorable characters, and startling adventures. However, despite the fact that it is full of fun and outrageous comic exaggeration, the book also contains vivid and authentic descriptions of western landscapes, frontier towns and mining camps and their inhabitants, and transportation in the days before railroads transformed the West that make it a valuable document of the history of the American frontier.

Roughing It is a big, complex book and a prime example of the difficulty, and perhaps pointlessness, of trying to pigeonhole Mark Twain's works. The book is generally classified as a travel work; however, it is also often seen as a work of autobiography and even as a novel. Is it possible for one book to fit all those genres at one time? Or, might the book shift from one genre to another as it progresses? Critic James M. Cox argues that the book "begins as autobiographical narrative and ends as a travel book." Could the book also be something else in between?

Regardless of the answers to those questions, it is important to keep the complex nature of *Roughing It* in mind while reading and writing about it. If you make the mistake of thinking that it is only one kind of book as you read it, you may get confused as it switches into a different mode. Perhaps the central question to ask during your reading is what it is really about, in other words, what interests its narrator more—talking about himself or talking about the regions through which he travels. Does he tend to hold the same interests throughout or do his interests shift as his narrative progresses? It may help you to begin by considering the basic genres into which the book seems to fall.

If we wish to read *Roughing It* as autobiography, the first thing to understand is that, although it follows the general outline of Mark Twain's experiences in the Far West between mid-1861 and late 1866, many of its descriptions of incidents and people are either embellishments or wholesale inventions. Moreover, some of the most significant experiences that Mark Twain had during those years are not even hinted at. For example, *Roughing It* says nothing about any of the famous hoaxes he perpetrated while writing for a Nevada newspaper or even the jumping frog story that made him famous while he was living in California in late 1865. In fact, it does not even mention his adoption of the pen name "Mark Twain" when writing for the Nevada newspaper in 1863. Even more significant, the book barely hints that the Civil War (1861–65) was raging in the East while he was in the West, let alone reveal what he thought about the war or what effect it was having on the West. Why the book deliberately ignores the war would make a good topic for an essay, but it would be one that requires some serious research into Mark Twain's life during that period.

Although *Roughing It*'s narrative voice is in the first person, it is not always certain that the narrator is meant to be Mark Twain or Sam Clemens. As with the narrator of the piloting chapters of *Life on the Mississippi* (1883), which recall Mark Twain's earlier steamboating years, the narrator of *Roughing It* is a young and naive greenhorn—a person very different from the nearly 26-year-old, well-traveled Sam Clemens who went to Nevada with his brother, Orion Clemens, in 1861. The first chapter of the book opens with a description of the narrator that immediately distances him from the real Sam Clemens. While expressing his envy of his older brother, whose new government job in Nevada Territory will take him into a land of adventure, he says, "I never had been away from home, and that word 'travel' had a seductive charm for me." This was written by a man who immediately before going west had been away from home on his own for eight years and had just spent four years piloting steamboats up and down the

Mississippi River. How different might *Roughing It* read if its narrator were a more realistic representation of its author, and what would it lose if it were?

Another important point about the narrator is that he never mentions his own name or that of his brother. Although his identity is not really a secret, he says almost nothing that might help identify him. That omission further distances Mark Twain from his narrator and allows him greater freedom in shaping his story. As you read *Roughing It*, look for clues to the narrator's identity and watch for a shift in his persona about halfway through the book, around the time that he becomes a newspaper reporter. In the book's first half, pay close attention to how the text exaggerates the narrator's youth and inexperience. An extreme example can be found in the narrator's description of his brother's meeting with the Mormon leader Brigham Young in Salt Lake City in chapter 13:

> When the audience was ended and we were retiring from the presence, he [Young] put his hand on my head, beamed down on me in an admiring way and said to my brother:
>
> 　"Ah—your child, I presume? Boy, or girl?"

Mark Twain obviously wrote that passage in an attempt at humor, not as a serious exercise in autobiography. Could he have written it the same way if he had identified himself as Sam Clemens or Mark Twain? (Incidentally, he and his brother never actually met Brigham Young, who was away from Salt Lake City when they passed through Utah.)

In 2002, when the Hallmark Channel aired a four-hour adaptation of *Roughing It*, the program's credits pointed out that the story was biography, not fiction. That seems an odd claim for the film to make, since its credits also say that the story is "based on the novel by Mark Twain." This confusion reflects the ambiguities of the book itself. Once you recognize that *Roughing It* cannot be read as reliable autobiography, what can you make of the book if you try reading it as a novel?

Novels are generally defined as fictional prose works of substantial length. *Roughing It* is clearly a lengthy prose work, and it does contain a great deal of fiction. Do these attributes alone make it a novel? Or do novels require other elements, such as developed characters, recognizable plotlines, or something else? Does *Roughing It* have any these elements? These are questions for you to consider, and they may even provide the basis for essays. Meanwhile, consider some of the elements of *Roughing It* that readers might *not* expect to find in novels—namely, elements found in travel books.

Mark Twain's first major book, *The Innocents Abroad,* is a true travel book describing his journey to Europe and the Holy Land on the cruise ship *Quaker City* in 1867. An immediate success when it was published two years later, it went on to become the best-selling American travel book of the 19th century; it was also Mark Twain's most widely read book during his lifetime. He also wrote other travel books and was probably better known as a travel writer than as a novelist. The fabulous success of *The Innocents Abroad* naturally made both Mark Twain and his publisher eager to come out with a similar book as soon as possible. The result was *Roughing It,* published in 1872.

Roughing It's chapters fall into three broad groups. The first 21 describe the overland journey that Mark Twain undertook with his brother to reach Nevada in mid-1861. The next 40 cover his experiences in Nevada and California over the ensuing five years. Most of the remaining chapters describe his months in Hawaii in 1866. Each section differs from the others in content, style, and tone, particularly in how it discusses the places through which its narrator moves. For example, the early chapters on the overland stagecoach journey say a great deal about the rigors of travel and the diverse characters whom the narrator encounters, but relatively little about the country through which the stagecoach passes. In the Nevada and California chapters, the narrator does less moving around. These chapters contain some descriptive material, but perhaps not as much as one would expect from a travel book, as the narrator's attention is taken up with his own doings. Nevertheless, you will find things in these chapters to suggest that travel writing was at least part of Mark Twain's purpose. By contrast, the 16 Hawaiian chapters are very much the kind of stuff one would expect to find in a travel book—rich descriptions of scenery, detailed statistics on Hawaii's economy, pithy analyses of Hawaiian people and politics, and fascinating anecdotes from local history. Indeed, these chapters are so different from the rest of

Roughing It, that some readers do not regard them as an integral part of the book.

There are reasons for differences among the book's sections, and you should keep them in mind as you read. They have a great deal to do with *how* Mark Twain wrote each section, and you may find that the essay topic on which you elect to write requires you to consider only one or two sections of the book, so you should be careful not to overgeneralize. When Mark Twain was working on the Nevada and California chapters, many incidents, people, and places he described were so fresh in his mind that he could move from episode to episode easily, picking and choosing from among his recollections what things to emphasize. By contrast, when he began writing about his overland journey, he discovered that he could scarcely remember a single detail of that trip. Given the vividness of many of the published chapters about that journey, that fact may seem astonishing. However, remember that the entire journey lasted only three weeks and carried Mark Twain rapidly over regions he saw only once. To recall details from that trip, he borrowed a detailed journal kept by his brother. It is therefore natural that the chapters that he wrote on the journey are sketchy and liable to be full of invention.

The Hawaiian chapters are of a very different nature for two reasons. First, when Mark Twain began writing *Roughing It,* he had no intention of covering his time in Hawaii and added the Hawaiian chapters only after discovering that the pages he had written on Nevada and California fell short of what his publisher expected. It happened that he had gone to Hawaii as a correspondent for a Sacramento, California, newspaper, for which he had written 25 letters. Much as he had done with his travel letters on Europe and the Holy Land when he wrote *The Innocents Abroad,* he drew on his Hawaiian letters to complete *Roughing It.* However, it would be a mistake to think that he simply copied those letters into his book. *Roughing It* includes entirely new material on Hawaii and contains many changes in the letters that it does use.

This brief description of *Roughing It'*s construction merely hints at the book's richness and complexity. It should, however, serve to make you appreciate the necessity of reading the book carefully and not taking anything about it for granted.

TOPICS AND STRATEGIES

The sections that follow discuss both general and specific ideas for essay topics on *Roughing It*. You certainly need not limit your choices to the subjects discussed here, but if you do select one of them, do not regard its discussion as an outline of what you should write in your own essay. In fact, you should not even assume that the points made here are necessarily entirely valid, and you certainly should not adopt anyone else's views unless you are satisfied you understand them and can advance arguments of your own to support them.

The discussions below raise many questions about *Roughing It*, but few of these questions necessarily have right or wrong answers. Be careful to avoid falling into the trap of getting stuck in fruitless efforts to prove points that may not be provable. The strength of your essay will come not merely from the decisiveness of the conclusions it reaches, but from the power and clarity of the arguments it advances to reach those conclusions. Whatever topics you choose to write about, use your imagination and try to consider all possible sides of every question. The keys to successful essay writing are originality of thought and clearness and force of argument.

A simple method of generating fresh ideas is outlining evidence supporting all possible points of view on the issues you discuss. For example, if you wish to argue that *Roughing It* makes a case for the futility of seeking easy riches, you would naturally begin by listing all the instances in the book in which the high hopes and get-rich-quick schemes of the narrator and others come to nothing. What you should do next is outline all the evidence you can find that supports the *opposite* point of view—examples of quests for riches that succeed. Whatever contrary evidence you find may not alter your original idea, but some of it may reveal weaknesses in your argument and thereby give you a chance to strengthen your essay. In any case, your goal should not be merely to win an argument, but to get at the truth, and doing that always requires looking at all sides of issues.

Themes

At its most basic level, *Roughing It* might be fairly considered a journey into a new world. Its subject is the western frontier of America during the mid-19th century—a time when the Far West was seen by most easterners as a lawless land populated by wild desperadoes and savage Indians and holding out the promise of fabulous mineral wealth for the taking. As *Roughing It* opens, its narrator presents himself as a naive tenderfoot anxious to experience adventure in the West, grab his share of easy riches, and return home a man of the world. The book's central themes revolve around the differences between what the narrator sets out to accomplish and what he actually achieves and the differences between his preconceptions of the West and its reality.

Sample Topics:

1. **Disillusionment on the frontier:** How does *Roughing It* develop disillusionment as a theme to debunk romantic notions about the western frontier?

   One of the strongest themes in *Roughing It,* especially the book's first half, is the constant disillusionment that the narrator experiences when the romantic notions he has brought to the West confront cold reality. Among the things he learns are that real Indians are not the Noble Red Men that he grew up reading about in novels, that ruthless desperadoes are not necessarily half-savage ogres, that gold and silver nuggets are not simply waiting to be scooped up from the ground, and even that one cannot ignite a fire with a pistol shot. Is a primary thrust of the book a conscious attempt to deromanticize the West? Or, does it exaggerate the narrator's näiveté and innocence in order to achieve comic effects by subjecting him to the repeated embarrassments and failures that disillusion him? The essence of the narrator's disillusionment may be a remark that Ballou makes in chapter 28, after telling the narrator that all the promising mineral specimens the latter has collected are worthless granite and mica (fool's gold). After the narrator observes that "all that glitters is not gold," Ballou goes further by saying "that nothing that glitters is gold." Might Ballou's remark serve as a metaphor for the narrator's entire experience, especially during his greenhorn period?

There are many different ways in which you might approach an essay on this subject. Whichever approach you follow, you should begin by taking notes on examples of the large and small forms of disillusionment that the narrator experiences. Look also for examples of ways in which the West lives up to the narrator's romantic preconceptions. Can you find meaningful patterns in the disappointments that the narrator experiences?

2. **Violence:** Does *Roughing It* glamorize western violence and desperadoes? Or does it use irony to satirize eastern conceptions of lawlessness on the frontier?

Although the narrator of *Roughing It* never lifts his hand in anger against another person, violence and threats of violence pervade his narrative. He often mentions how frontier disputes are settled with firearms, and his words sometimes seem to condone such violence. In chapter 12, for example, he says that "The commonest misunderstandings were settled on the spot with the revolver or the knife. Murders were done in open day, and with sparkling frequency, and nobody thought of inquiring into them." What might one infer from a passage such as that? Should the words "sparkling frequency" be read as a subtle endorsement of frontier violence? Or might they be meant to provide an ironic contrast to the word "murders," which one would not expect to be associated with anything that is "sparkling"? Can you find passages in the book to suggest that Mark Twain is deliberately playing on eastern conceptions of western lawlessness?

If you choose to write on this subject, you will doubtless start by cataloguing instances of violence and threats throughout the book. Pay particular attention to chapter 48, which opens with the assertion that "in a new mining district the rough element predominates, and a person is not respected until he has 'killed his man.'" You should also study chapters 9 through 11 closely, as they discuss the notorious desperado Jack Slade.

In an essay published in 1943, George Orwell—who would later become famous for his novels *Animal Farm* (1945) and *Nineteen Eighty-four* (1949)—expressed his disgust with *Roughing It*'s depiction of Slade. "It is perfectly clear," Orwell said, "that Mark Twain admires this disgusting scoundrel. Slade was successful; therefore he was admirable." Is Orwell's view accurate? If he is correct in saying that *Roughing It*'s narrator truly admires desperadoes and murderers? Is he also correct in saying that such admiration is a reflection of the importance of "making good" in America? As you consider these questions, keep in mind that the views of *Roughing It*'s narrator and those of Mark Twain may not be the same.

It might help you to evaluate *Roughing It*'s depiction of Slade and other desperadoes to know that the narrator's description of his encounter with Slade is significantly embellished. Mark Twain did, indeed, meet Slade during his stagecoach journey west in 1861. However, he knew nothing about Slade's violent reputation at the time he met him. Does this fact suggest that at least some of what he says about Slade is designed for comic effect?

Character

The primary character in *Roughing It* is obviously the narrator. Although we know that he is recounting many experiences that Mark Twain himself really had in the Far West, it is probably best to regard him as anonymous, for the same reason that we should be cautious about reading *Roughing It* as autobiography. Comparisons between the real Mark Twain and the book's narrator might provide fruitful material for an essay seeking to place the book in its historical context, but for the purposes of more purely literary discussion, you will find plenty to say about the narrator if you simply regard him as a literary creation. The best way to examine other characters in *Roughing It* might be to regard them as representatives of stock characters, or types, such as ruffians, greenhorns, and desperadoes.

Sample Topics:

1. **The narrator as a failure:** How does *Roughing It* use its narrator's inexperience and ineptitude to achieve comic effects?

An inescapable fact about *Roughing It* is that its narrator seems to fail at almost everything he undertakes, at least through the first 42 chapters of the book. His prospecting efforts all seem to come to nothing, he accidentally burns down his timber claim, he frequently gets lost, and he cannot even hold a job as an ordinary laborer at a quartz mill. His most spectacular failure comes when he and his partner blow their chance to become millionaires when they fail to do the token amount of work necessary to hold their claim to the "blind lead" in chapters 40 and 41. Is there a coherent pattern to the narrator's failings? Do they serve any larger purpose in the narrative than to get laughs? Are they necessary to maintain the narrator's pose as an inexperienced innocent seeking initiation into frontier culture? Is there a point in the book at which it can be said that the narrator has "arrived" and ceases to be a bumbling greenhorn?

To write on this topic, you will naturally want to begin by collecting notes on the narrator's various failures, as well as his successes. Pay particular attention to his self-evaluation in chapter 42. Look for patterns in the ways in which he fails and ask yourself how inexperience, bad luck, simple carelessness, or laziness might contribute to his failings. Do others seem to succeed where he fails? Does the narrator see himself as a typical greenhorn in the West? (See also the discussion about comparisons between the narrators of *Roughing It* and *Life on the Mississippi* in the Compare and Contrast section below.)

2. **Desperadoes and ruffians:** What do *Roughing It*'s depictions of these stock characters contribute to the book?

Two of the most interesting types of stock characters in *Roughing It* are desperadoes, such as Jack Slade and Bill Noakes, and stalwart ruffians, such as Arkansas, Scotty Briggs, Captain Ned Blakely, Jim Blaine, and the "Admiral" of the Hawaiian chapters. Slade (c. 1829–1864) was a real person, but Mark Twain made up the other names for characters whom he either modeled on real people or invented to represent types. An essay on desperadoes and ruffians might address a number of issues, such as what these and other characters similar to them have in common and how Mark Twain uses comic exaggeration to make them more vivid. A more important question, perhaps, is what each character contributes to the narrative. In some cases, the answer should be obvious. For example, chapter 50, in which Captain Blakely is introduced, opens by suggesting that Blakely's story is a representative illustration of how frontier justice works. (Mark Twain modeled Blakely on a real sea captain, Ned Wakeman [1818–75], who also inspired similar characters in several other Mark Twain stories.) Determining why Mark Twain used other desperado and ruffian characters will require a little more probing as you read *Roughing It,* but you should be able to explain the purpose of most of them. Another thing you should try to do is show how the role that each of these characters plays may have helped determine the individual traits that Mark Twain gave them. For example, he uses Scotty Briggs in a long anecdote about how funerals were conducted in Nevada in chapter 47. To emphasize the gulf between western and eastern customs, he has Briggs and the eastern pastor, whom he wants to preside over a funeral, speak in such rich language that neither man can understand the other. The point seems to be that an entirely new culture is arising in the West. The conversation between Briggs and the pastor is a masterpiece of comic dialogue, but it also serves as a vivid illustration of how different eastern and western cultures are.

History and Context

Like the early chapters of *Life on the Mississippi, Roughing It* recalls a period in American history that Mark Twain observed at first hand and that had essentially passed by the time he wrote about it. Whereas *Life on the Mississippi* recalls his steamboat piloting years during the late 1850s, *Roughing It* recalls the years immediately afterward, when he prospected for minerals and wrote for newspapers in the Far West. He arrived in the West after California's gold rush had slowed to a crawl but while western Nevada's silver boom was still in full swing. As his preface to *Roughing It* explains, part of his purpose was to record a "curious episode," about which little had been written by persons who "saw the happenings of the time with their own eyes." His book is therefore very much an attempt at a historical chronicle and might fairly be judged as such. At the same time, the book is full of tall tales, burlesque exaggerations, and pure invention. Just as it cannot be read as straight autobiography, it cannot be read as straight history. Perhaps the best way to regard the book is as a kind of impressionistic history. In this respect, the book is more properly a work of literature than one of history. Nevertheless, although its historical details may be sparse and occasionally questionable, its broad historical outlines are accurate. A more important question to ask, however, is whether the book succeeds in conveying the *spirit* of the period that it attempts to describe.

Sample Topic:

1. **The wild, wild west:** What kind of picture of the Far West does *Roughing It* convey?

This is an open-ended topic that could go in many different directions. You might, for example, survey *Roughing It's* depictions of lawlessness on the frontier and try to assess what the book says about its *effect* on frontier development. Be careful, however, to look at all sides of the issue. Although you might expect the book to suggest that the settlement and economic development of the West was retarded by lack of order, you may find ambiguities in the text. For example, what does the book say about the desperado Jack Slade's contributions to the success of the Overland stage? He imposed order, but did he do so lawfully?

Another subject on which you might focus is what the book's preface calls the "rise, growth and culmination of the silver-mining fever in Nevada." To what extent does that fever drive the narrator's actions? Does the book succeed in conveying the excitement that prospectors and investors felt during that era? If so, how? (Keep in mind distinctions between Nevada's silver boom of the 1860s and the California gold rush of the early 1850s.) Whichever aspects of the book you focus on, your overall goal should be to assess *Roughing It's* success in making the era it describes seem vivid.

Philosophy and Ideas

Another way to consider *Roughing It* is to explore the broad philosophical ideas that are expressed within it. This approach is related to the study of themes discussed above, but it operates at a more general level. However, that distinction need not affect what your essay will say if you choose to write on one of these topics. The primary purpose of these sectional headings is simply to help you direct your thinking.

Sample Topics:

1. **Civilization:** Does *Roughing It* present a consistent view about the desirability of civilization?

Civilization is a nebulous word that means different things to different people. However, it is typically applied to orderly and technologically advanced societies, generally those based around cities. *Roughing It* uses the word itself infrequently, except in ironic passages about the impact of Western "civilization" on native Hawaiians. Nevertheless, it is clear in other parts of the book that contrasts between what Mark Twain regarded as the orderly civilization of the East and the primitive and lawless conditions of the Far West were constantly on his mind as he was writing. Indeed, a case might be made that his book equates civilization with the rule of law, which was often absent in the West.

If you elect to write an essay on this topic, you will probably do best to restrict your discussion to the chapters of *Roughing It* pertaining to California and Nevada. Mark Twain's concern in the Hawaiian chapters is the interaction of Western civilization with the non-Western culture of native Hawaiians—a subject very different than the extension of civilization to the western frontier. (If you prefer to write on Hawaii, you would do well to approach the subject in the context of Mark Twain's later anti-imperialist writings. A good place to start your research on the latter subject is the collection of writings edited by Jim Zwick that is listed in the Bibliography below.)

To write an essay on *Roughing It*'s attitude toward civilization, you will need to reflect on the book's nuances. Before you start, you must be clear on how you define *civilization* and what are its key elements, such as law, stable political order, literacy, or urban centers. Reading a few general articles in good encyclopedias or social science reference works will help. Then, as you read *Roughing It,* stay focused on how your definition relates to the book's observations about the people, communities, and institutions of the American West. Watch for the narrator's comments on lawlessness and his use of such words as *half-civilized* and *savages.* Does he seem to condone the lawless conditions of the West? Or do you sense that he yearns for greater order? Are the views that he expresses consistent throughout the book? Does he convey any sense that greater order is on the way?

2. **Quest for riches v. the Protestant ethic:** What does *Roughing It* say about the relationship between work and rewards?

One of the most pervasive themes throughout Mark Twain's writings is the human desire to acquire easy riches. This theme is especially evident in his early novels. Indeed, the very title of his first novel, *The Gilded Age* (1874), which he coauthored with Charles Dudley Warner, suggests wealth, and quests for easy riches do, in fact, drive the book's central story lines. In *The Adventures of Tom Sawyer* (1876), Tom and Huck find a fabulous treasure, and then virtually everyone in their village turns out to look for more. In that novel's sequel, *Adventures of Huckleberry Finn* (1884), Huck renounces his fortune and attempts to flee from the problems caused by his father's greed, only to get mixed up with two con men who involve him in dishonest money-making schemes. *Roughing It* preceded all those books, and it, too, stresses the human impulse to seek easy wealth. In fact, the opening paragraph of the first chapter expresses the narrator's belief that all one has to do to get rich in Nevada is scoop up nuggets of gold and silver lying on the ground. That, of course, is comic exaggeration, but the idea that vast riches are ever within reach is repeated throughout the book, usually in connection with the narrator's prospecting efforts, investment schemes, and business opportunities. However, one point about all these schemes that should be obvious is that none of them ever succeeds. The only money the narrator ever makes comes from doing real work for wages.

Does *Roughing It* repeatedly dash its narrator's dreams of easy riches merely for comic effect? Or might the book be conveying the message that wealth can be obtained only by hard work, discipline, and thrift—the principles behind the Protestant ethic? An essay on this topic will require you to look for patterns throughout the book in the ways in which rewards and disappointments are distributed to those seeking wealth. Pay particular attention to the narrator's failed schemes. Does he—or anyone else—ever reap any rich rewards that he does not earn? Conversely, is he rewarded for honest work? The most telling incident in the book may be the "blind lead" story (chapters 40–41), in which the narrator and his partner, Calvin Higbie, stake a claim to a vein of ore that promises to make them both millionaires. What happens to their claim and why? Might that episode stand as some kind of metaphor for the book as a whole? Is it significant that the book's dedication, which is to Higbie, alludes to that episode?

If you wish to develop this topic further, you might read *The Gilded Age*, which appears to reach the same conclusion about the necessity of working to achieve wealth. However, getting through that long novel is a formidable challenge. You might find it more practical to read some of Mark Twain's later short stories, such as "The Man That Corrupted Hadleyburg" (discussed in another chapter in this book), "The $30,000 Bequest," or "The £1,000,000 Bank-note," all of which deal with the theme of easy riches.

3. **Hopes and dreams:** What does the motif of dreams and rude awakenings contribute to *Roughing It*?

Closely related to the topic of disillusionment discussed in the section on Themes above is the motif of hopes and dreams that runs through *Roughing It*. In the book's first chapter, the narrator remembers the hopefulness with which he planned his trip to Nevada and recalls how he "dreamed all night about Indians, deserts, and silver bars . . ." During the cross-country stagecoach trip that follows, the passengers—and even the drivers—were asleep much of the time, a fact suggesting that they traveled in something like a dream state. Other parts of the narrative return to the dream motif, especially when the narrator's subject becomes his hope of getting rich or experiencing adventure. However, almost every dream state is followed by a disappointing awakening.

Form and Genre

The opening section of this chapter questions *Roughing It*'s genre. It demonstrates that *Roughing It* has many of the characteristics of autobiography, fiction, and travel writing. Questions about whether the book properly belongs to any one of those categories might provide good topics for essays or you might write an essay that considers all three categories. Whichever approach you take, you will need to begin by defining what you mean by the terms you use.

Sample Topics:

1. **The narrator as a picaro:** Can *Roughing It* be considered a picaresque narrative?

   A classical picaresque novel is a satiric narrative—usually related in the first person—by an amiable rogue who travels from adventure to adventure, typically triumphing over the middle-class people he encounters along the way. Picaresque elements can be found in several of Mark Twain's novels, most notably *Huckleberry Finn* whose protagonist is clearly an amiable rogue. The first half of *Roughing It* also contains picaresque elements, but are there enough to justify labeling the book a picaresque?

   This should be a fun topic on which to write as it will require you to read *Roughing It* with an imaginative and perhaps slightly cynical eye with the aim of proving that the book's narrator is a rogue. Start by reading some discussions of the picaresque form in textbooks, literary reference works, or perhaps analyses of a work such as Miguel de Cervantes' *Don Quixote* (1605)—the most famous picaresque novel ever written. After outlining the essential elements of the picaresque form, review at least the first 40 chapters of *Roughing It*—to the moment when the narrator becomes a newspaper writer—to identify picaresque passages. Your essay should then discuss the components that make up a picaresque story and offer examples of those components from *Roughing It*. Finally, you should show the picaresque traits of the book are used to develop satiric observations.

2. **Southwestern humor and tall tales:** What do the tall tales in *Roughing It* have in common and what do they contribute to the book?

Like Mark Twain's other travel books, *Roughing It* is filled with anecdotal material, much of which is only marginally relevant to the main narrative. In view of the fact that the book concerns the Western frontier, it is not surprising that most of the anecdotes take the form of tall tales, a staple of what has been called 19th-century southwestern humor. Among the tall tales related in *Roughing It* are Bemis's account of being chased up a tree by a buffalo (chapter 6), Jim Blaine's unfinished story about his grandfather's old ram (chapter 53), Dick Baker's tale about the remarkable cat Tom Quartz (chapter 61), and the narrator's own story about Eckert and the coconut-eating cat in Siam (chapter 7).

Among the questions to address in an essay on this topic are what elements these tall tales and others in *Roughing It* have in common and why Mark Twain might have put them in this book. You should begin by doing some background reading on southwestern humor and the tall tale form. The chapter on Mark Twain's own jumping frog story in the present book would be a good starting point, as that story is regarded as a classic example of southwestern humor. Among the elements of tall tales to consider are their narrative form, their subject matter, and how the tales in *Roughing It* fit into the overall narrative.

3. **The Hawaiian chapters:** Should the section on Hawaii be regarded as an integral part of *Roughing It*?

When Mark Twain started writing *Roughing It,* he had no intention of carrying his story into the months that he spent in the Hawaiian Islands ("Sandwich Islands" in his narrative). In fact, he wanted to write about Hawaii in another book. However, because he was writing for a subscription book publisher, whose mostly small-town and rural customers expected their purchases to be big, fat books, he had to write enough to satisfy market expectations. When his Nevada and California chapters came up short, he added 16 chapters on Hawaii. Most of these chapters he adapted from letters that he had written for a California newspaper while he was in Hawaii, but they also include about 5,000 words of entirely new material. The resulting chapters are significantly different in content from the rest of the book. In fact, some scholars and critics consider them to be so different that they do not regard them as integral parts of *Roughing It,* and at least one publisher has issued an edition of *Roughing It* that omits the Hawaiian chapters altogether.

Apart from the fact that Mark Twain added the Hawaiian chapters as an afterthought, is there any basis for regarding them as something fundamentally different from the rest of the book? This may be a more complex question than at first appears. If the unifying theme of *Roughing It* is Mark Twain's years in the Far West, chapters on his time in Hawaii certainly seem to belong. Is there, however, a more subtle unifying theme that holds together all the chapters except those on Hawaii? To answer those questions, you will have to compare the content and style of the Hawaiian chapters with other parts of *Roughing It* to determine what is and is not different about them.

Language, Symbols, and Imagery

The language of *Roughing It*'s narrative is standard English, but it is rich in figurative expressions and comic exaggerations that reflect the book's debt to southwestern humor. The book also contains many passages that are rich in dialectal variations of English. A particularly interesting example is the Virginia City fireman Scotty Briggs's interview with the eastern pastor in chapter 47. The rich figurative language used by both characters might make a good topic for an essay that relates each character's imagery to his cultural background. Violence is a recurrent motif throughout *Roughing It,* and one of the most striking images used in the book is that of the firearms owned by different kinds of characters.

Sample Topics:

1. **Comic exaggeration:** How does *Roughing It* use figurative language and comic exaggeration to make its depictions of the West more vivid?

One of the great pleasures of reading *Roughing It* comes from savoring the rich figurative language and comic exaggeration in passages such as chapter 5's portrait of the "cayote" (coyote), "the living, breathing allegory of Want," a creature "so spiritless and cowardly that even while his exposed teeth are pretending a threat, the rest of his face is apologizing for it." It is impossible to read passages such as that without conjuring up vivid mental images. Much of the power of Mark Twain's writing comes from his ability to make readers see things as he sees them and remember them long afterward. Indeed, it was not by chance that *Roughing It*'s description of the coyote inspired animator Chuck Jones to create Wile E. Coyote for his Road Runner cartoons.

To write on this topic, collect as many examples of vivid figurative language and comic exaggeration as you can find and look for patterns in the types of language they use, their subject matter, and their comic effect. To show what they lend to the narrative, consider how they would read if Mark Twain had used more conventional language. For example, what would this description of a revolver lose if Mark Twain had simply given the gun's actual dimensions?

> I was armed to the teeth with a pitiful little Smith & Wesson's seven-shooter, which carried a ball like a homoeopathic pill, and it took the whole seven to make a dose for an adult.

That passage is funny because it exaggerates the gun's small size and ineffectiveness by comparing its bullets to homeopathic pills that are known for their almost microscopic quantities of medicine. Aside from getting a laugh, however, what purpose does such a passage have? Could it be designed to help describe the narrator as someone who has no intention of ever using a weapon against another person? Readers might forget what kind of gun the narrator carries and how many bullets it holds, but they are unlikely to forget the image of a homeopathic pill.

2. **Guns as symbols:** How does *Roughing It* use firearms as symbols?

Among the most obvious symbols throughout *Roughing It* are firearms. These range from George Bemis's hilariously ineffective Allen revolver and the narrator's own "pitiful" Smith & Wesson seven-shooter, to the more deadly shotguns, rifles, and heavy-duty revolvers of frontier desperadoes. Does the fact that many of the men mentioned in the book carry firearms confirm the frontier stereotype of gun-packing lawmen, cowboys, and outlaws? Perhaps a more relevant question to ask is what types of guns the various characters have and how they use them. Do references to firearms tend to work as symbols of their owners?

Compare and Contrast Essays

Compare and contrast essays can be both simpler and more challenging than other types of essays. They can be simpler because the range of topics from which to choose is immense and because their structure seems to define itself. At the same time, however, they can be more challenging because they may require more research and reading. These essays foster creativity on at least two levels: first, in finding aspects of one or more works to compare; then in finding significant points to make about the similarities and differences you observe. Perhaps your best chance of attaining true originality lies in writing this type of essay—particularly on a subject that may not be obvious to others. An obvious topic would be a comparison of *Roughing It* and *The Innocents Abroad* (1869), Mark

Twain's first travel book. That is a broad enough subject to allow wide scope for an interesting essay; however, your only chance for originality in such a subject would be in the arguments you make, not in the basic topic. A more original topic would be a comparison of *Roughing It* with a completely different kind of work, such as the novel *The Prince and the Pauper* (1881), that seeks to find common threads in Mark Twain's attitude toward violence. It is possible that no one—not even a scholar—has ever compared those two books.

If you opt to write a compare and contrast essay, you should begin by compiling lists of similarities and differences between pairs of characters, types of plots, different points of view, or other aspects of *Roughing It.* That would be the logical place to start, but do not assume that bare comparisons reveal anything. It is not enough to say that the narrative personas of the early chapters of *Roughing It* and the piloting chapters of *Life on the Mississippi* are both naive youths anxious to see the world and have adventures whose romantic dreams are dashed by reality and then list other similarities and differences between them. You would also need to explain why Mark Twain gave them such similar personas and how their personas help shape their narratives. If you find significant differences between them, you would also need to explain why they differ.

Sample Topics:

1. **Greenhorn narrators in *Life on the Mississippi* and *Roughing It*:** In what ways do the narrative voices of *Roughing It* and *Life on the Mississippi* resemble each other?

   Roughing It and the piloting chapters of *Life on the Mississippi* (1883) are similar in being works about periods in Mark Twain's life that he had to recall from memory. They also resemble each other in employing young narrators who leave home for the first time to travel great distances. In the opening pages of *Roughing It*, the narrator claims that he "never had been away from home, and that word 'travel' had a seductive charm for me." Thrilled by his older brother's appointment as secretary of the Nevada Territory, he packs and joins the brother on a journey to the Far West, a land of adventure. In *Life on the Mississippi*, the young narrator packs his valise, boards a steamboat headed for New Orleans, and exults in "being bound for mysterious lands and distant climes . . ."

The fact that Mark Twain embellished his real adventures in both these books should be evident, as he could not have twice left home for the first time. A question to ask of these books is what he hoped to achieve by making his narrators appear so young and inexperienced. At the start of their adventures, both are what are known as "greenhorns" or "tenderfeet"—newcomers who are unacquainted with the ways of the new worlds in which they are moving. As we read their narratives, we share in their sense of discovery as they learn about their new environments, and we laugh comfortably at the crises they survive and the processes of initiation through which they go.

An essay comparing the narrators of *Roughing It* and *Life on the Mississippi* need cover only the first 21 chapters of *Roughing It*, which describe the cross-country stagecoach journey, and chapters 4 through 20 of *Life on the Mississippi*, which cover the apprenticeship of the cub pilot. Perhaps the first point of comparison to look for is structural similarities between the two works, both of which are built around journeys into unfamiliar lands. With what expectations do the narrators begin their journeys? What types of incidents challenge their romantic illusions? When the cub pilot thinks he has mastered his new profession and starts to become cocky, something usually happens to drain his self-confidence; does the narrator of *Roughing It* have similarly deflating experiences? Are any of the major crises that the greenhorns survive in the two narratives almost the same? How does each narrator change and shed his greenhorn status?

Another thing to look for in both works is the author's consistency in his use of the first-person voice: Do the two narrators consistently speak in the voices of greenhorns? Or do they sometimes shift to the voice of the much older Mark Twain? If the narrators' voices do shift, are there discernible patterns to those shifts?

2. *Roughing It*'s **Indians v. Cooper's "Noble Red Man":** How do
   Roughing It's stereotypes of Native Americans compare with
   those in James Fenimore Cooper's Leatherstocking Tales?

It is generally acknowledged that Mark Twain was comparatively free of racial prejudices for a person of his time. If he had
one racial blind spot, however, it seems to have been his difficulty in finding positive qualities among Native Americans.
He seems eventually to have gotten past that, but *Roughing It*
repeatedly exposes his disdain for American Indians. The key
to his bias seems to have been his disillusionment with what he
called the "Noble Red Man" stereotype of the James Fenimore
Cooper novels he had read as a boy. He makes fun of Cooper's
writing in several of his published works, including *Roughing
It*. In chapter 19, the narrator describes himself as "a disciple of
Cooper and a worshipper of the Red Man—even of the scholarly
savages in the *Last of the Mohicans . . .*" In the same breath, he
expresses "disgust" with Nevada's Gosiute Indians ("Goshoots"
in the text); he then goes on to question whether he "had been
over-estimating the Red Man while viewing him through the
mellow moonshine of romance." He seems to blame Cooper for
fostering his highly romanticized view of Indians to which real
Indians cannot possibly live up. Is his criticism of Cooper's overromanticizing Native Americans valid? Does his disillusionment with the real Indians he encounters in the West account
for generally negative depictions of them?

   An essay on this topic will be especially rewarding but also
challenging, as it will require several lines of research. Its goal
should be to estimate how Cooper's fiction influenced *Roughing It* and whether, in its rejection of Cooper's Indian romantic
stereotypes, Mark Twain goes too far in the other direction.
Begin your research with a careful reading of *Roughing It* to collect notes on how it depicts Indians. That task is a challenge in
itself, as Indians are mentioned, or alluded to, in almost every
chapter on the Great Plains, Nevada, and California (pay particular attention to chapters 1, 5, 9, 19, and 38). To learn more
about Mark Twain's attitude toward Cooper, you should also

read his essay "Fenimore Cooper's Literary Offenses," which is great fun in itself. You might also read the posthumously published story "Huck Finn and Tom Sawyer Among the Indians," in which Tom Sawyer undergoes a disillusionment similar to that of *Roughing It*'s narrator. Finally, you should read at least enough of one of Cooper's Leatherstocking Tales to confirm or reject Mark Twain's charges against Cooper. *The Last of the Mohicans* (1826) is particularly apt because *Roughing It* mentions it by name.

Bibliography for *Roughing It*

Bassett, John E. "*Roughing It:* Authority Through Comic Performance." *Nineteenth-Century Literature* 43, no. 2 (September 1988): 220–34. Reprinted in Bassett's *"A Heart of Ideality in My Realism" and Other Essays on Howells and Twain* (1991).

Berkove, Lawrence I. "Nevada Influences on Mark Twain." *A Companion to Mark Twain.* Eds. Peter Messent and Louis J. Budd. Oxford, England: Blackwell, 2005. 157–71.

———. "No 'Mere Accidental Accidents': *Roughing It* as a Novel." *Mark Twain Annual* 1 (2003): 7–18.

Bridgman, Richard. *Traveling in Mark Twain.* Berkeley: U California P, 1987.

Camfield, Gregg. "*Roughing It.*" *The Oxford Companion to Mark Twain.* New York: Oxford UP, 2003. 521–28.

Gale, Robert L. "*Roughing It.*" *Masterplots, Second Revised Edition.* Ed. Frank N. Magill. Pasadena, CA: Salem Press, 1996. 10:5,730–803.

Melton, Jeffrey Alan. *Mark Twain, Travel Books and Tourism: The Tide of a Great Popular Movement.* Tuscaloosa: U Alabama P, 2002.

Messent, Peter. "*Roughing It* and the American West." *Mark Twain.* New York: St. Martin's Press, 1997. 44–64.

Plimpton, George. Introduction. *Roughing It.* By Mark Twain. New York: Oxford UP, 1996. xxxi–xliv.

Railton, Stephen. "Going West: *Roughing It.*" *Mark Twain: A Short Introduction.* Malden, MA: Blackwell, 2004. 18–31.

———. *The Life & Work of Mark Twain.* Chantilly, VA: Teaching Company, 2002 (Includes a lecture on *Roughing It*; available in audio and video formats).

———. *Mark Twain in His Times* (etext.virginia.edu/railton/index2.html) (Includes full text of *Roughing It* and numerous study aids).

Rasmussen, R. Kent. *"Roughing It."* In *Critical Companion to Mark Twain.* New York: Facts On File, 2007. I: 422–52.

Robinson, Forrest G. "The Innocent at Large: Mark Twain's Travel writing." *The Cambridge Companion to Mark Twain.* Ed. Forrest G. Robinson. New York: Cambridge UP, 1995. 27–51.

Rogers, Franklin R. "Burlesque Travel Literature and Mark Twain's *Roughing It.*" *Mark Twain's Humor: Critical Essays.* Ed. David E. E. Sloane. New York: Garland, 1993. 31–49.

Sloane, David E. E. *Student Companion to Mark Twain.* Westport, CT: Greenwood Press, 2001.

Twain, Mark. "Fenimore Cooper's Literary Offenses." *Collected Tales, Sketches, Speeches, & Essays, 1891–1910.* Ed. Louis J. Budd. New York: Library of America. 180–92.

———. "Huck Finn and Tom Sawyer among the Indians." *Huck Finn and Tom Sawyer Among the Indians and Other Unfinished Stories.* Berkeley: U California P, 1989. 33–81.

———. *Mark Twain's Letters from Hawaii.* A. Grove Day. Honolulu: U Hawaii P, 1966.

———. *Roughing It.* Ed. Harriet Elinor Smith, et al. Berkeley: U California P, 1993.

Wonham, Henry B. Afterword, For Further Reading. *Roughing It.* By Mark Twain. New York: Oxford UP, 1996. 1–20. (Back matter has separate pagination.)

———. *Mark Twain and the Art of the Tall Tale.* New York: Oxford UP, 1993.

Zwick, Jim, ed. *Mark Twain's Weapons of Satire: Anti-imperialist Writings on the Philippine-American War.* Syracuse, NY: Syracuse UP, 1992.

LIFE ON THE MISSISSIPPI

READING TO WRITE

MARK TWAIN'S *Life on the Mississippi* (1883) is a large, sprawling work that tries to do several quite different things. Its first three chapters offer a physical description and history of the Mississippi River and even include part of a chapter lifted from the then-unfinished *Adventures of Huckleberry Finn* (1884). Chapters 4 through 20 recall Mark Twain's years as an apprentice, or cub, steamboat pilot. The rest of the book describes Mark Twain's return visit to the river in 1882—a trip that he made primarily to gather material for this book. Here we shall focus on the piloting chapters of *Life on the Mississippi*. Those chapters might rightfully be considered a book within a book, and they are also the chapters that are most studied in literature classes. However, the fact that we are concentrating on those chapters need not stop you from reading the rest of *Life on the Mississippi*. Many of the book's other chapters expand on themes in the piloting chapters and help to place the earlier chapters in perspective with information on how the river and the piloting profession had changed since the earlier era. You may also find chapters 53 to 56 to be of particular interest, as they recall Mark Twain's youth in Hannibal, Missouri, before he became a pilot.

Life on the Mississippi's 17 chapters about cub piloting are different in content and tone from the rest of the book. That is not particularly surprising when we realize that those chapters began as magazine articles that Mark Twain wrote around eight years before writing the rest of *Life on the Mississippi*. In response to his friend W. D. Howells's request to write something for the *Atlantic Monthly* that Howells edited, Mark Twain eventually published seven articles under the series title "Old Times on the Mississippi." Apart from being broken into smaller chapters, those articles made the transition from the magazine to Mark Twain's book with few changes, and they make up chapters 4 to 17 of *Life on the Mississippi*. To complete the story of his cub piloting years, Mark Twain added three new chapters, 18 to 20.

The first question to ask of *Life on the Mississippi*'s cub pilot chapters is what Mark Twain's intentions were in writing them. Nothing in the book answers that question directly, so it will help you to know that his first goal was simply to recapture the glory years of steamboat piloting on the Mississippi River—a way of life that had changed almost beyond recognition since he left the river. Written in the first person in the form of a memoir, the chapters have a strongly autobiographical feel to them; however, it would be a mistake to regard them as autobiography in any strict sense of the term. Although the chapters follow the general outline of Mark Twain's cub piloting career and mention many real people and events, they also invent many incidents, embellish others, and give an exaggerated impression of their narrator's youth and inexperience. Consider this passage from chapter 5 describing the start of the narrator's first steamboat voyage:

> When we presently got under way and went poking down the broad Ohio [River], I became a new being, and the subject of my own admiration. I was a traveller! A word never had tasted so good in my mouth before. I had an exultant sense of being bound for mysterious lands and distant climes which I never have felt in so uplifting a degree since. I was in such a glorified condition that all ignoble feelings departed out of me, and I was able to look down and pity the untravelled with a compassion that had hardly a trace of contempt in it.

One might infer from that passage that the young narrator had never before left home. However, Mark Twain was 21 years old when he began the voyage that passage describes, and he was already an experienced traveler. Since leaving his Hannibal home nearly four years earlier, he had been on his own and had traveled widely in the Midwest and East. You might therefore ask why he deliberately distorted his persona in his narrative. Did he do it partly to enhance humorous effects or to make his narrator more sympathetic to the reader? As you read the cub piloting chapters consider how his narrative might differ if he had instead portrayed himself more realistically. For example, might his descriptions of the rigors of pilot training have been less vivid?

TOPICS AND STRATEGIES

The section that follows offers both general and specific ideas for possible essay topics on *Life on the Mississippi.* You certainly need not limit your choices to the subjects discussed here, but if you do select one of these topics, do not regard its discussion as an outline of what you should write in your own essay. In fact, you should not even assume that the points made here are necessarily valid, and you certainly should not adopt anyone else's views unless you are satisfied you understand them and can advance arguments of your own to support them.

The discussions below raise many questions about the piloting chapters in *Life on the Mississippi,* but few of these questions have right or wrong answers. If you are not careful, you may fall into the trap of becoming mired in fruitless attempts to prove points that may not be provable. The strength of your essay will come not merely from the decisiveness of the conclusions it reaches, but from the power and clarity of the arguments that it advances to reach those conclusions. Whatever topics you choose to write about, use your imagination and try to consider all possible sides of every question. The keys to successful essay writing are originality of thought and clearness and force of argument.

A method for generating fresh ideas that almost always works is outlining evidence supporting all possible points of view. Assume, for example, you wish to argue that Mark Twain deliberately made the narrator of his piloting chapters appear younger and less experienced than he himself had been as a cub pilot so that his narrator's eventual mastery of piloting would seem more impressive. You would doubtless begin by outlining all the points in *Life on the Mississippi* supporting that position. What you should do next is outline all the evidence you can find that supports the *opposite* point of view. Whatever contrary evidence you find may not alter your original idea, but some of it may reveal weaknesses in your argument and thereby give you the opportunity to strengthen your essay. In any case, your goal should not be merely to win an argument, but to get at the truth, and doing that always requires looking at all sides of issues.

Themes

If the cub piloting chapters of *Life on the Mississippi* have a central theme, is almost certainly the cub's struggle to "learn the river." Variations on that theme might provide the basis for many different essay topics. For example, "learning the river" might be taken as a metaphor for learning how to get through life. Or, the cub's painful initiation into piloting and his gradual mastery of the profession might be seen as a coming-of-age story—a subject discussed in the section on Form and Genre below. One might also treat as a theme the constantly changing *shape* of the river itself—the idea that however well one masters a body of knowledge, the body constantly reshapes itself, so that the process of learning never ends.

Sample Topics:

1. **Learning the river:** How might the cub pilot's struggle to "learn the river" be regarded as a metaphor for life generally?

   As we have seen, one of Mark Twain's goals in writing the "Old Times on the Mississippi" articles was to re-create a unique era in American history by showing what a glorious profession piloting on the Mississippi River had been during the heyday of steamboating. While repeatedly calling attention to the power and independence of pilots, Mark Twain shows why the pilots deserved their special privileges by demonstrating what extraordinary skills and knowledge they had to possess. He does that with a step-by-step reconstruction of the cub pilot's education. As the cub masters each seemingly insurmountable step in his education, his new-found pride is quickly crushed when he learns that another, and even more formidable, step awaits him. Moreover, he eventually learns that even after he qualifies for his piloting license, his education will never be complete, as the river itself never ceases to change. Do Mark Twain's ideas about the unending nature of education apply only to piloting or do they extend to life generally?

2. **Memory:** When the cub pilot first discovers how much information he must remember, he says that this "memory was never loaded with anything but blank cartridges." By the time he finishes his apprenticeship, however, he must have a prodigious memory. How do the piloting chapters develop the theme of memory?

The capacity of human memory is a subject that interested Mark Twain throughout his life. The subject is relevant to *Life on the Mississippi* in at least two ways. First, the piloting chapters are themselves exercises in recalled memory, as Mark Twain wrote them almost 20 years after the period in his life that they attempt to reconstruct. *The Adventures of Tom Sawyer* (1876) and *Adventures of Huckleberry Finn* (1884) are similar in being exercises in recalled memory that draw on their author's memories of even earlier periods. The trustworthiness of Mark Twain's memory and how the passage of time affected his views of the past might provide good subjects for essays. Of greater immediacy, however, is the more explicit use of memory as a theme in the piloting chapters of *Life on the Mississippi.* Throughout those chapters, Mark Twain repeatedly emphasizes the prodigious feats of memory that steamboat pilots were expected to perform. One of the cub pilot's first unpleasant surprises as he begins his training is the realization of the vast quantity of details concerning the river that he must remember. To his surprise, he actually masters the information. However, each time he thinks his memory is filled to capacity, he discovers that he must learn still more facts—sometimes double what he already knows. Moreover, not only must he carry in his head a stupendous number of details about the river, he must know them *perfectly*: "He cannot stop with merely thinking a thing is so and so; he must *know* it . . ."

To write an essay on this theme, begin by recording notes on all the references in the narrative to the demands placed on pilots' memories. How does the cub pilot react each time he learns of a new memory feat he is expected to master? Is there a discernible pattern in the rate at which these demands are placed on him? What observations does the narrative make about the ability of human beings to remember large quantities of information? Does the narrative suggest that prodigious memory feats are unique to the piloting profession? What, if anything, separates piloting from other professions in the demands placed on the memories of its practitioners? How do the narrator's criticisms of Mr. Brown's nearly photographic memory in chapter 13 fit into his overall views of memory?

Character

A basic question to consider while reading any work of literature is the extent to which its characters are, in fact, *characters,* and not merely one- or two-dimensional figures inserted simply to move the story along. True characters are complex, three-dimensional, and fully rounded people, about whom readers learn enough not to expect them always to behave predictably, just as real people are not always predictable. Although the main characters in *Life on the Mississippi*'s piloting chapters are, in fact, based on real people, you might be wise to disregard their real-life counterparts and consider them as you would fictional characters in any work of literature.

The piloting chapters may not offer a broad range of subjects for essays on character development, but the subjects they do offer are rich ones. Indeed, because the main story line is the education of the cub pilot, his character development is central to the narrative as a whole. The cub is as fully rounded a character as you will encounter in Mark Twain's writings, and after you have read the piloting chapters, you should understand him well enough to answer almost any question about him. The same cannot be said of other characters in the chapters. More "types" than characters, they are relatively flat and serve primarily to help develop the cub. For example, although the Mr. Bixby of *Life on the Mississippi* ("Mr. B." in "Old Times on the Mississippi") is based on the very interesting real-life Horace Bixby who trained Mark Twain as a pilot, it would be difficult to find many interesting things to say about the book's Mr. Bixby. A master pilot, he is a demanding but fair-minded teacher. What else can be said about him? The cub's other master is the belligerent Mr. Brown (also based on a real person), who provides a dramatic contrast with Bixby. There is not much more to say about him either. However, with some imagination, you might be able to work up an essay topic comparing Bixby and Brown that shows how their sharply contrasting personalities add interest to the narrative.

Sample Topics:

1. **The narrator:** Is the narrator of the piloting chapters more a literary creation or an autobiographical figure?

   The central character in the piloting chapters is, of course, the cub pilot himself. Although Mark Twain wrote the chapters in the first person and clearly based the cub's training on his own experience as an apprentice pilot during the late 1850s, it would be a mistake to regard the chapters as strictly autobiographical. The narrative corresponds fairly closely to Mark Twain's experience as an apprentice and mentions many real people, places, and events, but it also contains some pure fictions, such as the cub pilot's allusion to himself as an "orphan" in chapter 13. More important, however, is Mark Twain's deliberate altering of his narrative persona. As you read the chapters, what signs do you find indicating that the cub is more a literary creation than a real person?

2. **The river:** To what extent might the Mississippi River itself be considered a character?

   Scarcely a single paragraph in *Life on the Mississippi*'s piloting chapters fails to mention, or at least allude to, the Mississippi River. A central theme of the narrative is the river's constantly changing shape and sometimes unpredictable behavior. The river plays such a central role throughout the narrative that it is fair to ask whether it might be regarded as a character in its own right. An essay on this subject would offer your imagination wide scope. You would need to begin by defining what you mean by character. If a character must be a living, changing thing, can the river meet that definition? Is there anything in the narrative to suggest that the river has a personality or mind of its own?

History and Context

Among all the books that Mark Twain wrote, perhaps none comes closer to being a straight history than *Life on the Mississippi*. The book originated in the "Old Times on the Mississippi" articles that Mark Twain wrote in a conscious effort to record an earlier period of history. His subject was the pre–Civil War years of steamboating on the Mississippi River, when pilots enjoyed levels of power and prestige that almost vanished after the war. Mark Twain himself had piloted steamboats on the Mississippi during the four years leading up to the Civil War, so he was well qualified to write on the subject. His piloting career ended abruptly when the war closed down commercial traffic on the Mississippi. After the war, steamboats lost most of their passenger traffic to the rapidly expanding railroads, which offered cheaper and faster transportation up and down the Mississippi Valley. The steamboats also lost most of their cargo trade to huge barges pulled by towboats. Despite the relatively brief time between the period when Mark Twain was a pilot and his writing of "Old Times" during the mid-1870s, the piloting days he had known no longer existed. His goal, therefore, was to record that earlier era before it was forgotten completely.

If *Life on the Mississippi*'s piloting chapters were merely straightforward history, we would not be reading them as literature. That point raises a central question to consider as you read those chapters: *Why* are they considered literature, and not merely history?

Sample Topic:

1. **The majestic Mississippi:** How do *Life on the Mississippi*'s piloting chapters evoke changes on the river itself?

   History is about change over time, and *Life on the Mississippi* chronicles two fundamentally different processes of change on the Mississippi River. The first process is implied in the reasons behind Mark Twain's writing of the book's piloting chapters: his wish to document an earlier era of the piloting profession, which had been profoundly changed. The piloting chapters occasionally touch on historical changes in piloting and in steamboating, but that subject is more properly the province of the second half of the book, with which we are not primarily concerned here. The other process of change addressed by the piloting chapters is that which occurred in the river itself. A point stressed both in those chapters and throughout the rest of *Life on the Mississippi* is that the river is a powerful, living entity that constantly changes itself and refuses to be controlled. How effectively do the piloting chapters convey that idea? And what do they say about the effect of the river's changing nature on piloting work?

If you choose to write on this subject, pay special attention as you read *Life on the Mississippi* to references to how the Mississippi River changes. In addition to instances of specific major changes, such as the washing away of islands and the creation of new cut-offs, note allusions to more subtle changes, such as erosion of the river's banks and the appearance of new snags. What do these details contribute to the narrative? You should be able to find enough information within the piloting chapters alone to build an essay. However, you can find additional material on the river in later chapters of the book (see especially chapters 28 and 33).

Philosophy and Ideas

Another way to look at *Life on the Mississippi* is to examine the broad philosophical ideas that arise within it. This approach is related to the study of themes described above, but it operates at a more general level, applying to ideas that tend to transcend the works within which they are explored.

Sample Topics:

1. **The limits of freedom:** The narrator of *Life on the Mississippi* claims that the steamboat pilot of his era "was the only unfettered and entirely independent human being that lived in the earth." What does that statement really mean? Can it be true?

A pervasive theme throughout Mark Twain's writings is the quest for freedom in all its various forms. Within the cub pilot chapters of *Life on the Mississippi* that theme finds its strongest expression in frequent allusions to the power and independence of pilots, who did not even have to answer to the captains of their steamboats. In chapter 14, the narrator says that he "loved the [piloting] profession far better than any [he] has followed since" and then gives as his reason the statement quoted above—about pilots' being "unfettered and entirely independent." It is a bold statement, particularly because it comes from a man who had enjoyed a great deal of independence and freedom in his working life between the time he left piloting and the time he wrote those remarks. Could Mark Twain have truly meant what he said? Is it possible that his nostalgia for piloting clouded his judgment, making him overlook the harsh realities of what it really meant to be a pilot?

An essay on this subject needs to look closely at everything that *Life on the Mississippi* really says about the freedom and independence of pilots during Mark Twain's time on the river. You should have no trouble finding evidence that pilots truly did have a great deal of power and that they did not have to answer to other men while they were on the job. However, is being independent of human masters the only meaningful measure of freedom? Is it possible that pilots were actually slaves to a different kind of master, and one that could be more capricious and vindictive than any human being? That other possible master, of course, was the river itself. It was constantly changing and could never be taken for granted. Pilots might not have had to answer to other men, but they carried what Mark Twain calls the "staggering weight of all the responsibilities connected with the position"—the immense burden of having to protect the safety of their boats and passengers. Does the narrator of *Life on the Mississippi* express thoughts about the responsibilities and fears of pilots that might be interpreted as providing a view contrary to the one he expresses about pilots being "unfettered"?

2. **Romanticism and nostalgia:** How do the piloting chapters romanticize the past?

Mark Twain often wrote scathingly about authors whom he accused of overromanticizing the past and was particularly hard on Sir Walter Scott (1771–1832), the Scottish author of such popular medieval romances as *The Heart of Midlothian* (1818) and *Ivanhoe* (1819). Indeed, he blasts Scott in several of the later chapters of *Life on the Mississippi.* In chapter 46, for example, he accuses Scott of setting

> the world in love with dreams and phantoms; with decayed and swinish forms of religion; with decayed and degraded systems of government; with the sillinesses and emptinesses, sham grandeurs, sham gauds, and sham chivalries of a brainless and worthless long-vanished society.

In the cub piloting chapters of *Life on the Mississippi*, Mark Twain seems to work at debunking romantic illusions when he remarks on how the cub's growing mastery of his new profession gradually "knocked the romance out of piloting." Is it possible, that despite Mark Twain's protestations against romanticizing the past that what he wrote about the old days of piloting actually does just that? Think of how unusual his situation must have seemed when he started writing "Old Times on the Mississippi" in 1874. Then only about 39 years old, he had been away from piloting for less than 14 years; nevertheless, steamboating had already changed dramatically. During his time on the river, steamboats had been vital to the nation's commerce; pilots were kings on the Mississippi and earned as much money as the vice president of the United States. By the early 1870s, however, steamboats were almost inconsequential in national commerce, and pilots had lost most of their prestige. In chapter 22 of *Life on the Mississippi,* Mark Twain writes,

> Mississippi steamboating was born about 1812; at the end of thirty years, it had grown to mighty proportions; and in less

than thirty more, it was dead! A strangely short life for so majestic a creature. Of course it is not absolutely dead; neither is a crippled octogenarian who could once jump twenty-two feet on level ground; but as contrasted with what it was in its prime vigor, Mississippi steamboating may be called dead.

Was it not natural for Mark Twain to look upon his steamboating days nostalgically? Is it significant that when he wrote his articles, he titled them "*Old* Times on the Mississippi," thereby describing as "old" events less than 14 years in the past?

Writing an essay on this subject will require an especially thoughtful reading of the cub piloting chapters. You should also read some of the second half of *Life on the Mississippi*, particularly chapters 40 to 46, which criticizes the romanticism of the American South and lays much of the blame on Sir Walter Scott's novels. As you read the piloting chapters, take special note of passages conveying a wistful regret for the lost past. Some later chapters of *Life on the Mississippi* are more explicit in their expressions of nostalgia for the old days; reading them (especially chapter 28) will help you know what to look for in the cub piloting chapters. Keep in mind that your essay should focus on what the early chapters have to say. Mark Twain wrote most of those chapters before he returned to the river and wrote the rest of *Life on the Mississippi*. You should not mix up what he originally wrote in 1874–75 with what he wrote in 1882–83.

Form and Genre

The structure of *Life on the Mississippi*'s cub pilot chapters is simple and straightforward. After beginning with the narrator's recollection of his boyhood ambition to be a "steamboatman," they trace the course that led to his becoming a cub pilot and reconstruct—often in great detail—the long training that he went through. The moment that he completes his training, the narrative abruptly ends. What significance is there in the fact that Mark Twain chose not to write about the years that he was a licensed pilot? Could he have been more interested in the process of becoming a pilot than in actually being a pilot? Or did the cub's process of learning the river simply provide him with a better narrative frame-work than a licensed pilot's career would have? If Mark Twain had con-tinued his story into the later years, what more could he have said about piloting?

The cub pilot's narrative might justly be regarded as a nonfiction memoir, but it has many of the characteristics of a bildungsroman—a fancy term for a coming-of-age novel in which the hero matures and becomes ready to take on adult responsibility. The cub pilot chapters do not have everything one expects to find in a true novel, but do they have enough elements of fictional narratives to justify being considered a type of bildungsroman? The most obvious element is a narrative focusing on the cub pilot's gradually mastering his difficult profession until he quali-fies to join the ranks of full-fledged adults. His narrative ends abruptly— literally in the first sentence of chapter 21—at the moment that he gets his license; does this fact suggest anything about Mark Twain's intentions?

At the beginning of this chapter, it was pointed out that Mark Twain was much older and more experienced as a traveler at the time he became a cub pilot than the cub pilot in his narrative is. Whether you choose to write on this subject or not, you should keep these points in mind while you read and think about *Life on the Mississippi*.

The word *bildungsroman* was not coined until around 1910, so it could never have passed through Mark Twain's mind while he was writ-ing about his piloting days. Is it, however, possible that he nevertheless consciously attempted to craft a coming-of-age story and that he wanted his cub pilot to appear very young to make his maturation into a licensed pilot more interesting and dramatic?

Sample Topics:

1. **Coming of age:** How might the piloting chapters be regarded as a coming-of-age story?

The methodical exposition of the cub pilot's education in the piloting chapters does at least two things: It demonstrates the high level of skill and knowledge that were demanded of steam-boat pilots, and it also shows the maturing process through which apprentices went to complete their training. If Mark Twain's purpose had been merely to impress readers with how difficult piloting was, would he have taken so much trouble to develop his cub pilot's persona? Moreover, why did he end his narrative so abruptly, immediately before the cub becomes a licensed pilot? Mark Twain himself piloted steamboats for two years after getting his license; would his narrative have gained or lost something if he had continued it into those years? What other evidence in the narrative indicates that he consciously constructed a coming-of-age story?

As you are looking upon *Life on the Mississippi* as a literary work, you should be able to find all the information you need within its pages if you choose to write on this subject. You should not need to delve into biographies of Mark Twain. What you should look for as you read the piloting chapters are indications of the cub pilot's growing maturity. When the narrative begins, he is filled with romantic ideas of what it means to be a "steamboatman." What happens to cause him to change those ideas? Is there a moment at which it can be said that he ceases to be a naive boy and becomes a man? A more general question to consider is Mark Twain's purpose in deliberately exaggerating the youth and naïveté of his cub. What would the effect on his narrative be if his cub pilot were as old and experienced as he himself had been when he was an apprentice?

2. **Structure of the piloting chapters:** What is the relationship between the original "Old Times on the Mississippi" articles and *Life on the Mississippi*'s added piloting chapters?

As was discussed at the beginning of this chapter, Mark Twain wrote what became *Life on the Mississippi*'s chapters 4 through 17 as articles for the *Atlantic Monthly* in 1874–75. To flesh out the piloting story for his 1883 book, he wrote three additional chapters (17–20). How do these added chapters differ from the earlier cub piloting chapters? Does anything about their structure or style reveal that they were written about eight years later than the original chapters? Is there anything in their content to suggest why Mark Twain did not cover the same subjects in his original magazine articles?

Language, Symbols, and Imagery

The section on History and Context above raises the question of why *Life on the Mississippi*'s piloting chapters are regarded as a work of literature and not merely a history. Literature and history are not mutually exclusive categories, but literature is generally distinguished from other forms of writing by its use of such devices as symbolic language and vivid imagery, and *Life on the Mississippi* is rich in both.

Sample Topic:

1. **The language of sunshine and solitude:** How does *Life on the Mississippi* use language to evoke moods?

In his introduction to the Library of America edition of *Life on the Mississippi,* Jonathan Raban describes the book's piloting chapters as "suffused with the roseate style of *Tom Sawyer*"—an ornate way of saying that both works use language to create bright and optimistic moods. He quotes similar phrases in each: *Life on the Mississippi*'s "white town drowsing in the sunshine of a summer's morning" and *Tom Sawyer*'s "The sun rose upon a tranquil world, and beamed down upon the peaceful village like a benediction." Is Raban's observation about the piloting chapters generally valid? What other examples of roseate language can be found in those chapters? What effect on the reader does such language have?

You should also ask if the piloting chapters use other kinds of language to create different moods. An earlier chapter of *Life on the Mississippi,* for example, calls the river "an awful solitude . . . over most of its stretch" (chapter 2). Even now, in the 21st century, anyone who stands on a bank of the Mississippi River, away from towns, is apt to be awed by the river's immensity and the feelings of solitude that hang over it. To what extent do the book's piloting chapters impart similar feelings and what kinds of language do they use to convey those feelings? Are there patterns in the distribution of bright and dark images, and do such patterns relate to the progress in the cub pilot's training?

This subject may not be a simple one to write an essay on, as the evidence you would need to find is subtle. If you do choose to write on this subject, watch for words and expressions evoking images of emptiness, isolation, desolation, and loneliness, such as chapter 11's description of the "utter solitudes" of the chutes through which his steamboat passed. Keep in mind that much of what you are looking for may be written in language much less explicit than that in chapter 11.

Compare and Contrast Essays

Compare and contrast essays allow you to express your creativity on at least two levels: first, in finding aspects of one or more works to compare; then in finding significant points to make about the similarities and differences that are observed. One of your best chances of attaining true originality may lie in writing this type of essay—particularly on a subject that may not be obvious to others. For example, you might compare depictions of the various master pilots—Mr. Bixby, Mr. Ealer, and Mr. Brown—in the piloting chapters of *Life on the Mississippi* and ask what each contributes to the education and maturation of the cub. All three are based on real figures, but Mark Twain clearly took broad liberties in his depictions of them—particularly Mr. Brown, whose real-life model, William Brown, died in the *Pennsylvania* steamboat disaster described in chapter 20 of *Life on the Mississippi*.

While compare and contrast topics offer wide scope for developing original ideas, they also make it easy to fall into the trap of doing exactly the opposite. The danger lies in failing to develop your essay beyond a mere catalogue of similarities and differences between pairs of characters, types of plots, different points of view, or other aspects of the work or works you are analyzing. For example, it would not be enough simply to say that Mr. Ealer and Mr. Brown represent polar opposites as instructors of cub pilots and list their similarities and differences. You should also explain, so far as is possible with the evidence of the text, why they have their traits, how their traits affect their treatment of cub pilots, and what points Mark Twain may have been trying to make in using them.

Sample Topics:

1. **Prelude to *Huckleberry Finn*:** *Life on the Mississippi* is sometimes seen as a kind of warm-up to Mark Twain's masterpiece,

Adventures of Huckleberry Finn. What aspects of the book's piloting chapters anticipate that novel?

When Mark Twain wrote "Old Times on the Mississippi" during the mid-1870s, he had already made himself famous as an author with *The Innocents Abroad* (1869), about his journey to Europe and the Holy Land in 1867, and *Roughing It* (1872), which recalled his time in the Far West during the early 1860s. The "Old Times" articles turned his attention even farther back in time, to his years on the Mississippi River. He revisited those articles and added to them when he published *Life on the Mississippi* in 1883. He then completed his second great book about the Mississippi, *Huckleberry Finn,* which he had started about seven years earlier. That novel and the piloting chapters of *Life on the Mississippi* are very different kinds of stories, but both are about boys coming of age on the river. The fact that Mark Twain completed both books around the same time makes it reasonable to assume that each book may have influenced the other.

An essay on this subject would require that you read all of *Huckleberry Finn* and the piloting chapters in *Life on the Mississippi,* but you would not necessarily have to delve into other writings about Mark Twain's life. Perhaps the best way to approach this subject is to construct a list of questions to ask of both books and then to compare the answers that each book provides. There may be no limit to the range of questions that are possible, for example: What kind of figurative language does each book use to describe the Mississippi River? How is each book's narrator transformed by his experience on the river? What kinds of moods does each narrator's prose convey? To sum up your essay, try to answer the basic question of how Mark Twain's writing of the piloting chapters may have influenced his writing of *Huckleberry Finn.* However, if your arguments are based solely on comparisons of the texts of *Huckleberry Finn* and *Life on the Mississippi,* be careful to make that point clear. If you choose to bring additional evidence from biographies of Mark Twain, you should make that clear too.

2. **Greenhorns:** In what ways do the voices of the greenhorn narrators of *Roughing It* and *Life on the Mississippi* differ?

Roughing It and the piloting chapters of *Life on the Mississippi* are both works about periods in Mark Twain's life that he had to recall from memory. They are also similar in their use of young narrators who leave home for the first time to travel great distances. *Life on the Mississippi*'s narrator packs his valise, boards a steamboat headed for New Orleans, and exults in "being bound for mysterious lands and distant climes . . ." *Roughing It*'s narrator recalls that he "never had been away from home, and that word 'travel' had a seductive charm for me." Thrilled by his older brother's offer of a job in Nevada, he packs and joins his brother on a journey to the Far West, a land of adventure.

That fact that Mark Twain embellished his real adventures in these books should be evident, as he could not have twice left home for the first time. A question to ask of these books is what he hoped to achieve by making his narrators appear so young and inexperienced. At the start of their adventures, both characters are greenhorns—newcomers who are unacquainted with the ways of the new worlds in which they are moving. As we read their narratives, we share in their sense of discovery as they learn about their new environments, and we laugh comfortably at the crises they survive and the processes of initiation through which they go.

To write an essay comparing the narrators of *Roughing It* and *Life on the Mississippi*'s piloting chapters, you will need to read all the piloting chapters but only the first 21 chapters of *Roughing It,* which take the narrator from his Missouri home to Carson City, Nevada, on an exciting cross-country stagecoach journey. Perhaps the first point of comparison to look for is structural similarities between the two works, both of which are built around journeys into new worlds. With what expectations do the narrators begin their journeys? What types of incidents challenge their romantic illusions? When the cub pilot thinks he has mastered his new profession and starts to become cocky, something usually happens to drain his self-confidence;

does the narrator of *Roughing It* have similarly deflating experiences? Are any of the major crises that the greenhorns survive in the two narratives almost the same?

Another thing to look for in both works is the author's consistency in his use of the first-person voice: Do the two narrators consistently speak in the voices of greenhorns? Or do they sometimes shift to the voice of the much older Mark Twain? If the narrators' voices do shift, are there discernible patterns to those shifts themselves?

3. ***Life on the Mississippi* and *Tom Sawyer* as coming-of-age stories:** Mark Twain wrote both his "Old Times on the Mississippi" articles and *The Adventures of Tom Sawyer* (1876) around the same time. What parallels do the two works share as coming-of-age stories?

The sections on both Themes and Form and Genre above discuss the aptness of regarding *Life on the Mississippi*'s cub pilot chapters as a coming-of-age story. Mark Twain's novel *Tom Sawyer* is generally classified as a bildungsroman, or coming-of-age story, because its hero, Tom, matures morally and psychologically. When the novel opens, he is an immature rascal who shows little respect for authority, evades every kind of responsibility, and channels much of his energy into manufacturing adventures. By the end of the novel, however, he appears to have shed much of his earlier immaturity and placed himself on the threshold of adulthood. What elements of Tom's process of maturation can be seen in the development of the cub pilot of *Life on the Mississippi*?

If you write on this subject, you might begin by comparing this passage that concludes *Tom Sawyer* with the abrupt ending of the cub piloting chapters in *Life on the Mississippi*:

> So endeth this chronicle. It being strictly a history of a boy, it must stop here; the story could not go much further without becoming the history of a man. When one writes a novel about grown people, he knows exactly where to stop—that is, with a

marriage; but when he writes of juveniles, he must stop where
he best can.

Would that passage make a fitting conclusion to the cub piloting chapters of *Life on the Mississippi*? As with *Tom Sawyer*,
those chapters stop just as their protagonist is on the threshold
of manhood. The first paragraph of the next chapter (21) sum-
marizes Mark Twain's entire career as a licensed pilot in just
under 80 words: "In due course I got my license. I was a pilot
now, full fledged. . . ."

Bibliography for *Life on the Mississippi*

Bassett, John E. *"Life on the Mississippi:* Being Shifty in a New Country." *A Heart of Ideality in My Realism and Other Essays on Howells and Twain.* West Cornwall, CT: Locust Hill Press, 1991. 143–9.

Cox, James M. *"Life on the Mississippi* Revisited." *Mark Twain.* Ed. Harold Bloom. New York: Chelsea House, 1986. 153–67.

———. "Southwestern Vernacular." *Mark Twain: The Fate of Humor.* Princeton, NJ: Princeton UP, 1966. 156–84.

Dawidziak, Mark. *Horton Foote's "The Shape of the River": The Lost Teleplay About Mark Twain with History and Analysis.* New York: Applause, 2003.

Dix, Andrew. "Twain and the Mississippi." *A Companion to Mark Twain.* Eds. Peter Messent and Louis J. Budd. Oxford, England: Blackwell, 2005. 293–308.

Emerson, Everett. "Life on the Mississippi." *The Mark Twain Encyclopedia.* Eds. J. R. LeMaster and James D. Wilson. New York: Garland, 1993. 465–7.

Gerber, John C. "'Old Times on the Mississippi.'" *Mark Twain.* Boston: Twayne, 1988. 64–66.

Howe, Lawrence. Afterword. *Life on the Mississippi.* By Mark Twain. New York: Oxford UP, 1996. 1–18. (Back matter has separate pagination.)

———. "Transcending the Limits of Experience: Mark Twain's *Life on the Mississippi.*" *American Literature* 63 (1991): 420–39.

Kruse, Horst H. *Mark Twain and "Life on the Mississippi."* Amherst: U Massachusetts P, 1981.

LeMaster, J. R., and Kathryn Kalin Lee. "'Old Times on the Mississippi.'" *The Mark Twain Encyclopedia.* Eds. J. R. LeMaster and James D. Wilson. New York: Garland, 1993. 552–3.

Miller, Robert Keith. "Sailing a Shoreless Sea: *Life on the Mississippi.*" *Mark Twain.* New York: Frederick Ungar, 1983. 33–57.

Morris, Willie. Introduction. *Life on the Mississippi.* By Mark Twain. New York: Oxford UP, 1996. xxxi–liii.

Raban, Jonathan. Introduction. *Life on the Mississippi.* By Mark Twain. New York: Vintage Books/Library of America, 1991. xi–xvii.

Railton, Stephen. *The Life & Work of Mark Twain.* Chantilly, VA: Teaching Company, 2002 (Includes a lecture on "Old Times on the Mississippi"; available in audio and video formats).

Rasmussen, R. Kent. *"Life on the Mississippi."* In *Critical Companion to Mark Twain.* New York: Facts On File, 2007. I:296–315. (See also entries on Horace Bixby, Mississippi River, "Old Times on the Mississippi," Piloting, and Steamboats).

———. *"Life on the Mississippi."* *Masterplots, Second Revised Edition.* Ed. Frank N. Magill, Pasadena, CA: Salem Press, 1996. 6:3630–33.

Robinson, Forrest G. "The Innocent at Large: Mark Twain's Travel writing." *The Cambridge Companion to Mark Twain.* Ed. Forrest G. Robinson. New York: Cambridge UP, 1995. 27–51.

Sattelmeyer, Robert. "Steamboats, Cocaine, and Paper Money: Mark Twain Rewriting Himself." *Constructing Mark Twain: New Directions in Scholarship.* Eds. Laura E. Skandera Trombley and Michael J. Kiskis. Columbia: U Missouri P, 2001. 87–100.

Sloane, David E. E. *Student Companion to Mark Twain.* Westport, CT: Greenwood Press, 2001.

Twain, Mark. *Life on the Mississippi.* 1883. Facsimile reprint. New York: Oxford UP, 1996.

INDEX